Gift-Giving in Japan

Gift-Giving in Japan

CASH,

CONNECTIONS,

COSMOLOGIES

Katherine Rupp

STANFORD UNIVERSITY PRESS
STANFORD, CALIFORNIA

Stanford University Press
Stanford, California
© 2003 by the Board of Trustees of the
Leland Stanford Junior University

Printed in the United States of America

Library of Congress Cataloging-in-Publication Data
    Rupp, Katherine.
        Gift-giving in Japan: cash, connections, cosmologies /
        Katherine Rupp.
    p. cm.
    Includes bibliographical references and index.
    ISBN 0-8047-4703-2 (alk. paper) —
    ISBN 0-8047-4704-0 (pbk.: alk. paper)

1. Gifts—Japan. 2. Ceremonial exchange—Japan. 3. National characteristics, Japanese. 4. Japan—Social life and customs. 5. Japan—
Economic conditions. I. Title.

GT3040.J3R86 2003

394.'0952—dc21   2003008098
This book is printed on acid-free, archival-quality paper

Original printing 2003
Last figure below indicates year of this printing:

12   11   10   09   08   07   06   05   04   03

Designed and typeset at Stanford University Press in 10/13 Sabon

For Oma and Tante Ruth

Was du ererbt von deinen Vätern hast,
Erwirb es, um es zu besitzen.
Faust (lines 682–83)

⌢ Acknowledgments

The generosity of many individuals and institutions has made the completion of this book possible. I began study of Japanese and Japan as an undergraduate at Princeton University, and I remember well the dedication of my teachers there and at the Kyoto Center for Japanese Studies, especially Sogen Hori, Soho Machida, Earl Miner, Fumiko Nazikian, and Thomas Rohlen. Princeton's Department of East Asian Studies provided me with language-study grants.

My years at the University of Chicago provided extremely stimulating and enjoyable graduate training. I thank especially Norma Field and Marshall Sahlins for the very different ways they have opened and stretched my mind, for sharing their passion for and commitment to their respective fields of study, and for their warmth, generosity, and kindness. It is with much sadness that I acknowledge the debt I owe to Valerio Valeri, whose life was cut short before the completion of the dissertation on which this book is based. I will never forget his curiosity, rigor, and wide-ranging knowledge. Danilyn Rutherford provided critical insight in his stead. Nancy Munn made many helpful suggestions during my fieldwork. Anne Chi'en gave sound advice on numerous occasions. Rupert Stasch and Melissa Wender were my steadfast companions during our years together in Chicago, and learning from them and with them has been and continues to be an integral part of my life. Their work has enriched my own, and I deeply treasure our friendships. Melissa's presence at Yale during the final stages of writing has been a tremendous gift. My graduate studies were funded by the National Science Foundation and the University of Chicago, including one year of support from the Committee on Japanese Studies.

Twenty months of fieldwork in Japan have indebted me to many people. Osamu Mihashi's perspective has been significant. Machiko Aoyagi of Rikkyo University advised me during my stay in Japan, sharing many ideas for fieldwork strategies and facilitating numerous contacts. Mayumi Ariyoshi and Naoko Morita were both wonderful friends and enthusiastic teachers. This study would not have been possible without the people who, over the course of one year, recorded the gifts they gave and received and explained the circumstances of each of those episodes of giving or receiving to me. I greatly appreciate their generosity, and hope I have done justice to all they have taught me. In addition to these many individuals who, in order to protect their anonymity, cannot be named, I thank Keiko Kimura, who introduced me to many of the Tokyo participants in my study. Petra Kienle first suggested that I move to Warabi, and Kiichiro Hiramatsu, Shinya Ikegami, and Takahiro Sato greatly assisted me in all aspects of my fieldwork there. Seiichi Miura of Tobu Department Store provided me with much data and inside information of the gift giving industry. Lisa Brunckhorst and Eve Darian-Smith visited me during my fieldwork and helped me see my research through new eyes. I thank Robert Cheetham, Kenji and Donna Go, Mikiko Inoue, Mary Anne Jorgensen, Mami Maeda, Melissa Rinne, and Reiko Tanaka, for many interesting discussions related to Japanese practices of giving and receiving; it was Kenji who originally urged me to pursue the topic of gifts in Japan. The Japanese Ministry of Education provided the funding for my fieldwork.

My colleagues Christian de Pee and Conrad Schirokauer read parts of this manuscript when we taught together at Columbia University. I am grateful to them for their comments on my work and in particular for their guidance in developing a broader understanding of the history of East Asian social and cultural interchange.

I completed the manuscript for this book as a postdoctoral associate of the Council on East Asian Studies at Yale University; I thank the members of the council and, in particular, council chairs Valerie Hansen and Mimi Yiengpruksawan for this two-year period of research and teaching that has been so engaging and productive. I am very grateful to William Kelly of Yale University for his guidance and support, not only during my post-doc, but also during the period in which I wrote my dissertation while living in New Haven. Bill read both early and later drafts of chapters, offered excellent advice, and included me in various meetings and gatherings, making me feel welcome at Yale's anthropology department. Allison Alexy, Ian Condry, Sara Davis, Valerie Hansen, Hirokazu Miyazaki, Karen Nakamura, Helen Siu, Yohko Tsuji, and Gavin Whitelaw were very generous in providing comments on my research, some independently and some as part of the Japan Ethnography Reading Group and the Ethnography and Social Theory Colloquium.

I thank Muriel Bell, John Feneron, and Martin Hanft of Stanford University Press for their editorial expertise, as well as Joy Hendry and one anonymous reviewer for careful readings of the manuscript and valuable suggestions.

The sketches (mostly drawn from photographs I took during my fieldwork) are by Chika Sato MacDonald, and I treasure these beautiful illustrations.

The Breslauer-Royzman, Farrell, Mohnen, Walker, and Walsh families have been sources of strength, joy, and companionship throughout the writing of this book. Irina Royzman staunchly encouraged me to focus on the task at hand, and Maya Walker gave many detailed and insightful comments on an earlier version of the manuscript.

My parents, George and Nancy Rupp, my sister, Stephanie Rupp, and our close family friends, Bud and Donna Ogle, have read successive iterations of this book; they have given me more than I can put into words. My husband's parents, Bruno and Maria Coppi, and his siblings, Maddalena and Andreas Coppi, have repeatedly offered helping hands. I am especially thankful for the way in which our families, despite other pressing demands, have taken care of our son Alex Rupp-Coppi. My mother in particular has devoted much time and energy in this regard, much to Alex's delight. I am grateful to our families and to the teachers at the

Yeladim Childcare Center of the Jewish Community Center of Greater New Haven for giving me time to write. My husband, Paolo Coppi, urged me to work hard at my research; I thank him not only for his encouragement and assistance during my stay in Japan and throughout the writing of this book (including the arduous job of scanning my fieldwork negatives and formatting the figures) but also for his many contributions to the shaping of our life together. I finished this manuscript just a few weeks after the birth of our son Leo Rupp-Coppi; it is with great joy that we welcome him as the youngest member of our family.

I dedicate this book with deep love and gratitude to our extended family's two most senior members: my grandmother, Erika Braunöhler Rupp and her twin sister, Ruth Braunöhler Schulte. Even as they encounter the last and most difficult stage of their lives, in which old age extracts a heavy toll from their bodies and minds, I clearly remember and at times still recognize their strength, generosity, discipline, good humor, ability to think critically, willingness to defy authority, and compassion. May my own children embrace these qualities and values and make them their own.

                                                                          K.R.

New Haven, Connecticut
June 2002

☞ Contents

⌒ Illustrations

Gift-Giving in Japan

1 ⤢ Examples of Giving

In Japan, as in many other parts of the world, the giving of gifts is extremely important. To note one measure of its significance: people invest substantial amounts of money in gift-giving. Many people feel burdened by their giving obligations. It is not uncommon for people to avoid visits to their hometowns because of the gifts those interactions would entail, to hide travel plans from friends and neighbors so as not to have to bring back presents from trips, or for close friends to agree not to invite each other to their children's weddings.

Gift-giving is very important, not only at personal and household levels but on national and macroeconomic levels as well. For example, *ochūgen* and *oseibo*, summer and winter gifts, provide 60 percent of the annual profits of most Tokyo department stores.

A major avenue for social mobility in Japan is through bribery and patronage. The distinctions and continuities between "gift" and "bribe" are subtle and complicated. People give summer and winter gifts to their bosses, to the teachers of their children, to their doctors. Parents give large sums of money to the bosses of their sons when those bosses serve as go-betweens at their sons' weddings. Parents and spouses pay the equivalent in yen of thousands of dollars to the doctors, particularly to the surgeons, who care for their loved ones. Bureaucrats in Japan have wide authority to form policies, grant licenses, and dispense lucrative contracts, sometimes with very little accountability, and people in industry seek their favors. Politicians receive donations from industry, and they in turn intercede with the bureaucracy to secure projects on industry's behalf.

In short, not only do individual Japanese people spend a lot of time, worry, and money on gift-giving, but gift-giving is also a crucial part of the overall workings of the macro-economy. The question this book seeks to answer is why that is the case. Why do people give as much, as often, and in the particular ways that they do? Why do some people reject giving and receiving? How do attitudes toward and practices of giving relate to considerations of age, class, gender, geographic area, occupation, and religion? How have these practices changed over time? How have they been used for political ends? In what way can the study of gifts in Japan contribute to the broader field of gifts and exchange in anthropology?

This book is based on eighteen months of fieldwork in the Tokyo metropolitan area, as well as on short-term research in other parts of Japan. The core of my study is sixteen family representatives of different ages, classes, genders, occupations, neighborhoods, and religions. This principal network maintained records of all gifts given and received over the course of one full annual cycle. In ongoing intensive meetings, family representatives elaborated on the circumstances and motives of each gift transaction. I also interviewed experts, including the author of books on proper gift-giving etiquette, Buddhist and Shintō priests knowledgeable in the religious and historical underpinnings of gift-giving, department store and funeral company employees who advise customers on gifts, and elderly workers at Tokyo's Tsukiji fish market who are familiar with intricate rules for the giving of various kinds of fish, seaweed, and other ocean creatures and plants. I participated in neighborhood festivals, election rallies, house-building rites, and other ceremonies in which gift-giving was an integral part, and collected information from print and electronic media and other public sources.

Those (all referred to by pseudonyms) who taught me about the practices of giving can for the most part be divided into two distinct groups. I became acquainted with the people in the first group through the mother of a Japanese family who had stayed in the United States. She had lived in the apartment next door to my family when I was a child, and my sister and I had played with her son and daughters. These people whom I met through this neighbor resided either in the wealthier sections of Tokyo or in its suburbs, were upper middle class, and were well educated. Many of these families had annual incomes of ten million yen and more. (The exchange rate during my time in the field, 1994–96, was roughly 100 yen to U.S.$1.)

The people in the second group were my friends and neighbors from a place called Warabi. Warabi is located in the southern part of Saitama prefecture, and it is about thirty minutes by train from central Tokyo. It has a population of about 72,000 people. In the Edo period, Warabi was a relay station on the Nakasendō, a highway that still stretches from Tokyo to Kyoto. Inhabitants were primarily weavers and farmers until the late 1950s, when rice fields were filled in and houses and apartment buildings were built at a rapid pace. The incomes in Warabi, especially in the neighborhood in which I lived, were lower than those in Tokyo; the average income for a family of four or five was between five and six million yen. Almost everyone I knew had completed high school, but many adults had not gone to college.

I begin with some concrete examples that will structure the analytical themes of the chapters that follow.

1. Mrs. Ueda is a housewife in her midfifties. She and her husband, a company employee, live in an upper-middle-class neighborhood of Tokyo. They have two children. She and her family are part of the small minority of Japanese who are Protestant Christians. In the two years before I met Mrs. Ueda, her son and daughter each married, and her mother-in-law passed away. She agreed to teach me about the gift exchanges connected to these life cycle events. She spoke animatedly and at length about various aspects of her children's weddings, and so it is the marriages on which I will concentrate. I attended two other weddings during the time I was in Tokyo, watched videos of several more, and interviewed many people about their wedding experiences. Gift exchanges associated with the two weddings that Mrs. Ueda described did not differ markedly from those of people who were not Christian (giving at weddings and funerals seemed to differ more starkly along geo-

graphical than religious lines), and her command of the details of various kinds of gift-giving and her patient explanations were invaluable.

Before the marriages of each of Mrs. Ueda's children, about twenty relatives and close friends came on various auspicious days to offer their congratulations and elaborately decorated envelopes of cash. Etiquette dictates that these gifts should be brought to the home of the bride or groom on an auspicious day, calculated in accordance with the lunar calendar, even though most people now simply bring the envelopes with them to the wedding. The guests who presented their gifts before the wedding were served salted cherry blossom tea, and they received small gifts: dry sugared sweets in the shape of cranes, turtles, pine branches, and chrysanthemums; and *kaishi*, paper folded in such a way that the opposite ends rest inside each other.

Whether the wedding guests belonged to the minority who went to the bride's or groom's house to offer their gifts before the day of marriage, or the majority who brought their gifts with them to the wedding reception, all people invited to the wedding (and even some who were not) gave gifts. At the entryway to the reception hall were two tables, one for receiving envelopes from people related to the bride and one for envelopes from people related to the groom. Some people approaching these tables would carefully unwrap the envelopes they had carried in *furoshiki*, cloths for covering and wrapping. Others would simply remove the envelopes from suit pockets or purses. Bowing with both hands outstretched, the givers handed their envelopes to the table attendants, who received the envelopes in the same way. The monetary amounts of these gifts were technically supposed to be odd numbers of 10,000 (*man*) yen units: one man yen (10,000 yen), three man yen (30,000 yen), five man yen (50,000 yen), or seven man yen (70,000 yen). Even gifts of cash that were technically even—such as 10,000 yen or 100,000 yen—were seen as odd numbered units of one. The bills were crisp and new, placed face up in the envelopes. The *mizuhiki* (dyed paper cords used to tie the envelopes) came in three strands, five strands, seven strands, and eleven strands, although five strands was the most common thickness. The mizuhiki were tied with the *musubikiri* knot, which cannot be undone (the literal meaning of musubikiri is "to tie completely"). When passing their envelopes to the attendants, the givers turned the envelopes so that, from the attendants' point of view, the ends of the mizuhiki pointed up.

Mrs. Ueda described those gifts brought by wedding guests to her daughter's wedding as follows: There were three gifts of 100,000 yen. These came from Mrs. Ueda's parents, Mrs. Ueda's elder brother, and Mr. Ueda's elder brother. If Mr. Ueda's parents had been alive, Mrs. Ueda said, they also would have given 100,000 yen. There were two gifts of 50,000 yen. These came from Mrs. Ueda's younger brother and Mr. Ueda's younger brother. There were three gifts of 30,000 yen, which came from the two daughters of Mr. Ueda's elder brother. There were gifts of 20,000 yen from Mr. Ueda's mother's younger sister and the eldest son of Mrs. Ueda's eldest brother. There were also half a dozen gifts of 20,000 yen each from Mrs. Ueda's daughter's friends. There were many other gifts given by guests at the wedding, but Mrs. Ueda never saw the records of those received by the groom's family; she had no interest in discussing those given by business associates of her husband.

Mrs. Ueda described exactly the same gifts given from the same people at her son's wedding, with four exceptions: Mr. Ueda's eldest sister and eldest brother's son gave 30,000 yen at the son's wedding, 10,000 yen more than they gave at the daughter's wedding. Mrs. Ueda's younger brother gave 100,000 yen at the son's wedding, twice what he had given for the daughter's wedding. Finally, there is the matter of the gift from the go-between. A marriage is made possible through the go-betweens, or *nakōdo*. The nakōdo is a married couple. Their names appear on the wedding invitation. At the reception, they sit on either side of the newly married couple at a long table facing the guests, whereas the parents of the bride and groom sit in the very back of the wedding hall. In the past, go-betweens may have played a role in arranging the marriage, although that is less often the case in present-day Japan.

Usually, the male nakōdo will be in a position to help the groom in his future career. From the time her son entered the company, Mrs. Ueda had sent gifts to the male nakōdo, the vice president, who had been instrumental in her son's initial employment at the company, both at *seibo*, the winter gift-giving season, and *chūgen*, the summer gift-giving season. Before the wedding of Mrs. Ueda's son, the nakōdo gave the couple 100,000 yen as a wedding present. The go-between at Mrs. Ueda's daughter's wedding was the groom's boss. Although she spoke much about the nakōdo of her son, Mrs. Ueda did not remember the gift exchange with her daughter's nakōdo.

People who gave gifts even though they were not invited to the weddings were mostly neighbors. These gifts ranged from 10,000 yen to 30,000 yen. There was one such gift with an especially long and complicated history. These neighbors, who owned a local supermarket, gave 20,000 yen at the marriage of the Uedas' daughter and 30,000 yen at the marriage of their son. Several years earlier, the son of the supermarket family had married. Mrs. Ueda was not invited to the wedding, but because she was a close friend of the family, she had brought over a gift of 30,000 yen before the wedding. After the marriage the newly married couple came many times to Mrs. Ueda's apartment, but they never found her at home. Finally, the son came alone, and catching Mrs. Ueda at home, he thanked her many times for her kindness, then handed over a bag. After he had left, Mrs. Ueda looked into the bag and saw that it contained gift certificates worth 30,000 yen, and an assortment of fancy plates. She described her shocked reaction in these terms: "I thought to myself, exactly the same amount of money that I gave to them came back to me, plus a set of plates! What meaning, then, did it have for me to even try to give a gift in the first place?" Mrs. Ueda found the fact that the money was returned as gift certificates, a form so close to the original cash, particularly disconcerting.

About a year after the wedding, the son of the supermarket owner got divorced and married another woman. Mrs. Ueda debated whether or not to give another gift. She did not really want to, as the money would probably just come straight back to her. But then she discovered that the couple would be moving into her apartment building, on the floor below the Ueda household. In this case, she decided, she did need to give a gift. She brought 20,000 yen to the parents. While the son was on his honeymoon with his new wife, his father visited with a bag containing 20,000 yen in gift certificates and a sesame seed grinder worth about 3,000 yen.

The 30,000 yen given to the Uedas' son and the 20,000 yen given to their daughter exactly mirrored the 30,000 yen given to the supermarket owner's son on his first marriage and the 20,000 yen given on his second marriage. The 10,000 difference in gifts between a first marriage and a second marriage was not surprising; nor was it unusual that the marriage of a daughter would elicit smaller monetary gifts than the marriage of a son, Mrs. Ueda said.

The Uedas sent return gifts to the homes of people who gave money but did not attend the festivities. These return gifts were almost always worth half the value of the original gifts. For the son's wedding, the Ueda family gave sets of either three or five forks, and for daughter's wedding, vases and sets of five place mats.

Gifts and hospitality extended to the wedding guests were as follows: The cost of the meal, Mrs. Ueda explained, was 20,000 yen. Each guest received a bag containing food as well as more expensive keepsakes. The kinds of gifts selected were different for the son's wedding and for the daughter's wedding, because the son's wedding was in Tokyo, and the daughter's wedding was in Niigata, and gift-giving customs in the two places are not the same. However, the cost of these gifts was 7,000 yen, both at the daughter's wedding and at the son's. In addition to the *hikidemono*, or bags of gifts given to the departing wedding guests, guests who had come from far away were given envelopes of money to cover the cost of transportation to the wedding: *kurumadai*. Friends of the bride and groom gave about 20,000 yen each. Many friends came from Osaka (the Ueda family had lived in Osaka when the children were growing up). In the case of the son's wedding, which was in Tokyo, these guests received 20,000 yen from the Ueda family to cover transportation costs. In the case of the daughter's wedding in Niigata, they each received 30,000 yen, because the trip from

Osaka to Niigata is much more expensive. Givers at the lowest end
of the scale ended up receiving more than their original gift. (At one
Osaka wedding I attended, many young people came from Tokyo,
and I observed the same pattern. Young guests gave 20,000 yen and
received 20,000 yen in the form of kurumadai. The meal they
enjoyed at the wedding cost about 15,000 yen, and the gifts they
took home were worth 10,000 yen. The hosts paid 45,000 yen for
each guest and received 20,000 yen in return.)

Kurumadai was offered to all guests who traveled a great distance. Some close family members (Mrs. Ueda's two elder brothers
and their families and Mr. Ueda's elder and younger brother and
their families) made it clear before the wedding that they did not
wish to receive kurumadai. There were also two instances at Mrs.
Ueda's daughter's wedding where kurumadai was returned. Mrs.
Ueda was full of praise for the manner in which one of the guests
returned the kurumadai; she did not care for the method used by
the other guest. In the latter case, a seventy-year-old woman who
had been the high school teacher of Mrs. Ueda's daughter sent Mrs.
Ueda a wallet, worth about 10,000 yen (half the amount of money
she had been given by the Ueda family for kurumadai). Accom-
panying the wallet was a letter saying that she could not accept so
much reimbursement for transportation, as she had gotten a senior
citizen discount on her train ticket. In the former case, an eighty-
year-old man who was an old friend of the family returned the unopened envelope containing the money with a letter saying that he
did not want it, as he had come as a representative of the dead
grandparents of the bride. As will be explored in the conclusion,
Mrs. Ueda spoke at some length about the reasons for her favor-
able assessment of the man's action and her unfavorable assessment
of the woman's.

All of the wedding guests returned home with bags of gifts, and
many received reimbursement for transportation costs. The one
return gift that was different from all the others, however, was the
one made to the go-between. Mrs. Ueda did not remember the
details of the return gift she had made to the go-between at her
daughter's wedding, but she clearly recalled that she had returned

her son's go-between's gift threefold. Several weeks after the wedding, the bride and groom gave Gucci plates they had purchased on their honeymoon in Hawaii, and the parents of the bride and groom 300,000 yen, to the nakōdo. Mrs. Ueda stressed that this money was not made with the direct intent of helping her son get ahead in his company; rather, it was to show their gratitude to a busy man of high social standing who had kindly done them the favor of associating with them for this private matter of their son's wedding. In addition, she was sure that in the future her son would become indebted to him at the company; all they wanted was for their son to be promoted regularly and normally. At this point her voice wavered a little. Mrs. Ueda said hesitantly that she was not sure how to express herself; it was probably the case, she said, that embedded in their gift to the nakōdo was a request that he take care of their son.

Gifts to the nakōdo are usually sent for at least three years after the wedding, at both the summer and winter gift-giving seasons. Sometimes only the couple sends gifts, and sometimes the couple and both sets of parents send gifts. After three years, it is customary for the nakōdo to write a note saying: "Please don't trouble to send gifts any longer"; sometimes the gifts will stop, and sometimes they continue indefinitely.

For the first gift-giving season after her son's wedding, Mrs. Ueda sent an Alaskan king crab worth 10,000 yen to the nakōdo (Figure 1.1). She has recently been sending slightly less expensive gifts, around 7,000 to 8,000 yen. However, she is sending gifts only until her son and his wife return from Cairo, where his company has transferred them temporarily. She expects her daughter-in-law to take over the responsibility of giving gifts to the nakōdo when they return to Japan.

From this sketchy description of only a small portion of the exchanges that occurred during the weddings of the son and daughter of the Ueda family, several points should be marked for further investigation. Why are gifts supposed to be given only on certain days, in odd numbers of new bills, which are inserted face up into envelopes that are bound with cords whose odd number of

FIG. 1.1. Alaskan king crab at department store year-end gift display. Photograph by author.

strands are tied in special knots? What is the meaning of the cherry blossom tea, various forms of dried sweets, and paper? How do givers determine the cash amount they will present to the families of the couple getting married? How are the amount and form of the return gifts decided? Why did Mrs. Ueda react negatively when her gift of cash was returned in a different form, in the instance when the high school teacher made a return gift of a wallet? Why was a partial return by changing the form of the initial gift, the standard pattern for making return gifts, considered in this instance to be petty and calculating? Mrs. Ueda was shocked when her wedding gift of cash to the neighboring family was returned in a form almost equivalent to cash—that is, gift certificates. But she was impressed by the old man who returned unopened the envelope of money; he returned cash for cash and was the object of Mrs. Ueda's unending praise. Why? What are the different ways in which gifts of money are viewed? What are the different views of the calculations that people must make when they give gifts? When is it good to calculate carefully, and when is it damaging to a relationship? What is the difference between a gift and a bribe (for example, in the case of presents to a son's boss)?

2. Mr. Hoshino is a fuel dealer. He lives in Warabi. The houses in Warabi are heated with small kerosene stoves, and Mr. Hoshino's job is to deliver fuel. He is a tall man with a gentle smile who dresses in worn, oily clothes. He, his wife, his father, and his youngest daughter (who is twenty) live on the Nakasendō, one of the five important highways the Tokugawa shogunate (1600–1868) controlled. The Nakasendō started at Nihonbashi, a bridge in Edo (now Tokyo) where the five main roads administered by the shogunate came together, and ended in Kyoto. Warabi was one of the sixty-seven way stations on the 500-kilometer-long route. Mr. Hoshino's family has lived on this same spot on the Nakasendō for generations, as have most of the other families who have homes on the Nakasendō. The relationships between these families go back for hundreds of years.

Mr. Hoshino and his family decided to rebuild their home, and I was privileged to be a witness to two of the ceremonies that accompanied that event. Mr. Hoshino's father repeatedly told me how the building of a house happens once in a lifetime, and even then, only if a person is very fortunate. Their old and rickety house was demolished. When the debris had been carted away, a ceremony called *jichinsai* was held in order to purify the site and to pacify the spirits of the earth, spirits who might be angered by the digging and the construction. The date for this ceremony was carefully selected by Mr. Hoshino's father, who knows a great deal about divination, or *eki*. He also chose the date for the *tatemae* (also called *muneageshiki* or *jōtōshiki*), the celebration of the completion of the framework for the house.

A Shintō priest officiated at jichinsai, with the members of the crew who demolished the old house and representatives of the con-

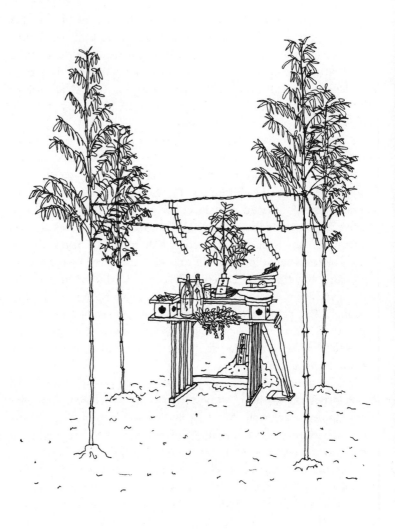

FIG. 1.2. *Jichinsai* altar. Drawing by Chika Sato MacDonald.

FIG. 1.3. Shintō priest officiates at *jichinsai*. Photograph by author.

struction crew who would build the new one, Mr. Hoshino's family, and myself attending. A Shintō altar was constructed in the middle of the site (Figure 1.2). The priest performed *harae*, Shintō purification rites, and made offerings of rice, sake, fish, and vegetables (Figure 1.3).

Key members of the construction crew and Mr. Hoshino's family took turns digging in the ground with a special shovel; sake and rice were sprinkled on the four corners of the lot, and then we all drank sake together. Mr. Hoshino's father gave envelopes of money to the head of the demolition crew and the head and the second-in-command of the construction crew. Each envelope contained 10,000 yen. The priest took the envelope that was placed on the altar; it contained 30,000 yen.

Tatemae was celebrated several weeks later, with about sixty people attending. Mr. Hoshino's father carefully prepared the altar

FIG. 1.4. *Tatemae* purification rites and offerings. Drawing by Chika Sato MacDonald.

inside the frame of the house. For some weeks, Mr. Hoshino's neighbors had been asking when the tatemae would be held; he told them, and they remembered, bearing gifts of sake, whiskey, beer, and sometimes money when they arrived for the ceremony. Relatives, friends, neighbors, business associates, members of the

FIG. 1.5. Table of *tatemae* offerings. Drawing by Chika Sato
MacDonald.

construction crew, electricians, and an interior decorator all were
present. Mr. Hoshino's father, resplendent in beautiful green robes,
performed the purification rites and made the offerings of rice; sake
(he carefully laid out rows of small cups on a tray so that everyone
afterward could partake); various delicacies from the ocean, such
as seaweed, squid, and fish (wrapped in white paper labeled with
the character for "up, above," as they were being offered up to the
gods); and vegetables (Figures 1.4 and 1.5). A branch decorated
with red and white paper hung from the ridge beam.

   Part of the reason for rebuilding the house was to accommodate
three or four generations. Mr. Hoshino and his son, who will, when
he eventually marries, move into the new house with his wife, went
to the north, south, east, and west corners of the lot and sprinkled
rice and sake on the ground. Most of the guests were men. They
made small talk while the Shintō rites were conducted, bowed and

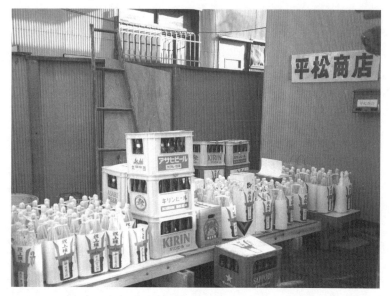

FIG. 1.6. Gifts of alcohol brought by *tatemae* guests. Photograph by author.

clapped, and then drank together of the sake, which had first been offered to the gods. The carpenters stood up after the Shintō ceremony and sang an ancient song that no one understood because it was not in modern Japanese. There were a few female guests, but most of the women were there to work; female friends and relatives prepared and served a banquet, which they then spread on boards laid inside the frame of the house. The Hoshino family did not sit down to eat at all. Mrs. Hoshino and her daughters refilled the guests' cups, and Mr. Hoshino and his father recorded the mounds of gifts that guests deposited in front of the construction site. There were many cases of beer and bottles of sake, decorated with red and white paper and tied together with string (Figure 1.6).

Partway through the Shintō ritual, the fishmonger, a close friend of Mr. Hoshino's, pulled up in his van, which was stuffed with white bundles. Several of us helped him unload these return gifts. Each was wrapped in a square white plastic sheet decorated in red with drawings of cranes, turtles, bamboo plants, pine branches, plum blossoms, and the character *kotobuki* ("congratulations"). Inside was a small box wrapped in red and white paper and tied with a red and white cord. The box was filled with *sekihan*, a special dish made from white glutinous rice and red beans. There was also a tray, wrapped in clear plastic emblazoned with the gold character kotobuki, which contained a variety of canned goods, including tuna, salmon, and asparagus, and a red plastic sea bream (*tai*) filled with white sugar (Figure 1.7). This tray was topped with a thin wooden lid, which was wrapped in red and white paper and decorated with the character kotobuki and drawings of a pair of cranes and a pine tree. Each guest, upon departure from the party, received one of these white packages and a plastic bag of mandarin oranges.

The Hoshino family also gave the construction crew *goshūgi*, which means both gratuity and congratulatory gift. The master carpenter and his second-in-command were given 30,000 yen each. The other fourteen workers were each given 10,000 yen. Each of

FIG. 1.7. Contents of *tatemae* return gifts; sugar is contained inside plastic red fish (*tai*). Photograph by author.

these men had brought either two or three bottles of sake (except for two who brought cases of beer) worth between 3,000 and 6,000 yen for the Hoshino family.

There were forty-six gifts of two bottles of sake, thirteen gifts of three bottles of sake, eleven gifts of one case of beer, two gifts of 5,000 yen, twelve gifts of 10,000 yen, two gifts of 20,000 yen, and one gift of 30,000 yen. Gifts of cash were in the form of new, crisp bank notes placed face up in red and white envelopes. People who gave two bottles of sake included construction workers, neighboring families, businesses, shopkeepers, the parents of Mr. Hoshino's eldest daughter's husband, as well as the campaign headquarters for the city council election of one of Mr. Hoshino's elementary school classmates. Two of these two-bottle gifts were unusual. The family living behind the Hoshinos' house gave 30,000 yen in addition to the two bottles of sake, and the Tokuguchi family living down the street gave two bottles of a very special kind of sake. Most sake comes in one-liter bottles worth between 1,500 and 2,000 yen. This unique sake comes in two-liter bottles worth 5,000 yen each, and the Chinese characters of its brand name can be read, by altering the pronunciation, as "May your household flourish." People who gave three bottles of sake included senior construction workers, neighboring families, businesses, shopkeepers, a cousin of Mr. Hoshino, and Mrs. Hoshino's parents. Mrs. Hoshino's parents live in Niigata, and in Warabi three bottles of the famous Niigata sake they sent would be worth 10,000 yen. Cases of beer were worth 6,000 yen, and they came from such donors as the concrete company from which concrete for the foundation would be purchased, the rice cracker shop across the street from Mr. Hoshino's house, Mr. Hoshino's friend from elementary school (beer was her personal gift; the sake was the gift from her campaign), and Mr. Hoshino's mother's elder brother, who gave two cases. One of the gifts of 5,000 yen was from me, and the other was from a neighbor who did not attend the tatemae. The gifts of 10,000 yen were from such people as Mr. Hoshino's younger brother and sister, and from Mr. Hoshino's friends, including Mr. Shūji Ishiyama, the rice dealer; Mr. Tomoyasu Ishiyama, the rice cracker maker (the 6,000 yen case of beer was the gift from his shop, and the 10,000 yen gift was his personal present); and the fishmonger. The gifts of 20,000 yen came from Mr. Hoshino's father's younger sister's son and the head priest of the local Shintō shrine.

Many questions emerge from this example of Mr. Hoshino's tatemae. How may gifts reflect, reinforce, or change the relationship between two families or between two individuals? How is giving related to social status? How is it related to expressions of gratitude or obligation, to feelings of closeness between families or individuals? When can giving too little or giving too much be damaging to a relationship? When Mr. Hoshino explained to me that his neighbors had been asking when the tatemae would be held, the literal translation of his words was: "They did me the favor of worrying when we would have tatemae (*itsu tatemae o yaru ka shinpai shite kureta*)." How is worrying, being careful to bring the right gift at the right time, and the like encouraged? Why is it encouraged? In explaining who gave what, why did Mr. Hoshino lay such emphasis on the fact that it was a family, or *ie*, that made the gift, rather than an individual person? What are the symbolic meanings of the gifts offered to the gods and given to the guests upon their departure? Why do people partake in the offerings to the gods? How is giving between people connected with giving between people and gods?

When I asked Mr. Hoshino why some neighbors brought two bottles of sake and other neighbors brought three, he answered in terms of Japanese people as a national entity being considerate of others and always fearing they are giving too little; it was very hard for me to learn why one person gave three bottles and another gave two. Customs of gift-giving were often explained to me as something purely Japanese; if I spoke of the origins in other parts of Asia of these traditions, my words were sometimes not very well received. In what ways is the giving of gifts connected with ideas about national identity? What is the meaning of the wrapping of gifts, of the writing on the wrapping paper, and on the envelopes, and, in the case of money, whether the bank notes are new or old, face down or face up? What are the meanings of the red and white colors, and the drawings of certain plants and animals? Why are certain kinds of objects appropriate offerings? Why are some days auspicious and others not?

3. Mr. Ishiyama Shūji is short, slight, about fifty years of age; he is generous, warm with children, has an expressive face and a quick wit. His manner is impatient, almost direct. He is a rice dealer, although he has converted his shop from one that sells only rice to a convenience store that sells other items as well. Ishiyama Shūji knows everyone in Warabi and everything that goes on there, and he works tirelessly at many different projects. His wife, mother, son (age twenty-five, a newspaper company employee), and daughter (age twenty, a restaurant worker) all live with him just above the family store.

In 1991, Ishiyama Shūji's father died. Hundreds of mourners brought *kōden* (literally, "incense money," or in the Kantō area, specially decorated white-and-black or white-and-purple envelopes of cash) to the funeral; as is the custom in Warabi, they were given the *kōdengaeshi* (return of kōden) as they left the funeral. Regardless of the kōden given, the kōdengaeshi were the same; this pattern is very different from the way in which return gifts from funerals in Tokyo are calculated, according to the amount of the mourner's kōden. Mr. Ishiyama, who is the family's eldest son, allowed me to copy the twelve notebooks containing the records of the kōden and then patiently detailed the circumstances of many of these gifts.

Mr. Ishiyama's father's wake and funeral were both held in a low building next to the old neighborhood temple. A local funeral company made the necessary preparations. Mr. Ishiyama arranged for me to interview workers in this funeral company, and to attend a funeral in the same building where his father's funeral was held. These experiences, together with Mr. Ishiyama's written records and his and his mother's recollections, allowed me to reconstruct what his father's funeral had been like.

Arrangements for the wake and funeral were as follows: The wake took place on the evening of the day that Mr. Ishiyama's father died. In the same way that the days for weddings and the days for bringing gifts to the bride or groom's home before the wedding are carefully selected, the funeral was held on the day that was as close to the death as possible while still being appropriate for funerals. Some days, such as *tomobiki* (the character for "friend" and the character for "pull"), are lucky for weddings, as friends might also be pulled along the road of matrimony, but unlucky for funerals, for fear of inviting another death. Most people went either to the wake or to the funeral, although those who were closest to Mr. Ishiyama's father attended both.

The majority of mourners walked past a row of white funeral wreaths standing outside, handed their kōden to people who sat at long white tables, passed into the building with the flower-surrounded coffin, stayed for the long Buddhist service at which they made offerings of incense, picked up their return gifts, and left. The attendants who had volunteered to collect the incense money were relatives and friends of Mr. Ishiyama's. The mourners bowed while presenting their envelopes, which were tied by black cords with musubikiri (the same knot used for weddings). In some cases, black lines representing cords and knots were printed onto the envelopes. When passing their envelopes to the attendants, the givers turned the envelopes so that from the attendants' point of view, the ends of the cords pointed up. The people at the long white tables gave each mourner a small numbered card. This card was to be used later for picking up kōdengaeshi. Toward the middle of the service, the priest called for offerings of incense to Mr. Ishiyama's father. Narrow tables containing incense stood before the coffin. First the relatives closest to Mr. Ishiyama's father offered incense in order of the depth of their relationship to the dead man, with the person with the closest bond making the first offering. (Deciding the order in which these offerings are made sometimes results in family quarrels, the funeral company employees told me.) Then came the offerings by the other mourners. They bowed to the family of Mr. Ishiyama's father. The family of Mr. Ishiyama's father returned the bows. They bowed to the coffin. Then they took from a shallow dish pebblelike incense between thumb and two forefingers, brought the incense toward their foreheads, and finally let it fall back into the dish, repeating the procedure three times. They bowed to the coffin, and again to the family. The family bowed in return. Some mourners left after offering incense, although the service was not technically over.

At the conclusion of the service, the mourners lined up to exchange their numbered cards for bags of gifts. These bags were somber colors, such as white, black, and purple. Each bag contained a small bottle of sake worth about 300 yen, a package of salt, and a blue, purple, or green futon cover. Mr. Ishiyama had ordered these gifts from shops in Warabi whose relationships with the Ishiyama family were centuries old. The futon covers cost 4,000 yen each, and the bottles of sake cost 300 yen each. Mr. Ishiyama laughed as he told me that, unlike Warabi, where return of kōden takes place immediately, people in Tokyo give all the mourners a token gift of sugar, salt, sake, and maybe a telephone card, and then they send return gifts equivalent to half the value of the original gift via department store forty-nine days after the death. In Warabi, he emphasized, regardless of the size of the original kōden, the return gift is the same. "We don't discriminate against poor people," he stated.

Flowers were an important part of the funeral-related gift-giving. In contrast to the gifts of money, no return gifts were made for flowers. Many of the people who gave flowers also gave kōden. There were two types of flowers given: "outside" flowers and "inside" flowers. The white wreaths of artificial flowers that stood outside the building where the wake and funeral were held were one meter in diameter and rested on stands two meters off the ground. White ribbons attached to the wreaths contained the names of the donors, who included neighborhood and citizens' associations, as well as shops and companies with business relations with the Ishiyama family. These fifty-three wreaths cost 10,000 yen each.

The wreaths of flowers inside the building came in pairs, with the giver's name printed on a wooden slat placed in the center of each wreath. Each of these thirty pairs cost 30,000 yen. They surrounded the coffin and were from people who were personally *inside from family.*

close to Mr. Ishiyama's father. Unlike the artificial outside flowers, the inside flowers were genuine chrysanthemums, mostly white with a few splashes of yellow and purple. The inside flowers from relatives were given by the parents of the wives of Mr. Ishiyama's father's three sons, the brothers of the wives of the sons, Mr. Ishiyama's father's siblings, or, if the siblings were also deceased, the spouses or children of Mr. Ishiyama's father's siblings. Inside flowers were also gifts from less close relations, such as Mr. Ishiyama's distant cousin (his father's father's father's brother's child's child), who sent one pair of wreaths, and that person's brother's wife, who sent another, as well as the three children of Mr. Ishiyama's distant cousin, who together sent a pair of wreaths. Donors of inside flowers who were not relatives included two neighbors, members of Mr. Ishiyama's high school band, the president of the Warabi Lion's Club, the president of Warabi's Sister City Club, two of Mr. Ishiyama's friends from the German town of Linden, with which Warabi has a sister city relationship, the president of a large rice company, the owner of a local sake shop, and the owner of a local flower shop.

There were four gifts of 2,000 yen, twenty-two gifts of 3,000 yen, 421 gifts of 5,000 yen, 310 gifts of 10,000 yen, twenty-seven gifts of 20,000 yen, eighteen gifts of 30,000 yen, three gifts of 50,000 yen, and one gift of 200,000 yen. All were old, slightly crumpled bank notes placed face down in black and white or back and purple envelopes. Here are some examples of the kinds of people who made these gifts: Gifts of 2,000 and 3,000 yen came from people in the neighborhood who had little social interaction with others, elderly people, six of Mr. Ishiyama's friends from city hall (all six of whom refused return gifts), Mr. Ishiyama's daughter's friend, and Mr. Ishiyama's mother's singing class from the local community center. Gifts of 5,000 yen came from other acquaintances of the Ishiyama family. Some of the friends of Mr. Ishiyama's mother, wife, and brothers' wives also gave gifts of 5,000 yen. Mr. Ishiyama's friends, and friends of his father, mother, wife, brothers, and brothers' wives gave gifts of 10,000 yen, as did business associates and some of the children of his cousins. Gifts of 20,000 yen

gifts go to specific people depending on what they did.

came from cousins, the children of Mr. Ishiyama's distant cousin, a vegetable store owner, a close friend of Mr. Ishiyama's father, a priest from the nearby temple, a man who had been a fellow patient when Mr. Ishiyama's father was in the hospital, a neighbor, families living on the Nakasendō, and the son of the deceased accountant who kept the books for Mr. Ishiyama's rice store. Gifts of 30,000 yen came from Mr. Ishiyama's wife's younger brother and his brothers' wives' brothers, the three children of Mr. Ishiyama's mother's elder sister, the parents of Mr. Ishiyama's close friend, and the wife of the deceased accountant (this gift was not kōden, but rather was in lieu of flowers, and was marked "flower money"). Gifts of 50,000 yen came from Mr. Ishiyama's mother's elder sister, Mr. Ishiyama's wife's elder brother, and the wife of the late accountant. The gift of 200,000 yen came from Mr. Tomoyasu Ishiyama, the local rice cracker maker and Mr. Ishiyama's cousin's son.

After the funeral, the body of Mr. Ishiyama's father was taken to a crematorium. One of the workers from the funeral company took me on a tour of that place. There were three rooms. The ovens in each of the rooms were the same on the inside, but the price for cremation differed according to room. In the least expensive room, there were twelve ovens with bronze doors; in the next most expensive room, there were six ovens with silver doors, and in the most expensive room there were two ovens with gold doors. Close friends and family members waited while the body was cremated, and then, using long wooden chopsticks, carefully picked up the bones from the ashes and placed them in an urn. The urn was kept on the Buddhist altar in Mr. Ishiyama's home.

Prayers and offerings to Mr. Ishiyama's father's spirit continued in the weeks, months, and years after his death, and still continue today. One week after the death of Mr. Ishiyama's father, a Buddhist priest came to offer prayers for his spirit. Every seven days, the family gathered to make offerings. The priest officiated at these ceremonies on the twenty-first and thirty-fifth days after Mr. Ishiyama's father's death, and performed a special service for relatives and close friends on the forty-ninth day, at which point his

bones were placed in a grave. Memorial services were held on the
third, fifth, seventh, and thirteenth anniversary of his death. Mr.
Ishiyama's mother makes daily offerings of rice and water to Mr.
Ishiyama's father's spirit, as well as to the spirits of his parents and
ancestors.

These examples of gifts given on the occasion of Mr. Ishiyama's
father's funeral bring up many interesting themes that later chapters will explore in depth. How do people decide what to give?
How do they calculate the appropriate amount of money for
kōden? Why do they place the bank notes face down? When do
they give funeral wreaths to be placed outside and when inside, and
when do they give no funeral wreaths at all? How do they decide
whether to accept a return gift? Why are certain objects, such as
those made from cloth, selected as return gifts for money received
at funerals? What cycles govern the selection of the day on which
to hold the funeral, and what cycles determine when offerings must
be made to the dead? What is the significance of multiples of the
number seven? How and why are the customs of returning kōden
different in Warabi and in neighboring Tokyo? Are there other
ways in which customs of giving vary with region? A number of
Warabi residents mentioned to me that in the past, people gave
much less: a five-kilogram sack of sugar or rice was the standard
kōden. They said that recently, giving has become more showy
(*hade ni natte shimatta*). How have practices of giving changed
over time, and why?

4. Mr. Tanabe is a retired stockbroker, and Mrs. Tanabe is a
retired housewife. They are in their early seventies and live in a
modest house in an old and beautiful part of Tokyo. Inside their
home it is fairly dark, because the houses in their neighborhood are
built so close together. I know the Tanabes' daughter Reiko, who is
a surgeon. I met her while she was working as a researcher at the
University of Chicago.

Reiko gave me her parents' address and phone number and told
me to call on them when I arrived in Tokyo. I knew I would need
to bring a gift, and on my first visit, when I handed over a carefully wrapped present—a box of cards from the Art Institute of

Chicago—Mr. Tanabe received it politely and set it on the table in front of him. After I had returned to my apartment, the telephone rang, and Mr. Tanabe thanked me for the gift; he explained that it would have been childlike (*kodomo mitai*) to open it in my presence. At the time of my visit he would have thanked me even more, he said, if he had known it was a set of cards: he had been afraid that it would be chocolate (beef jerky, cowboy hats, and chocolate are considered by some to be the most appropriate gifts from the United States), and neither he nor Mrs. Tanabe could eat chocolate. The second time I visited the Tanabes, again my gift was not opened until after I had left. But the third time, Mr. Tanabe hurried upstairs, offered it to the photographs of their dead parents, hastened back downstairs, and opened the gift. Because Mr. Tanabe is not an eldest son, there is no Buddhist altar containing ancestral tablets in their home, but there are photographs of their parents on the second floor. I was formally introduced to Mr. Tanabe's dead parents a few weeks later, when we went to the Zen Buddhist temple where they are buried. Mr. Tanabe made offerings of flowers and incense, and then poured water over the stone grave marker. "This is Kathy, Reiko's friend," he said. He gave me water to pour, too, and nudged me to respond. Confused, I bowed and mumbled, "Nice to meet you."

Mr. and Mrs. Tanabe taught me a great deal about gift-giving, because Mr. Tanabe dislikes the custom very much. Although I brought small gifts the first few times I visited them, I stopped after they repeated many times that my offering of gifts was not necessary. I asked them to participate in my research by recording gifts given and received, and Mrs. Tanabe was interested. Mr. Tanabe, however, said, "I'll do it if you really think it's important, but I'd much rather not." Mr. Tanabe was one of many people who felt oppressed by these customs of gift-giving. When Mr. Tanabe told me that he would prefer not to participate in my survey, I was interested to hear his reasons. He answered with a story.

Before he retired, Mr. Tanabe had been a stockbroker. The owner (*mama-san*) of a bar he occasionally patronized after work asked him to help her with her investments. He invested some of her money for her. She sent him gifts in summer and winter, and once, in a winter gift-giving season, she made him a present of live shrimp—a real delicacy. At that time, the stocks he was investing for her were not doing very well. When the delivery man came with the gift, Mr. Tanabe refused it and asked him to return it to the sender. A day later the package was redelivered to Mr. Tanabe; it had not been possible to return it to the sender. Now all the shrimp were dead.

At this point, Mrs. Tanabe interrupted his story: "You stubborn old guy! She sent the gift because she was grateful to you; after all, you are a customer of her shop, and even though the stocks weren't doing so well, you still took a lot of time with them! The normal thing to do would have been to accept the gift; what you tried to do in sending the gift back was very rude!" Mr. Tanabe defended himself, saying that there had been no reason to accept the gift. I asked why, and he answered sharply, "Because the stocks were doing badly!"

Mr. Tanabe elaborated on his discomfort with gift-giving. In his company, the wives of all his colleagues had gone to select gifts during the summer and the winter, when their husbands' bonuses were given out, to send to various superiors in the company. "We never sent gifts," said Mr. Tanabe. "Not once. The wives of the other employees would use over half of the winter and summer bonuses for sending gifts. These wives would go over to the boss's house at New Year's to help the boss's wife with the cooking and serving. Even with questions like the education of the boss's children, they would scurry around and find out information about the best cram schools and make suggestions. . . . [T]hese kinds of gifts and favors were all given with a certain objective in mind: advancement at the company. How odious [iya] and troublesome [mendokusai]! It should be enough to do one's best job at work."

"In the case of the live shrimp, however, wasn't that gift given without calculation?" I asked him. "After all, the stocks were doing badly. The gift was not a reward because the bar owner had made money, but an expression of gratitude even though the market was not doing well. Isn't that a good kind of present?"

"No," Mr. Tanabe answered.

Questions arise from the story of the live shrimp: How do people's attitudes toward the giving and receiving of objects vary? For example, do they vary according to age? Class? Education? Family background? Gender? Place of residence? Occupation? Religion? How do people interpret the meaning behind a gift? Why are some gifts received without any reservations, whereas others are not gladly received? What happens when some gifts contain multiple layers of meaning, or when the meanings are not clear? Do people distinguish between gifts and bribes? What are the words people use to talk about-giving and -receiving, and what are the connotations of those words? How do people divide these words into categories?

5. Mrs. Inoue is a housewife. She is in her late fifties and has raised two daughters, the elder of whom recently gave birth to her first child. Cheerful, funny, interested in everything, Mrs. Inoue is the founder of a study group for housewives in her area. These women concentrate mainly on social and environmental issues, and they publish a monthly newspaper. Mrs. Inoue lives with her husband, who is the president of a family machine tool company, and her younger daughter, who works in a fabric store. They have a large, traditional Japanese house. For our first few sessions, Mrs. Inoue used very polite Japanese, but as the months passed, she gradually switched to a more informal style of conversation, laughing and teasing.

The exchanges outlined so far in this chapter (those related to Mrs. Ueda's children's weddings, Mr. Hoshino's tatemae, Ishiyama Shūji's father's funeral, and Mr. Tanabe's career as a stockbroker) have been confined to certain points in time. Some patterns of giving and receiving, however, emerge only after examining gifts given and received over an extended period. Mrs. Inoue approached the task of recording exchanges and teaching me about them with a great deal of generosity, energy, and organization. When I visited her home to go over her records, she set an entire day aside, and I usually stayed from ten in the morning until ten in the evening. What follows is a compilation of three important categories of gifts that emerged from her faithful records. These three categories are "meaningless" gifts, travel gifts, and seasonal gifts.

Every day, Mrs. Inoue gave and received a large number of gifts that she termed "meaningless"—so many, she said, that it was impossible to keep track of them all. These gifts included freshly dug bamboo shoots, other vegetables, fruit, different kinds of Japanese sweets, tea, an apron, a handbag, a cooking pot, rice crackers, sake, wine, chestnuts, jam, butter, cooking oil, and so on. Mrs. Inoue divided all "gifts of no meaning" into the following categories: *miyage* (gift), *temiyage* (visiting gift), *susowake* (distribution of surplus), and *purezento* ("present" written in *katakana*). It was also used to describe gifts of nonperishable things given not because one was visiting a person's house, not because one had extra of something, but simply because one saw something that one thought another person would like or might need: an apron that Mrs. Inoue's friend gave her fits into that category. Susowake literally means "dividing the edge or bottom of something" (*suso* is the cuff of trousers, the hem of a skirt, or the foot of a mountain; *wake* means "divide"). Saying something is susowake is a way of lessening the feeling of obligation of the receiver. It implies that one has such an overabundance, it is necessary to share. Miyage is the product of a particular local area (the characters are based on meaning rather than pronunciation: the first character signifies "earth, soil"; the second, "to produce, to give birth"). However, miyage connotes "gift" in a much more general sense. Oftentimes, Mrs. Inoue told me that she was uncertain whether to classify gifts as susowake or miyage. An example would be when she would hand guests small gifts on their departure, saying, "This is unusual (*mezurashii*), so please eat it." That kind of gift would be miyage, a word commonly used to describe the gifts given to guests upon their return home. At the same time, it would also be susowake. Temiyage is miyage with *te*, the character for hand; it means miyage carried by hand, and thus a visiting gift offered to the host or hostess.

Ryokōmiyage are gifts brought back from trips to be given to friends and relatives who stayed at home. In the six months be-

tween March and August 1995, Mrs. Inoue received eighteen ryokōmiyage from various people; she recorded two gifts that she herself gave, although the actual number of presents she gave was
probably much higher. She had gone with her husband on a trip to
France, Germany, and Austria, and had returned with pens containing small towers and moving swans from the castle of Neu-
schwanstein, beautiful washcloths woven with many colors of
thread and wrapped in paper from the Mitsukoshi department
store in Munich, and many other souvenirs. However, with the
birth of her daughter's child, she became very busy and was unable
to keep track of the many people to whom she had given presents.
The travel gifts she received were almost all delicacies from various
parts of Japan, such as salmon eggs from Hokkaidō (famous for its
salmon and its dairy products), sake from Niigata (famous for its
delicious rice, and thus also for its sake), and eggplants from Sendai
(Sendai is famous for long eggplants). Prices ranged from 1,000 to
6,000 yen. The 1,000 yen gift was from Mrs. Inoue's tea teacher,
who had brought her some ice cream from Hokkaidō (packed in
dry ice), and the 6,000 yen gift was a variety of sweets and pickles
from Kyoto from a friend to whom Mrs. Inoue had extended hospitality on various occasions. Most of the other gifts ranged in
price from 2,000 to 3,000 yen. Often these gifts were given through
third parties (*kotozuke*).

At least seventeen of the gifts that Mrs. Inoue recorded in the
six months between March and August could be considered seasonal. A small minority were associated with gift-giving practices
imported from Western Europe and North America: Mother's Day
presents of flowers and Father's Day gifts of a compact disc from
the Inoue daughters, small presents of infant formula (for her
grandson), socks (for her daughters) at Christmas, and the purchase of white chocolate and scarves to be given as return gifts on
White Day, March 14, to the women who had given her husband
obligatory Valentine's Day dark chocolates on February 14. Mrs.
Inoue purchased White Day gifts for a total of 15,000 yen, but for
the purposes of record-keeping those White Day gifts were all considered one exchange.

Chūgen (summer or midyear gifts) were the largest category of seasonal gifts. They generally consisted of such items as canned fruit and curry sauce, sent from the investment firm that manages some of the savings of the Inoue household, eggplants from a close friend, watermelon from the farmer from whom Mrs. Inoue buys organic fruits and vegetables, gifts of staples such as coffee, oil, and seaweed from companies that make the parts used by Mr. Inoue's company to make machine tools, and cheese from the parents of her son-in-law. The Inoue family sent summer gifts (specialty items carefully procured in advance from specialty shops in old parts of Tokyo) to the neighborhood doctor, to the landlord, and to the family temple. When Mrs. Inoue's mother-in-law had been alive, she had given gifts at the summer and winter gift-giving seasons to the same doctor, who is now very old but is still practicing medicine, to the same family that owns the land on which their house is built, and to the temple where Mr. Inoue's parents and other family members are buried.

Gifts to ancestral spirits were given at *higan* (the autumnal equinox) and *bon* (a Buddhist observance honoring ancestors, held either in mid-July or mid-August). These gifts often included melons, pears, or some other kind of luxury fruit. Fruits were considered luxury items because of the especially high cost of fruits intended for gift-giving; some melons that Mrs. Inoue gave or received each cost 10,000 yen (see Figure 4.10), and the less expensive ones were usually given in sets of five or six, so that the total cost came to 10,000 yen. Gifts to ancestral spirits often included wine and sweets, following the rule of thumb, Mrs. Inoue explained, that one should offer as a gift something that the deceased had particularly liked. If the offering was to the collective ancestors of a household, a gift that the people living in the house would enjoy was more appropriate. Alternatively, gifts to the ancestors could be flowers (for example, a white lily was offered to the spirit of Mr. Inoue's younger sister, who had just recently passed away). As the years since the death increase, the color of the flowers may become more vivid. One gift of particular interest to me was a telephone card with the photo of Mrs. Inoue's husband's younger sister's *jūdō* teacher. (This younger sister had been divorced; for that reason her ancestral tablet was at the home of her elder brother rather than that of her husband.) One of her friends from jūdō class had brought it to offer to her spirit during higan. I noticed the card on the Buddhist altar and asked Mrs. Inoue what it was; that small telephone card was an example of the kind of "meaningless" gift she usually did not record. Sometimes Mrs. Inoue made offerings of money to the departed spirits, as was the case when she went to pay her respects to the spirit of the only daughter of one of her close friends. This was to be the first bon (*niibon*: literally, "new bon") after the death of her friend's daughter, and thus the first time her friend's daughter's spirit would return home. In these instances in which she visited a family's home and made offerings at the Buddhist altar, Mrs. Inoue received gifts of sweets or sometimes towels upon her departure.

A final example of Mrs. Inoue's seasonal gift-giving is a gift that was made outside the six-month period discussed here, although it is part of an important category of seasonal gifts. On May 5, 1996, or Boys' Day, she made a number of different presents. (Technically, May 5 is "Children's Day"; it is a holiday for both boys and girls. Gifts to girls, however, are given on March 3, which was not turned into a national holiday.) Because it was her new grandson's first Boys' Day, she gave him a wind-sock flag shaped like a carp, which his parents will hang outside their door. She also gave her grandson a warrior doll, and *kashiwamochi* (rice cakes filled with sweet bean paste and wrapped in oak leaves). Mrs. Inoue noted that gifts given on Boys' Day often are wrapped in paper with an iris motif, and the leaves of irises are added to bath water on the evening of May 5.

Examination of even this limited portion of Mrs. Inoue's gift-giving records raises many questions. What are the different cycles of seasonal gift-giving, and how do they relate to one another? Seasons and life cycle events played important roles in the giving that Mrs. Inoue, as well as some of the other people introduced in this section, described. How might cosmic values be transacted through giving? What is the relationship between gifts given at certain times of the year (summer and winter) and at certain points in a person's life (birth, marriage, death)? How are certain kinds of numbers, colors, animals, birds, plants, ways of tying and wrapping gifts, lucky days and unlucky days, seasonal cycles, life cycles, and hierarchical relationships, interconnected? Mrs. Inoue's description of traveling gifts also suggests the underlying presence of a larger cosmic process. There is a hierarchical ranking system that encompasses all wondrous and different things, whether they are the long eggplants from Sendai or the towels purchased at Mitsukoshi department store in Munich. Why is so much energy expended in categorizing and receiving the specialty items of each far-off place? Why is so much attention paid to the ranks of stores, particularly of department stores and specialty shops? What is the history behind these rankings? How are department stores connected with travel and relations to faraway places? Finally, how does the fact that Mrs. Inoue is a middle-aged woman from a well-to-do family influence her attitudes toward gift-giving and the sheer volume of exchanges in which she participates? How does her giving compare with the giving of people of other ages, occupations, family backgrounds, and regions?

The next chapter begins to answer these questions by examining how issues of strength of relationship, gratitude, and hierarchy influence giving and receiving. Chapter 3 describes how giving and receiving are connected with major turning points in the life cycles of human beings, and Chapter 4 investigates their relation to seasonal cycles. Chapter 5 explores how practices of giving and attitudes toward giving differ according to class, gender, location, occupation, and religion. Chapter 6 situates this particular study of gifts in Japan within the larger anthropological literature on gifts and exchange.

2 ⌒ Strength of Relationship, Gratitude, and Hierarchy

Giving is never simply the result of prior conditions. While giving reinforces human relationships, it also changes them. In order to comprehend the many different issues involved in giving and receiving, it is necessary to explain the critical factors that people say they use in deciding what amount of money to give: strength of relationship, gratitude, and hierarchy. First, these will be examined with reference to examples of gifts where only one or two such variables are at work. Then, a more complicated example of a gift that contains all three underlying variables will be explored.

Strength of Relationship

When people explained why they had given a certain amount of money or a particular object, expressions they frequently used were: "Our relationship is *chikai* (close)" or "Our relationship is *tōi* (far)." The words *fukai* (deep) and *asai* (shallow), as well as *koi* (strong, thick) and *usui* (weak, thin) were also mentioned often. The differing temporal and special referents of the related adjectival pairs chikai/tōi (close/far), koi/usui (strong/weak), and fukai/asai (deep/shallow) index subtle differences in kinds of relationship. Chikai is used in describing relationships governed primarily by external circumstances such as living near one another or working at the same place; tōi would indicate that one rarely has the chance to see the other person. Koi/usui is generally used to describe blood relationships. Parent/child relationships are koi; those between third cousins once removed are usui. Fukai/asai connotes depth of feeling. One may have a friend who lives far away and whom one rarely sees, but the relationship is very deep, or koi; an asai relationship would be with a person with whom one has only a superficial friendship. Mr. Hoshino, the fuel dealer who gave the house-building ceremony, spoke about the connection between the monetary amount of gifts and strength of relationships:

> Mr. Hoshino: Giving things is difficult because, in the end, you must look at what degree of interaction two people have with each other. . . . [Y]ou may meet with a person frequently, but you have to think to yourself, is it [this relationship] shallow or deep? Is it that we have an especially good relationship, or is it a relationship that only looks good on the surface, and then when it comes to a time of association [kōsai], things are completely different?
> Rupp: Can you tell the relationship between two people from a gift?
> Mr. Hoshino: Pretty much.
> Rupp: How?
> Mr. Hoshino: For example, at times of celebration, that person doesn't bring anything, or even if he/she does bring something, the amount of money is low. . . . [Or] if a person with whom you truly have a good relationship dies, you bring more money than usual. The gift tells you the depth of the relationship, because a friendship truly from the heart is different from a superficial friendship. . . . [W]hen my daughter had a baby, there were people who brought gifts and people who didn't. . . . [T]he way of giving differs according to true friends and superficial friends.

The receiver usually assumes the monetary value of a gift has at least partly been calculated in accordance with the giver's perception of the strength of relationship that exists between giver and receiver.

There are different criteria for judging strength of relationship. One of these criteria is the level of friendship that exists between two people. As Mr. Hoshino explains, his "true friends," those people with whom he associates from the heart, will give more than his "superficial friends." In the case of his house-building ceremony, those people he considered his closest friends—the rice dealer, the rice cracker maker, and the fishmonger—did in fact give 10,000 yen, two to three times as much as the other people who attended. Similarly, at Mr. Ishiyama Shōji's father's funeral, Ishiyama Shōji's friends gave 10,000 yen each, and two close friends of the deceased each gave 20,000 yen.

There are some cases in which people give generous gifts in order to create a stronger relationship, but such giving can be precarious, as the following example demonstrates. In the two year period before I met Mrs. Ueda, her son and daughter each married, and her mother-in-law passed away. At the funeral of her mother-in-law, there was one instance of a gift of 10,000 yen from a woman who was not a neighbor but who lived in the same building. Mrs. Ueda was not at all happy with this gift, because she had been trying to distance herself from interaction with this woman. Mrs. Ueda had once done a few activities together with her, but then decided she did not care for the woman's personality. Mrs. Ueda had not expected her to come to her mother-in-law's funeral. She interpreted the gift from this woman, who had not known Mrs. Ueda's mother-in-law at all and who now had almost no contact with Mrs. Ueda, as an attempt to force Mrs. Ueda back into social relations with her.

Gifts at the lower end of the spectrum in many cases were tied to lack of close friendship between giver and receiver. At the funeral of Mr. Ishiyama's father, three of the four gifts of 2,000 yen were from people who hardly knew the Ishiyama family. In these cases, gifts of little money may have also suggested stinginess or social ignorance; gifts of 2,000 yen were far less than was appropriate even for a very superficial friend or acquaintance. Mr. Ishiyama's mother hinted that some people take advantage of the fact that in Warabi, return gifts are the same regardless of the amount of incense money. She said that sometimes very little money is given so that a profit can be made on the return gift. Mr. Ishiyama disagreed; he said that such gifts of very little money came from people who were elderly and were not aware of current prices. When I pointed out that prices for kōden had not changed very much in the last couple of decades (for example, one of the 20,000 yen gifts from a neighbor was the exact same amount of a 20,000 yen gift the Ishiyama family had given at the funeral of a member of the neighbor's family some twenty years before), and that the people who gave the least money were not elderly, but in their forties and fifties, Mr. Ishiyama said that they were probably people without much social contact.

A second criterion for judging strength of relationship is the number of intervening links of people between giver and receiver. At Mr. Ishiyama's father's funeral, for example, close friends of the son of the deceased were considered to have weaker relationships with the deceased than close friends of the deceased. Close friends of the son of the deceased gave 10,000 yen, while close friends of the deceased gave 20,000 yen. The gifts from the people with more direct relationships to the deceased were higher than the gifts from the people with less direct relationships to the deceased.

The same pattern generally holds true for intervening genealogical links. For example, at Mrs. Ueda's children's weddings, the siblings and parents of Mr. and Mrs. Ueda gave 100,000 yen, and almost all other relatives gave between 30,000 yen (20,000 yen by a few who did not attend) and 50,000 yen. Those who gave 20,000 yen or 30,000 yen were the furthest removed genealogically from the person getting married. At Mr. Ishiyama's father's funeral, cousins of Mr. Ishiyama in general gave 20,000 yen. The closest relatives to the deceased, namely his wife, sons, and sons' wives, paid for the funeral expenses. They therefore brought no gifts. But the younger brother of Mr. Ishiyama's wife, as well as the brothers of his brothers' wives, gave 30,000 yen. The reason for this, Mr. Ishiyama's mother told me, was that they were considered *kyō-daidōshi* (fellow siblings) to the children of the deceased. Living siblings of the deceased gave 50,000 yen. They were considered to have the strongest, or most koi, relationship to the deceased of the relatives who gave money.

Sometimes a relationship that should be strong and therefore entail a relatively large gift is not. Mrs. Ueda's mother's elder brother gave only 10,000 yen at each of Mrs. Ueda's children's weddings. In this case, the relationship between Mrs. Ueda's mother and Mrs. Ueda's mother's eldest brother was bitter. The strained personal relationship, Mrs. Ueda explained, weighed against the close genealogical relationship. Thus, the amount of the gift was very low for an offering from a close relative. This gift of relatively little money crystallized Mrs. Ueda's dislike for her uncle.

At Mr. Hoshino's house-building ceremony, relatives gave more than most people who were not relatives. Giving on the occasion of house-building ceremonies is less elaborate than giving at weddings and funerals, and so all gifts from relatives were roughly the same: 10,000 yen, two to three times as much as was given by most other guests, and the same amount as was given by especially close friends. The parents of Mr. Hoshino's daughter's husband gave only two bottles of sake. Mr. Hoshino said this gift was very little, as they are considered *oyadōshi* (fellow parents), but guessed that his daughter's in-laws were planning to make a larger present once the house was built.

A third criterion for judging strength of relationship is place of residence. In one interview with a woman about the incense money given at her mother's funeral, she explained that two neighbors, to whom she felt equally close, gave two different amounts. The one living immediately next door gave 10,000 yen, whereas the neighbor down the street gave 5,000 yen. I asked whether it was not the case that the basis for calculating the amount of the gift was the feeling of closeness at the personal level, for there might be more opportunities to interact with a next door neighbor. I was told definitely not. The depth of friendship with both people was the same. As a rule, she said, next door neighbors must give more than neighbors who live down the street, and people who live in apartments above, below, and to either side must give more than people who live in other parts of an apartment building, regardless of personal feeling. One can have a close (chikai) relationship based solely on geographical proximity.

There are of course examples of gifts, such as the 30,000 yen from a neighbor at the marriage of Mrs. Ueda's daughter, in which a neighbor is also a close friend. In this case, the woman had lived for fifteen years in the same building with Mrs. Ueda in Osaka. When Mrs. Ueda's husband and the neighbor's husband were transferred at the same time from Osaka to Tokyo, both families moved to the same apartment building in Tokyo. This friend did not live in an apartment above, below, or next to the Uedas, and she and Mrs. Ueda had agreed not to ask each other to their children's weddings because of the trouble and expense such invitations entail. Her gift of 30,000 yen was therefore very high, especially compared with the 20,000 yen from the family who lived directly above the Uedas. There were three reasons for this generous present, Mrs. Ueda explained: the long history of living in the same building, even in different cities; the close friendship between the two women; and the neighbor's special affection for Mrs. Ueda's daughter.

In giving connected with place of residence, not only the price of the gift but also the place of giving differs according to strength of relationship. For example, a woman named Mrs. Kosugi explained to me that she had received two gifts related to moving. A woman who had lived next door for twenty years moved away. She came with a box of cookies bought from a famous bakery in order to say good-bye and to thank Mrs. Kosugi for being such a good neighbor for so long. This woman who was about to move went into Mrs. Kosugi's house and stayed and chatted. The cookies she brought were worth about 5,000 yen. The man who later moved into the woman's house also stopped by with a box of cookies, but these were worth 1,000 yen and were given to Mrs. Kosugi at the house's outermost extremity, the gate. He bowed and asked Mrs. Kosugi to treat him favorably. Mrs. Kosugi said, "When you don't know someone at all, you give at the front gate. Then, when you know someone better, the person may come to the *genkan* [the area for removing shoes before stepping up into the house]. Only someone who is pretty close would bring expensive cookies and come up into the house!"

A fourth criterion for judging the strength of relationship is the historical connection between giver and receiver. Recall that at his house-building ceremony, Mr. Hoshino received from the Tokuguchi family, down the street, two two-liter bottles of special sake worth about 10,000 yen whose name could be read, by altering the pronunciation of the Chinese characters, as "May your household flourish." One of the reasons for this gift was that Mr. Hoshino's family and Mr. Tokuguchi's family both live on the Nakasendō, and the relationship between their families has continued since the Edo period. In general, relationships based on historical connections between families are referred to as deep (fukai) even though particular individuals of those families may not know each other very well.

In the same way, the gift of 20,000 yen from the head priest of the local Shintō shrine presented to Mr. Hoshino at his house-building ceremony was in part the result of a historical relationship between Mr. Hoshino's family and the shrine. In the Edo period, a priest who practiced both Buddhism and Shintō was traveling on the Nakasendō. He stopped to rest for the night with Mr. Hoshino's family. The priest extended his stay to teach the Hoshinos about various forms of religious practice, in particular about the climbing of mountains. Every year from that time forward, the head of the Hoshino family, in cooperation with the local shrine, has led a group of pilgrims from Warabi to the mountain Ontake-san.

A statement by Mr. Ishiyama's mother made the significance of historical connections between individuals and families clear. Mr. Ishiyama's mother takes part in a community center class on traditional Japanese songs. The thirty-odd members of this class made a token present of 3,000 yen when her husband passed away. Two members of this class made an additional present of 10,000 yen. I asked why. Mr. Ishiyama's mother responded that they lived on the Nakasendō. I asked if the fact that they lived on the Nakasendō meant that she knew them better than the other students. She said no; she felt no more familiar with these two women than she did with the others in her class. But as they lived on the Nakasendō, their families had known hers for hundreds of years, and therefore they made this extra gift.

Gratitude

Many of the offerings of money at Mr. Hoshino's house-building ceremony and at Mr. Ishiyama's father's funeral were motivated in large part by gratitude. For example, at Mr. Hoshino's house-building ceremony, Mr. Hoshino's father's younger sister's son gave 20,000 yen. This gift was larger than gifts from other relatives because in the months preceding the house-building ceremony, Mr.

Hoshino's wife had been caring for Mr. Hoshino's father's younger sister, who was seriously ill.

At Mr. Ishiyama's father's funeral, the wife of the deceased accountant who had kept the books for the Ishiyama family store presented a kōden of 50,000 yen. When the accountant had died some years ago, Mr. Ishiyama's father helped out with the arrangements for the accountant's funeral. The wife and son of the accountant heard only some days after the funeral of Mr. Ishiyama's father that Mr. Ishiyama's father had died. They therefore came with 30,000 yen in lieu of the wreaths they would have sent, as well as 20,000 yen from the son and 50,000 yen from the wife.

Other gifts motivated by gratitude were as follows: The gift of 20,000 yen from the vegetable dealer was because Mr. Ishiyama's father helped this vegetable dealer receive his license, and also employed the vegetable dealer's younger brother at his rice store. The gifts from Mr. Ishiyama's distant cousin and his children were especially generous, because during World War II, he and his mother had been taken in by Mr. Ishiyama's family. The Buddhist priest offered 20,000 yen because he had discussed many of the temple's problems with Mr. Ishiyama's father, who had been a good listener and good advisor. The parents of Mr. Ishiyama's close friend gave 30,000 yen because Mr. Ishiyama's parents had been go-betweens for their son and his wife.

Hierarchy

Hierarchy is also a factor that influences giving. In general, people who are of higher status are given larger amounts of money or objects of higher value than people of lower status. They are also under obligation to give more than people of lower status. Chapter I contains several examples of gift-giving that become more understandable when their hierarchical components are explored.

The supermarket family returned Mrs. Ueda's congratulatory presents of 20,000 yen and 30,000 yen with gift certificates equivalent to those amounts of money plus a sesame seed grinder in the case of 20,000 yen, and a set of fancy plates in the case of 30,000 yen. In the past, it was sometimes the practice at happy occasions, such as weddings, to make a return gift of twice the original gift. However, now a return gift equivalent to half the value of the original gift is the norm. Mrs. Ueda received slightly more than she gave because she was a customer of the store. Mrs. Ueda herself was initially shocked by this return gift, because it surpassed her initial present; she came to the conclusion that the reason for this return gift was that she was a customer of this store only after some consideration of different possibilities. When I later consulted shopkeepers about the possible reasons for this kind of gift in this particular situation, they immediately responded that it is the customer who stands in hierarchically superior relation to the store owner, and thus the store owner must make a return gift worth more than the original gift.

At Mrs. Ueda's son's wedding, the nakōdo (go-between) gave 100,000 yen to the couple before their wedding, and received Gucci plates and 300,000 yen from the couple and their parents after the wedding. In addition, the go-between received gifts from the Ueda family twice yearly. In this case, the vice president of Mrs. Ueda's son's company was a social superior to Mrs. Ueda's son. He had been one of the people who made the decision to hire Mrs. Ueda's son, and he would have the power to influence the course of Mrs. Ueda's son's career in the future. Embedded in this gift to the nakōdo, Mrs. Ueda said, was gratitude for his past action of hiring her son, his present action as a crucial participant in her son's marriage, and a request for his future support of her son.

Mrs. Ueda's son is in a social position superior to that of Mrs. Ueda's daughter. As the eldest son, it is he who is responsible for continuing the Ueda family. In many households, when a daughter marries, she legally and symbolically leaves her family. If her husband is an eldest son, it is she—the wife of the eldest son—who is responsible for making offerings to his deceased parents and relatives. When she dies, her bones will be placed in her husband's family grave, whereas a son's bones will be placed with his parents. These practices are slowly changing among younger people in some areas, as women make arrangements to avoid being buried with their in-laws and as ancestor worship becomes more bilateral in nature. However, Mrs. Ueda noted that it is still customary that the most money from relatives comes at the marriage of the eldest son, and that it was not at all surprising that some relatives gave more money at the marriage of her son than at the marriage of her daughter. She feels that her two children are the same, she said, but that especially her husband's relatives place more value on her son than on her daughter.

In the examples of giving related to the construction of Mr. Hoshino's new house, hierarchy was also an important underlying variable. At jichinsai, the ceremony held in order to pacify the spirits of the earth, the only people who received gifts were those highest in the hierarchy. The head of the demolition crew and the head and second-in-command of the construction crew each received 10,000 yen. Ordinary workers did not receive anything. At tatemae, the ceremony to celebrate the construction of the frame of the house, the master carpenter and the second-in-command were given 30,000 yen each, and the ordinary workers were each given 10,000 yen. Higher ranking people received more than lower ranking people.

Lower ranking people are expected to give less than higher ranking people. The gift of 2,000 yen at Mr. Ishiyama's father's funeral from Mr. Ishiyama's daughter's friend was acceptable because she was probably the lowest ranking person at the funeral. Mr. Ishiyama's daughter is the youngest member of the Ishiyama family, and her friend was then a young girl of about fourteen years of age.

Women are expected to give less than men, and gifts made in a man's name when the intervening link between giver and recipient is a woman are less expensive than when the intervening link is a man. For example, Mr. Hoshino described a gift of 5,000 yen given in his name, as the head of household, at the funeral of his wife's friend's husband. If the gift had been intended for the funeral of the wife of one of his own friends, he said, the amount would have been doubled: 10,000 yen rather than 5,000 yen. He stated that when the link was a woman, it was forgiven if the amount of money was not very high. Women, he said, could "get away" with giving less than men.

Some other people I asked concurred with Mr. Hoshino, saying that links with men are generally more important to the well-being of the family than links with women. They stated that men's relationships with bosses, colleagues, and customers influence the financial stability of a family, whereas a woman's friendships are merely sources of support and pleasure for her as an individual. The people most likely to agree with Mr. Hoshino's statement were in married relationships in which the husband worked outside the home and the wife ran the household and raised the children. Even though people in these situations stressed the greater importance of male connections over female connections, examination of gift-giving records usually indicated that there were at least as many gifts to people connected to the wife as to people connected to the husband, although the cash amounts of each individual gift of the latter category tended to be higher.

Often relationships between men result in higher exchanges of money than relationships through women; it is also common for senior people to give more than junior people. At Mrs. Ueda's children's weddings and at Mr. Ishiyama's father's funeral, elder brothers, who either would succeed or had succeeded their fathers as heads of household, gave more than their younger brothers. A newspaper reporter told me of an incident at the wedding of a fellow newspaper employee. This reporter's elder colleague (elder by two years) was upset to realize that they were both planning on making a gift of the same amount. Just before approaching the table and presenting his envelope, the elder colleague argued with his wife, who finally opened her purse and handed him an additional 10,000 yen to insert into the envelope.

Here are some other examples of higher status people who give larger amounts of money or objects of higher cash value than people of lower status. When Mrs. Inoue purchased gifts to be given on White Day, March 14, to the office ladies who had given her husband obligatory chocolates on Valentine's Day, the cost of the return gifts was twice the cost of the original gifts. Young women

told me that it is the general practice for male workers, particularly those high up in the company hierarchy, to make twofold return
gifts on White Day. When the professors and the students from the
anthropology department with which I was affiliated in Tokyo
went out for dinner together to celebrate the beginning of the new
school year, new first-year graduate students paid nothing, second-
and third-year graduate students paid more, fourth- and fifth-year
graduates still more, and professors the most. One of the second-
year graduate students told each person how much to pay, and
when I asked him how he decided the amount for each person, he
said that there were two basic rules: the new first-year graduate
students must not pay anything, and professors must pay more
than the most advanced graduate students.

The giving of more money or a gift with a high monetary value
by persons of higher status is not only an obligation; it is also a
right. For example, Mr. Tokuguchi, who gave the special sake
worth 10,000 yen at Mr. Hoshino's tatemae, is from the oldest family of the Nakasendō. He is ten years younger than Mr. Hoshino,
but his family stands above Mr. Hoshino's family in the neighborhood hierarchy. At neighborhood festivals, Mr. Hoshino is always
careful that his gift of money is lower than Mr. Tokuguchi's. To
give the same amount of money or a higher amount of money
would be an insult to Mr. Tokuguchi, Mr. Hoshino explained.

Gratitude and hierarchy are often intertwined. At Mr. Hoshino's house-building ceremony, the neighbor living behind the
Hoshino house gave 30,000 yen and two bottles of sake. This
neighbor rents land from the Hoshino family. People who own land
are higher ranking than the people to whom they rent land. When
I asked Mr. Hoshino why this particular neighbor gave so much
more than all the others, he responded, "Because he is indebted to
us, as we are letting him lease our land. His generous gifts are signs
of his gratitude."

Other combinations of giving influenced by both gratitude and
hierarchy are as follows: When Mrs. Ueda sent summer and winter
gifts to the vice president of her son's company, she was expressing
her gratitude toward him, but was also signaling that she wished

him to continue his support of her son in the future. Mr. Tanabe refused to send gifts to the superiors in his company or accept the gift of live shrimp from the woman whom he helped with stocks because he knew that when a person in a position of higher status accepts a gift from a person in a position of lower status, the person of higher status may incur an obligation to take care of the person of lower status. Mr. Tanabe wanted to avoid relations of hierarchy in which people granted favors out of feelings of obligation.

Mr. Tanabe stood in a position of hierarchical superiority to the woman who had sent him live shrimp, because Mr. Tanabe had been a customer at her bar, and because he had used his financial knowledge to help her. When she sent him the particularly lavish gift just when the stocks were not doing well, and during a time when many people feel compelled to give to social superiors, he felt burdened by her gift. He would have been able to accept a present if the stocks had done well and she had sent him something to share her joy. But because he had done "nothing good," the gift of the live shrimp made him feel obligated to reciprocate at some point in the future, and this expectation, he said, gave him an extremely painful feeling.

It was not that he would not do his best to help the bar owner profit from her investments, but rather that he did not like to feel that he was obligated to do so. To explain further, Mr. Tanabe gave me another example of gifts that made him uncomfortable. A friend from university days who is now a lawyer asked him for help with stocks, and Mr. Tanabe was glad to be of assistance. This friend has since sent gifts of *tsukudani* (preserved food boiled down in soy) during summer and winter every year since Mr. Tanabe performed what he saw as a small task. He would have been glad to help his friend without receiving anything in return, but because this man is older than he and was ahead of him at the university, he was unable to refuse the gifts. Also, in this case involving his university friend, he felt that he had been useful; the bar owner had lost money, but the lawyer had not. He said that from the point of view of his friend the lawyer, "He is not sure when the next time is that he will need to ask me for help, and so in this way, he keeps up a connection." Mr. Tanabe does not like this situation because he would of course be glad to help his friend whenever possible, and he does not feel that gifts are necessary for ensuring his future cooperation.

Strength of Relationship, Gratitude, and Hierarchy: Mr. Ishiyama Tomoyasu's Kōden

At Mr. Ishiyama Shōji's father's funeral, most gifts from cousins were 20,000 yen. But Mr. Ishiyama Tomoyasu, the local rice cracker maker, and Mr. Ishiyama Shōji's cousin's son gave a gift of 200,000 yen. I had examined many kōden registers, but this amount, roughly equivalent to two thousand dollars, was the highest I had seen. I was especially surprised, because Ishiyama Tomoyasu seemed to be a man of relatively modest means. But because Mr. Ishiyama, who usually explained things to me in a focused and energetic way, seemed unwilling to discuss the matter any further, I decided to wait until another time.

I returned a few days later to ask him again why this particular kōden was such a large amount of money. In the meantime, I had been wondering whether the reason was connected to the fact that these two Ishiyama families shared an unusual combination of relations through blood and marriage. I had taken down their family tree some months earlier (Figure 2.1). Ishiyama Shōji 's mother's sister's son had been adopted by Ishiyama Tomoyasu's mother's family in order to marry Ishiyama Tomoyasu's mother, an only daughter, and thus carry on the family name. Since the Meiji period (1868–1912), the most prevalent form of adoption is *muko-yōshi*, in which a family withour a son adopts a son-in-law, who is an adult, often a relative's second son or grandson. However, my questions were in vain; Ishiyama Shōji still told me that he had no idea why Ishiyama Tomoyasu had given so much. If I was really so curious, he said, I should go and ask Ishiyama Tomoyasu directly.

The opportunity presented itself several weeks later at a neighborhood party at which Ishiyama Tomoyasu was present but Ishiyama Shōji was not. Ishiyama Tomoyasu spoke about the rea-

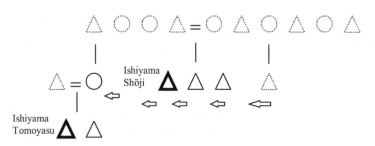

F I G . 2 . 1 . Ishiyama family tree. Solid black lines indicate living people.
Dotted lines indicate people who have died. Arrows indicate adoption.

sons he gave the kōden he did, claiming that of course Ishiyama
Shōji knew; Ishiyama Shōji had probably been feigning ignorance
out of modesty. Ishiyama Tomoyasu began by explaining how his
family is *honke* (main family) and Ishiyama Shōji 's family is *bunke*
(branch family), because Ishiyama Shōji's father was a second son.
At the funeral of Ishiyama Tomoyasu's father, Ishiyama Shōji's family (under the name of Ishiyama Shōji's father) had given 100,000
yen. The main family, being of higher status than the branch family, was obliged to give more, and thus gave 200,000 yen at the
death of Ishiyama Shōji's father. In addition, Ishiyama Tomoyasu
stated, the two families were very close, in terms of friendship,
geography, and kinship. They were constantly visiting each other.
They used to live next door until Ishiyama Shōji decided to build
his house on top of his store (at that time, Ishiyama Shōji's store
was in the middle of the rice fields, and Ishiyama Shōji's house was
on the Nakasendō). They were also related to each other through
both their fathers and their mothers.[1] As he continued speaking,
however, Ishiyama Tomoyasu modified the statement he had made
at the beginning of our conversation. Although it is in general true,
he said, that main families should give more than branch families,
in this particular case, he felt that the underlying reason for his gift
was the gratitude (*kansha*) he felt toward Ishiyama Shōji and
Ishiyama Shōji's father. Ishiyama Tomoyasu's father had been a
very difficult man, partly because he had been adopted and was

therefore insecure in his position as head of the family. When Ishiyama Shōji's father was alive, Ishiyama Tomoyasu would come to him for advice on how to deal with his father. After the death of Ishiyama Shōji's father, he would discuss these issues with Ishiyama Shōji. For these reasons, he feels deeply grateful.

Although for the most part this chapter has investigated how giving is determined by factors such as strength of relationship, gratitude, and hierarchy, giving is much more than a reflection or outcome of various circumstances. Giving both presupposes and affects variables such as strength of relationship, gratitude, and hierarchy, and is at the same time determined by these factors. Ishiyama Tomoyasu's kōden is a case in point. Numerous circumstances prompted the giving of the 200,000 yen, but this giving in turn influenced the relationship between the two families. Ishiyama Shōji's modesty in refraining from explanation of the reasons behind the gift seemed to indicate that he was well aware that this gift was motivated in large part by gratitude for his deceased father's kindness as well as his own. If the main reason for this gift had been that the main family stood in hierarchical relation to the branch family and thus was obligated to make a larger gift than the 100,000 yen given by Mr. Ishiyama Shōji's family at the passing of Mr. Ishiyama Tomoyasu's father, an amount slightly higher than 100,000 yen might have been given, not double the amount. The gift of 200,000 yen stressed the close relationship between the two families and the feelings of gratitude. At the same time it de-emphasized the traditional relations of hierarchy between the two houses. This gift was not merely a result of past circumstances, but rather a force that softened the hierarchical relations between the two families, and solidified their close relationship. Usually, superiors give support and inferiors offer material objects as a token of their gratitude. In this case, it is the other way around. This substantial gift of money is an indication that the head of this particular main family does not see his family's relationship with the branch family as one of superiors to inferiors. The party in need is helped by the party who is able to assist, regardless of social position; it is an egalitarian friendship based on mutual affection and respect.

Three critical factors that people use in determining the monetary amount of gifts are strength of relationship, gratitude, and hierarchy. Understanding how these variables often express themselves in relationships of giving is crucial in interpreting meanings of gifts. Generally, the closer the relationship (in terms of kinship distance, friendship, place of residence, and historical connection) the higher the cash value of the gift. Gratitude for past deeds of the recipient or the recipient's family also increases the amount of the gift. Hierarchy influences giving in the sense that people of higher status are obliged to give more than people of lower status, and people of higher status are also given more than people of lower status. Accordingly, women both give less and are given less than men, and gifts in which the intervening link between giver and recipient is a woman are less than when the intervening link is a man. Precise calculations of monetary value indicate the giver's perception of the relationship with the recipient and can signal or effect changes in the social position of the giver, the receiver, and the relationship they share.

3 ᐸ Life Cycles

This chapter and the next describe life and seasonal cycle practices. Many of the details come from the way these events are observed in Warabi by families that have lived there for generations. People who live in Tokyo, or people who moved to Warabi only after World War II, were often unfamiliar with many of the ways in which seasonal and life cycle events in Warabi were celebrated. I describe these rites of passage in detail in order to have a rich and nuanced basis for understanding the larger symbolic systems that inform practices of giving and receiving.

I am not implying that all Japanese people observe or are even aware of all of the different practices contained in these next two chapters. It is my contention, however, that even young, highly educated residents of Tokyo who consider many aspects of the giving and receiving I detail cumbersome, old fashioned, and largely irrelevant are themselves influenced both directly and indirectly by these larger processes. For example, as part of the grant I received to do fieldwork, I was assigned two graduate students from the anthropology department of Rikkyo University, which I was affiliated with during my stay in Japan. They were to help me with my research, but they insisted that they not engage in the giving of gifts, and explained that they saw gift-giving as ridiculous. However, the parents of one of these men sent gifts every summer and winter to the professor who was their son's main advisor. The other young man was successful in convincing his parents not to send gifts to his professor, but his parents still insisted on sending seasonal gifts to his landlord. Partly as a result of these gifts, this man explained, his landlord had installed an air conditioner in his apartment.

In addition, when the mother of our advisor passed away, these two men were preoccupied with proper behavior at the funeral. All the graduate students in our department (even though none of the students had ever met our professor's mother) attended the funeral, and all gave gifts of incense money. But it was the two students who had expressed gentle amusement at my fascination with these quaint gift-giving customs who went out and rented black mourning clothes because they had no black suits. They were very concerned about the clothes I would wear, and one had his wife telephone me—she had worked as an office lady in a major corporation and so, I was told, was more familiar with rules for proper behavior than were graduate students—to make sure that I did not show up in gray or purple by mistake. The amount of time and energy spent on gathering money for joint gifts and making individual offerings was considerable. When I filled out my name and address on the envelope containing my offering of incense money, one of the students quickly intervened, because I was writing with a blue pen rather than a black pen, and for a funeral the ink must be black. On the train to the funeral, my two friends debated what they should tell our professor when it came time to bow and express condolences. They settled on a set phrase that had been suggested by the graduate student's wife. At the funeral, they watched the other mourners carefully so that they would know how to offer incense to the deceased in the correct way.

My two friends paid attention to all of these details that, when applied to other people and to other people's lives, they had deemed absurd. Their heightened concern was partly because they were fond of our professor, sorry for her at the loss of her mother, and anxious to show proper support and respect for her and her family in this time of crisis. Their interest in correct manners was also because our professor had a great deal of influence in the directions their lives would take, and they wanted to make sure that their relationship with her would be good.

Ways of giving and receiving relate to conceptions of larger cosmic forces, including ideas of souls, deities, auspiciousness, and inauspiciousness. People do not necessarily have to think that these entities or qualities actually exist in order to be influenced by them. Neither the professor nor the graduate students imagined that failing to say the appropriate words, give the incense money in the appropriate way, or select the appropriate items as return gifts would have any direct or immediate results. For example, our professor did not schedule the funeral on a day known as tomobiki because she thought that to do so would allow a second death to occur, but because to do so would be disrespectful to the funeral guests. The descriptions in the next pages of souls, deities, auspiciousness, and inauspiciousness are important not because the majority of Japanese people consciously believe in them, but rather because these ideas are the basis of larger symbolic structures that in more subtle ways inform their daily lives.

Before Birth to After Death

The life cycle of human beings stretches from before birth to after death. Beliefs of course vary from one individual to another, but in general the souls of babies are said to come from another world, and those of dead people are said to go to that world.[1] After birth and after death, there are successive stages at which the soul becomes either more or less attached to the body of the human being. The distance between these points is often measured in increments of seven. For example, on the seventh night after an infant's birth, its soul is considered relatively firmly anchored in its human body, and the baby is given a name.[2] Similarly, the seventh night after a person dies is the first step of separation of the soul from the body. During this never-ending cycle, the human soul enters into relationships with other souls, and changes those relationships, sometimes even severing them.[3]

Giving at rites of passage both marks and even initiates transitions. For example, in the past, there were three events at which bowls were piled high with rice packed into a mound. The first was at the birth of a child. The second was at marriage. The third was at a person's death. In daily life, etiquette dictated that a rice bowl should never be completely filled, and that the person consuming the rice should leave one mouthful of rice in the bowl when asking for more. It was only at major life cycle junctures that these rules were turned upside down. When a child was born, the bowl of mounded rice was offered to the tutelary deity, the family's shrine or Buddhist altar, and in some instances to the baby. This offering of rice cut the relationship of the child to the world of the dead from which it was reincarnated. When a woman left her own home to enter into her husband's home, she completely consumed one bowl of rice that had been piled high, thus cutting her ties with her natal house. When a bowl of mounded rice was offered to a corpse it both symbolized and effected the end of the deceased's relationship with the world of the living.

Why does a mounded bowl of rice cut ties?[4] These mounds are created by first filling one bowl with rice. A second bowl identical to the first is moistened with water and then packed with rice as well. The second bowl is placed upside down on the first, and the shaped mound of rice slides out from the second bowl and rests on the filled first bowl. When a person consumes a mounded bowl of rice, he or she eats an entire sphere-shaped unit. This underscores that consumption is total, that a complete whole has been eaten. Total consumption breaks a relationship.

The principle that giving and receiving must be continuous in order to keep a relationship strong and that total consumption in many cases breaks a relationship is evident in many practices of giving. The ideal is never to consume a gift completely; one should receive, give a little back in the form of a return gift, but never give enough back to cancel the value of the original gift. A portion of the original gift should always be retained and a portion should always be given back.

Historical Change

There have been many changes over time in practices of giving and receiving related to major life cycle events. Today, in most parts of Japan, the mounded offering of rice occurs only at funerals. There are more people whose actions suggest that they might believe the souls of the dead continue to exist for a while in our world than there are people who act in ways indicating they believe that babies and small children are not firmly planted in this existence. People show much care and affection for dead people, or for the souls of dead people. For example, during my fieldwork in the Tokyo area, Chieko, the daughter of a family with which I lived for a year during college, suddenly died. I went to Kyoto for the service forty-nine days after Chieko's death. I arrived the night before the service. A container with Chieko's bones stood before the family's Buddhist altar. Chieko's mother asked me to sleep in the room with the Buddhist altar rather than my usual place, for she said that Chieko would want to be with me; she did not want Chieko to be lonely. Similarly, when I was shown the Buddhist altar of the president of a major company, it was piled high with magazine articles about him. He wanted his deceased father to see how well he had done in his career (see Smith 1974 for analysis of similar practices).

But few people spoke of children as not firmly planted in the world of the living. Although Embree reports in *Suye Mura* that the term for a baby's soul being finally secured in a human body is the same word for the separation of a dead person's soul from the corpse (Embree 1939: 183), everyone I asked was familiar with the latter concept but very few people with the former. It is hardly surprising, then, that offerings of mounded bowls of rice are still presented to corpses but no longer given to newborn babies.

The natal family of a woman about to be married no longer gives her a mounded bowl of rice to eat; other rituals indicating the woman's cutting of ties to her natal family and her incorporation into her husband's family are gradually being omitted from wedding celebrations.[5] The majority of newly married couples live alone rather than with the husband's parents, and ties to both the husband's and the wife's families remain more or less equal. Some women are even making arrangements before their deaths so that their bones will not be placed in their husbands' families' graves.

Offerings presented to corpses but no longer to babies and brides provide an example of one particular historical change in practices of giving. There are other more general trends as well.

Gifts of money have to a large degree replaced gifts of goods such as food, cloth, and alcohol. Additionally, as Japanese society has grown wealthier, giving has become much more extravagant. Giving relationships now tend to be concentrated in the workplace rather than in extended families or neighborhoods, especially in urban areas. The work of holding funerals and weddings is usually no longer borne by neighbors and relatives but rather is contracted out to funeral companies, wedding palaces, and hotels. Finally, the Meiji government fashioned some of the present forms of rites of passage for reasons relating to national unity, ideological persuasion, and social control.

Auspiciousness and Inauspiciousness

Life cycle events are divided into happy events related to life and sad occasions connected with death; practices of giving differ accordingly. For example, living people wear kimono with the left side over the right side. At funerals, the corpse is dressed in a kimono so that the right side is laid over the left side. (Note that in life, the yang side is dominant; in death, it is the yin side that is dominant.) Similarly, at funerals, right is folded over left when wrapping money before inserting it into an envelope, and when wrapping an envelope in a cloth; at funerals when paper is folded vertically instead of horizontally, the bottom edge is always laid over the top edge. At weddings, the reverse is true; left is folded over right, and top over bottom.[6] At weddings, bills should be new and shiny and lying face up; at funerals, they should be old, crumpled, and lying face down.

Envelopes containing money for betrothals, weddings, births, and other celebrations are very different from the envelopes for funerals and memorial services. Envelopes for weddings and other auspicious occasions are marked with a small decoration in the upper right hand corner that symbolizes abalone. Originally, a slice of dried and flattened abalone was attached to gifts for auspicious occasions to indicate that the event was unconnected to death, and therefore Buddhist abstinence from flesh was not required.[7] Today this symbol is simply printed on the envelope, although some more elaborate envelopes use origami decorations, and some still do use dried abalone (Yanagita 1970: 45; Edwards 1989: 107; Hendry 1993: 15). Cords used to tie the envelopes for funerals and memorial services are white, black or silver. If black is used, one side of the envelope may be tied with a white cord, although sometimes only a black cord and rarely only a white cord is used; if silver is used, both sides will be tied with a silver cord. These envelopes are sometimes decorated with black, purple, and gray lines instead of real cords. Cords tying envelopes for celebrations are usually the auspicious combination of red and white (*kōhaku*) or gold and silver, although sometimes a single color, usually either red or gold, will be used. Two separate colors of cords tied together, such as white and red, black and white, and so on, may be related to the symbolic function of these gifts of reinforcing ties between different individuals or groups of individuals (Edwards 1989: 106).

In addition to the two categories of celebration and bereavement, there is differentiation between events that happen only once in the lifetime of an individual and events that are repeated. The cords for wedding and funeral gifts are tied with the special musubikiri ("to tie completely") knot, which cannot be undone. Gifts to people recovering from illness should technically be tied with a red and white cord using this same kind of knot, in order to indicate that the sickness will not come back. Most other occasions, such as the birth of children, construction of homes, birthdays, graduations, long life celebrations, and so forth are tied with a *chōmusubi* ("butterfly knot"), which is supposedly readily untied, indicating that these events may occur more than once. An employee at Mitsukoshi Department Store told me that when he first started working, he was shocked at how angry customers become if a clerk made a mistake in the kind of knot used. A funeral present tied with a butterfly knot is very inauspicious, as it indicates a recurrence of death. A wedding gift tied with a butterfly knot is considered unlucky because it indicates the marriage will not last. If a gift at a birthday is tied with the knot that cannot be untied, this is also very ominous, as it suggests that this birthday will be the person's last. Therefore, some people can be extremely sensitive to the tying of these knots. Once a mistake is made, there is a feeling that it cannot be undone, even if the knot is retied; it is a bad omen.

Certain kinds of gifts are appropriate for happy occasions, and others for sad ones, although there is a certain amount of variation according to geographical area. For example, when a woman who had been raised in Kagoshima, Kyūshū married a man from Tokyo and had a child, the couple sent green tea as a return gift for each baby gift they received. According to the woman's family's traditions, green tea was an item appropriate for all kinds of gifts.[8] However, in many parts of Japan, including the Tokyo area, tea is associated with gifts at funerals and memorial services. At events connected with weddings, a drink made from hot water and cherry blossoms preserved in salt is served instead of tea. Some people explained to me that the association between tea and death is because tea blooms facing downward. (Seaweed is also a gift associated with funerals and memorial services, and so perhaps the green color is significant.) When the relatives living in Tokyo received tea, they thought that something may have gone terribly wrong with the new baby, and telephoned the man's parents to find out if the child had died.

Return gifts at funerals include two different categories: token items for purposes of purification, and more substantial gifts. In Tokyo, all guests receive a small bag containing a package of salt (to be sprinkled on the mourner to remove impurities before entering his or her home), sake, sugar, and sometimes a telephone card decorated with an image of lilies or leaves wet with rain. Afterward, return gifts calculated to be roughly half the value of each mourner's original gift are sent through the mail. In Warabi, everyone receives exactly the same gift at the time of the funeral: a larger bag that contains both the symbolic items for purification, as well as the main item.[9] The main item is often tea, seaweed, or something made from cloth, although there are endless possibilities in department store and funeral company catalogues. In the past, sugar and soap were often given as return gifts at funerals, but with the overall increase in affluence, these items are now less common.

Before World War II, five kilograms of sugar was a typical return gift at funerals in Warabi.

In many parts of Japan, objects made from thread, such as sheets, towels or furoshiki, are typical return gifts at funerals. The colors are usually muted, such as white, navy blue, and gray. People accumulate such items, and then sell them at bazaars to raise money for schools or neighborhood associations. When I moved to Warabi, neighbors gave me towels and sheets that had originally been return gifts from funerals. Cloth is appropriate for funerals because it does not last forever; cloth wears out and is eventually discarded. Because presents associated with funerals are inauspicious, people do not want to keep them indefinitely.

Return gifts for joyous occasions such as weddings will usually contain one item that will last a long time. This enduring gift may be some kind of ceramic or lacquerware, metal or wooden item, such as a vase, a set of flatware, a tray, or a music box; return gifts for these festive occasions will also include some food. This long-lasting gift becomes a souvenir of the happy event, and the food is often shared among family members who did not attend. (In the past, only the head of household would be invited to important life cycle functions such as weddings, unless it was the wedding of a close relative, in which case other family members might attend.) The kind of food included in this return gift is carefully selected for its auspiciousness. Often, the colors red and white are important. Red beans and glutinous white rice, pink bonito flakes, or pink and white rice cakes are common presents for return gifts at happy occasions.

There are certain kinds of objects that are associated with happy or auspicious events. As in the case of the red beans and white rice, many of these objects are red or white or a combination of red and white. Even animals not naturally only red and white will be drawn with red and white colors, such as the decorations of cranes and turtles that decorate many gifts and gift wrappings given out at auspicious occasions. Cranes and turtles, symbols of longevity, are said to live one thousand and ten thousand years, respectively (Hendry 1981: 156).

In November, on *tori no ichi* (the day of the rooster), shrines sell

FIG. 3.1. Auspicious items on rake.

rakes decorated with many auspicious items, so that purchasers will "rake in" good luck in the coming year (Figure 3.1).

Identifying some of the auspicious representations on this rake provides a sense of the kinds of lucky items used in gifts given at auspicious occasions. *Kabu*, a kind of turnip that looks a little bit like a radish, is visible in the center right of Figure 3.1. It is red on the outside and white on the inside, and it is round. Round things have no edges, and therefore they symbolize smooth interpersonal relationships. To the left of the kabu are two small fans, considered auspicious because they open out, indicating that good fortune and happiness will spread out like an unfolded fan (*suehirogari*). In the past, some gifts were offered on fans, and fans still are an important part of wedding attire. (The shape of a rake is also very similar to the shape of a fan, as is the character for the number eight, which will be examined shortly.) Toward the bottom of the rake are two large sea bream, or tai. They are red, an auspicious color, and their name tai echoes the word *omedetai*, which means "auspicious." Toward the top of the rake are two carp, famous for their strength and bravery as they swim upstream, sometimes up waterfalls, to spawn. Also near the top of the rake are pine branches and plum blossoms, and toward the bottom, bamboo leaves. Chapter 1 mentions briefly how Mrs. Ueda served sweets formed in these shapes to the guests that brought wedding gifts to her home. Pine, bamboo, and plum (*shōchikubai*) are three plants considered very auspicious. In the Nara period (710–784), pine, bamboo, and plum were adapted from China as symbols of long life and happiness. Pine and bamboo stay green throughout the winter, and plum is the first flowering tree to bloom in spring.

As the examples in Chapter 1 demonstrate, the days for special events, whether weddings, funerals, or house building ceremonies, are carefully selected. The days on which it is safe to go through with certain life cycle rituals and appropriate to give gifts in relation to those events are determined by designations known as *rokuyō* (literally, "six days"; also called *rokki*). Originally, these were divisions of each day, but in the Tokugawa period (1600–1868), they began to mark entire days (Iwashita 1993: 11). The names of these six days are *senshō* ("early victory"), tomobiki ("pull friend"), *senbu* ("haste loses"), *butsumetsu* ("Buddha's death"), *taian* ("great safety"), and *shakku* ("red mouth"). Senshō is a day on which ventures concluded early are successful. Tomobiki is auspicious for a wedding, as good things will multiply on this day; it is bad luck for a funeral, as it invites another death. Senbu is a day on which early morning activities will result in failure, but a desired end will be attained later. Butsumetsu is an inauspicious day for happy events. Weddings held on this day are given roughly a 30 percent discount by hotels and wedding halls. Taian is always an auspicious designation, except for noontime. Weddings, engagements, the handing over of wedding or betrothal gifts prior to a wedding, the first visits of babies to shrines and temples—all should ideally occur on this day. Shakku is inauspicious, except for noontime. These six ritual designations of days have been correlated with the Western seven-day week, and appear on almost all Japanese calendars.

Thus all giving, but in particular giving connected with rites of passage, follows specific rules related to ideas of auspiciousness and inauspiciousness. Giving related to life cycle events, as with many other kinds of giving, emphasizes odd numbers, in particular odd numbers greater than one. When money is given, it is usually offered in odd increments. The cords used to tie the gifts are made from odd numbers of strands; a nine-stranded cord is the one with the highest number of strands, and it is appropriate for a very auspicious event, such as a wedding. Giving is connected with rites of passage of children aged three, five, and seven years; odd numbers also determine other times at which giving takes place. The following discussion will bring out such examples in more detail. Before entering into further descriptions of the different life cycle and afterlife-cycle events, the significance of odd numbers must be explained.

Every odd number greater than one contains within it both an odd and an even number (for example, 3=1+2). It would therefore seem that odd numbers are superior to even numbers because a hierarchical principle is at work, in which "the elements of a whole are ranked in relation to the whole" (Dumont 1980: 66). The inferior becomes a member of the superior; the even is subsumed within the odd.

In accordance with the philosophy of yin and yang as found in the *I ching*, even numbers are yin and odd numbers are yang.[10] Yin and yang emerge from an absolute existence that is the root of everything (*taikyoku*). Yin is moon, female, negative, disorder. Yang is sun, male, positive, order. Neither yin nor yang on its own has the power to create anything, but in combination with each other, they give birth to everything in existence. Yin and yang are not absolute principles. Yin is contained in yang, and yang within yin. Thus the relationship between yin and yang, in purely philosophical terms, is not hierarchical (Yoshino 1983: 57–58; Granet 1934: 115–48).

In some forms of practice, however, yang is superior to yin, and can even be seen as subsuming yin. P. Steven Sangren, in his work *History and Magical Power in a Chinese Community*, argues that in contrast to ancient Taoist philosophy's emphasis on the equal importance of changelessness and chaos, modern Taoist practice privileges order over disorder. For example, in a rite of cosmic renewal known as *chiao*, Taoist practitioners compel disorder (yin) to submit to order (yang) so that nature will flourish and social relations will be proper and harmonious.

Dumont's "encompassment" is expanded in Chinese yin/yang thought into what first appears to be an infinite series; yang encompasses yin, which encompasses yang, and so forth. But in the chiao this entire framework is itself encompassed at a transcendent or "meta" level by the principle of changelessness, order. This principle is no longer termed yang, but it occupies the same position in the structure of categories, relatively speaking. (Sangren 1987: 172)

It is plausible that preference for odd (yang) numbers in Japanese practices of giving and receiving is related to the hierarchical relationship between yin and yang in Chinese rituals. Although from a philosophical perspective, neither yin nor yang is superior to the other, in practice, the side that is identified as male, order, sun, and positive subsumes the side identified with female, disorder, moon, and negative. As the previous chapter demonstrated and those that follow will pursue in more detail, practices of giving often reinforce relations of hierarchy. It is hardly surprising, then, that the number of strands used to tie gifts, the numbers of objects given, and the amounts of cash placed inside the envelopes are themselves determined by a hierarchical principle.

There are some indications that even numbers were once used for gifts at inauspicious occasions. An expert on etiquette informed me that it once was the case that gifts given at funerals were tied with even numbers of strands; odd numbers of strands were used only for celebratory presents. In Warabi, gifts of rice cakes passed out at the first time a spirit returns home for the festival of the dead known as bon are given in even numbers.

In many parts of China and Taiwan, however, odd numbers are associated with gifts to the dead,[11] and even numbers are considered lucky and auspicious. Whereas virtually all Japanese people I interviewed stated that even numbers are unlucky because they can be divided, it seems that in China, the character for even number is the character for "pair" (sō) and even numbers are auspicious because good things will be doubled or brought together.[12] Experts on seasonal and life cycle events state that the emphasis on odd numbers is Chinese in origin (Tokoro 1986: 182; see also Okada and Akune 1993: 105). It is possible that thousands of years ago, the Chinese people who transmitted these customs to Japan did prefer odd numbers, and that Japanese numerological rules of giving and receiving trace their roots back to Chinese practices that have changed in the intervening centuries. What is more interesting (and relevant) than the historical development of number preferences is the status of the old Chinese model in present day Japan.

Although in Japan odd numbers are considered better for giving than even numbers, there are other rules related to numbers that are sometimes at odds with this general principle. Nine (ku), which sounds like the word for pain (ku), is considered bad luck, particularly for gifts to sick people. In other instances, however, it is considered auspicious, for 3 x 3 is the Chinese totality. A cord composed of nine strands is the most auspicious cord with which to tie a gift. The most elaborate set of lucky items that accompanies the presentation of the formal engagement gift (yuinō) has nine parts (less elaborate sets have three, five, and seven parts). Eight, although it is an even number, is considered auspicious. Most people say the reason why eight is lucky is that the Chinese character for eight widens at the bottom, indicating that good things will multiply.[13] Four is considered a very unlucky number, perhaps because it is even, but primarily because one of the pronunciations for the character for four is shi, which is the same as the word for death.

Numbers are one example of the way in which the structural characteristics are thought to convey auspicious and inauspicious qualities. In the descriptions of auspiciousness and inauspiciousness as related to practices of giving at life cycle events, there were other examples as well. To mention one: bills should be crisp, new, and face up for weddings, and old, crumpled, and face down for funerals. Fresh, new bills are to a young couple about to marry as old, crumpled bills are to a corpse; the human faces on the bills are clearly visible for the wedding gift to the living couple, but are not visible for the gift made in behalf of the human being who has passed away. New bills, I was told, indicate joyful anticipation and careful preparation on the part of the giver; old bills connote surprise, dismay, and hasty gathering of money. The gifts not only convey the sentiments of the giver but also ensure that the rite of passage will progress normally, that what is dead will remain dead and that what is living will be celebrated and enhanced. When discussing the improper giving of gifts, people recounted stories of corpses getting up from their coffins, or souls continuing to cling to this world rather than moving on to the next. Giving is more than a matter of conveying joy at life or grief at death; it is through giving that both states of existence are symbolically reinforced.

The categories of objects that are a part of this system of meanings include not only numbers but also colors, shapes, plants and animals, perishable and nonperishable items, homonyms, and uneven pairs. Red is an extremely important color for auspicious occasions related to life and reproduction. Red is the color of life, of blood and fire; it is noteworthy that, in the past, sea bream (a bright red fish) was often given at celebrations. Red beans are almost always given at celebrations. In Warabi, recipients of food at auspicious events would bring the red beans and white rice or red bean sweets home with them. They would clean the trays on which these auspicious foods had been placed, and then would return the trays with boxes of matches. Matches often have red tips and create fire, another symbol of life. Shades of red, such as pink, are also auspicious. For example, pink shavings of dried fish are a common return gift at weddings (Figures 3.5–3.7).

White by itself is a color that indicates the cutting of relationships. In Warabi, the sweets given out forty-nine days after a person's death, when the soul of the deceased separates from the world of the living, are made from white beans. Flowers at funerals are overwhelmingly white. A white envelope with a white cord is used at memorial services for people who have long been dead. Corpses, like babies and brides, are dressed in white clothes. White in combination with other colors seems to be an unmarked sign: red and white are considered auspicious, because red is auspicious; black and white are considered inauspicious, as black is inauspicious. White by itself has different meanings in different contexts. For example, flowers at funerals are white, but flowers at memorial services some years after death may be more vibrant colors. White here is seen to represent extreme and total grief, while colors other than white indicate the gradual return to normalcy. Thus white flowers are most common relatively soon after a death. However, a white envelope with a white cord might be more appropriate for a memorial service a longer time after the death, once the soul has completely departed from the world of the living.

Black is the color of death, and subdued shades such as gray and purple are also appropriate for occasions related to dying. In general, black is the only color that can be worn at funerals. Mourners at funerals appear all in black, and no other color is tolerated, especially in Tokyo, which explains why my two friends rented special black clothes for the funeral of their professor's mother.

At wakes it is acceptable to wear subdued colors such as gray or purple, because wakes are held on the first night after a person's death, and mourners may not have had time to prepare appropriate all-black outfits. Envelopes for funeral offerings of incense money are generally tied with black and white cords, or are decorated with black lines. For memorial services, gray or purple lines or cords are more common. As grief gradually subsides with time, the color becomes less severe. As the soul of the dead person becomes more and more removed from this world, it becomes less necessary to symbolically reinforce the state of death to keep the soul from staying in the world of the living.

Gold and silver are also sometimes the colors of cords used for tying envelopes. Gold and silver take on the same symbolic roles as red and white. An envelope tied with a gold and silver cord is a more elaborate version of an envelope tied with a red and white cord.

Especially auspicious shapes are those that are long, rounded, or outward- reaching. Long noodles and long sticks of candy suggest long-lasting relationships and long life spans. Rounded objects, such as tangerines and radishes, indicate never-ending, smooth relations. Shapes that spread outward, such as the shape of fans and the shape of the character for the number eight, connote ever-increasing happiness and good fortune.

In the same way that red, a color signifying life, is considered to be lucky, animals that live longer than other animals, or that are associated with reproduction, or plants that are blooming and vigorous when other plants are not, or that have preservative properties, are auspicious. As mentioned earlier, plum blossoms open in February amid the snow; bamboo and pine are green in winter when all other vegetation is dead. Bamboo is also used to store food because it helps prevent spoilage. Carp (besides being red in color) are associated with strong and enduring qualities that allow them to procreate, and are often portrayed swimming up waterfalls to spawn. Turtles and cranes are said to have life spans of a thousand years.

Auspicious foods are those that are either very fresh or those that will keep indefinitely. Sea bream was once given at auspicious occasions, and this blood-red fish may have represented life, vigor, and freshness. Sugar, sake, rice, and beans all keep for a very long time without going bad. Sake has purifying and preservative properties, as do dried squid, seaweed, and fish flakes. All of these items are considered lucky.

Auspicious objects often have names that are homonyms for lucky words and phrases. For example, the tangerine known as *dai dai* is not only round, indicating smooth, ongoing, relations, but, in addition, dai dai is a homonym for the phrase "generation to generation," indicating that the family will stay connected and flourish from one generation to the next. Dried seaweed, *konbu*, is said to be auspicious because it sounds like *yorokobu*, the word for "rejoice." Bonito flakes are not only an auspicious pink color but also a homonym for the phrase "samurai wins."

Auspicious objects are often pairs of unequal parts. For example, bonito flakes are made from bonito that has been dried and cut into two parts; the top part is the male part and the bottom part is the female part. Sometimes the top and bottom pieces are then further divided (Figure 3.5). Cups, chopsticks, rice bowls, chopstick holders, and so on are also given in pairs composed of a male and female part. These items are usually gifts intended for couples, with the object for male use larger than the object for female use. As was demonstrated in the section on numbers, unequal pairs cannot be divided into two equal parts, and thus symbolize togetherness over and against separation. Just as odd numbers subsume even numbers, larger male parts encompass smaller female parts.

All of these auspicious categories signify what is taken to be crucial for maintaining or enhancing life and maintaining or enhancing connections with other people. They also assert the hierarchical order of male over female. Emphasis on unequal pairs of male and female underscores the importance of reproduction, because it is through the symbolic combination of male and female in unequal relationships that life is believed to be created.

People pay particular attention to auspicious symbols at times of transition: when someone is leaving for a trip or returning from a trip; leaving a neighborhood or moving into a neighborhood; entering school or graduating from school; being born or dying. Implicit in these practices is the idea that giving can actually influence how completely and successfully these major boundaries are crossed.[14] Gifts to the traveler followed by reciprocation of these gifts ensure that the traveler returns safely home; gifts of odd-numbered units of money (with the bills face up in the envelope and tied with a knot that cannot be untied with a cord of a certain odd number of strands) signal a happy and fruitful marriage; a gift of a sash of a certain color (wrapped in white paper and tied with a red and white cord of an odd number of strands with a particular knot) to an expectant mother from her natal family ensures a healthy child; offering a bowl of mounded rice to the guardian deity cuts the ties of an infant to the other world and anchors it firmly in the realm of human beings. Mistakes, such as using the wrong kind of knot, placing money face down for a wedding or face up for a funeral, giving cash in units of four at an auspicious occasion, are disturbing not only because they convey a lack of consideration and therefore seem to indicate that the giver does not value the relationship with the receiver, but also because they may negatively influence a crucial point of transition. Through these symbols of auspiciousness and inauspiciousness, givers and receivers align themselves with a larger cosmic order to ensure the flourishing of the natural and social worlds. Those who do not consciously believe in this larger process still tend to act in accordance with its rules in order to show respect to the recipients of their gifts.

Department Stores and Travel Gifts

Gifts from particular department stores or localities also express respect to the recipient and link him or her to a larger hierarchical order. A woman explained to me that cookies she gave to a craft teacher at a final lesson were bought from a well-known shop; if she had baked them herself, the gift would have looked careless and sloppy. When I asked her why, she offered the following series of explanations. If the gift is bought from a famous bakery, everyone knows the price. As the last class was a formal occasion, it was important for the gift to be *kichinto shita* (exactly, scrupulously, properly done). Buying cookies from the well-known shop meant "putting up, elevating" the teacher. Giving a gift that is too familiar can be rude, as would have been the case if this lady, at her last class, had given the teacher cookies she had baked herself.

Similarly, a gift wrapped properly in the paper of a famous department store is an indication that the giver is treating the relationship with the receiver carefully, with respect. In order to protect their reputations, department stores insist on doing the wrapping in the store; they will not give out paper and let customers wrap gifts themselves. New employees spend days practicing wrapping. It is not only the name of the department store that is important, but also its location, which is stamped on the wrapping. A gift bought at the Nihonbashi branch of Mitsukoshi Department Store means that much care has been taken with one's relationship to the other person; the same gift purchased at the Ikebukuro branch of Mitsukoshi connotes less consideration. Rankings of department stores are connected to networks of transportation. Nihonbashi is the location of the original Mitsukoshi building, and it is an important place historically. The two roads linking Edo and Osaka, the Nakasendō and the Tōkaidō, end at Nihonbashi. Mitsukoshi was originally a maker of very high quality kimono, and the combination of its age, its original location, and its link with such a prestigious kind of good are all reasons why it has long been considered one of the highest ranking department stores in Tokyo. Takashimaya, an Osaka department store, is famous for exactly the same reasons; it is historically a maker of kimono located at Nipponbashi, the place in Osaka where the two highways linking Edo and Osaka end.[15] Railway companies built lower-ranking department stores, such as Tobu and Seibu, in order to sell goods to people traveling on their train lines. Tobu is the lowest ranking of all, apparently because its train lines go through areas that are the least valuable in terms of real estate.

In the same way that the selection of department store may convey respect or consideration for the giver's relationship to the recipient, the kind of present a traveler brings back from a particular place is very important. Miyage (the first character means "earth" and the second means "give birth to, produce") is the word for something produced in a particular place. A related term in English would be the French-derived "souvenir," although the connotation is different in that miyage must necessarily be given to someone who has not participated in one's journey, whereas a souvenir can be kept to remind the traveler of the trip.[16] Also, miyage are often food, which is generally not the case for souvenirs; it is because souvenirs are nonperishable that they may be kept as memories. Travelers bring back these specialty items to their families, friends, neighbors, teachers, fellow students, bosses, and colleagues. Buying presents for all the necessary people often takes up a major part of any trip. Train stations and airports offer miyage from different places, and there are companies that specialize in procuring appropriate miyage and sending them to the customer's home to relieve the burden of incessant gift buying while traveling.

Each region of Japan, and increasingly, each country of the world, is known for a particular specialty. In Chapter 1, Mrs. Inoue's traveling gifts included such items as long eggplants from Sendai and towels purchased at a Munich branch of the Mitsukoshi Department store. Why is so much energy expended in categorizing and obtaining specific items of far-away places? (See Figure 3.2 for specialty items of particular countries in a department store display.) In his master's thesis "Gift Exchange in Japan: The Role of the Foreigner," James Holland notes that miyage are appropriate if they are unique to a distant place and if the recipient recognizes the relationship between the gift and the place:

> [An] informant warns foreigners in Japan that if they should decide to buy Japanese things as gifts for Japanese, they should know which makers are famous for that product. . . . [Another] informant explains the apparent failure of certain gifts given by Americans in Japan in these terms. The Americans were from Texas, and decided to take bottles of wine made in Texas as souvenirs, but the gifts seemed poorly received. This, it appears, was because Texas is not famous for wine, and because the gifts ignored the image Texas is famous for . . . cowboys and the Old West. Leather goods, beef jerky, or cowboy hats clearly would have been more successful. (Holland 1989: 29)

Even in the case of novel items from places the recipient has never been, there is a framework that determines which items are noted or famous and which are not. In the example of the Texas wine, the gift recipients did not seem to be interested in learning about the image their guests wished to project of Texas. They would have preferred what they considered a *meibutsu*, a famed or noted product. A local item recognized by them would have ranked as a better gift than the wine prized by their guests.

In trying to determine why one gift would be valued over another gift, it is useful to see the context in which the gifts are appreciated and perhaps consumed. Miyage become conversation pieces not only between foreign visitor and Japanese host but also between the host and other people who may come to visit at a later time:

> Some *omiyage* are things that can be displayed, perhaps in the living room of a house, to serve as handy, *mezurashii* [novel, rare, unusual] triggers for conversation. Other *omiyage* are *mezurashii* things that can be served to

FIG. 3.2. European specialty items in department store display.
Photograph by author.

guests, such as whiskey or sweets. [Bottles of prestige brands of whiskey
are also prominently displayed.] Two informants volunteered the information that no matter how bad the taste, food or drink that is truly
mezurashii will be served by some Japanese because of its conversational
value. Another informant talked about the conversational value of
mezurashii whiskey when the recipient plays host to others. (ibid.: 27)

Novelty must be balanced with recognition because if a gift fits
into a well-known framework, the special status of an item can be
readily determined.[17] In much the same way that a gift from a high-
ranking department store conveys status to the recipient, meibutsu
demonstrate to others that the recipient is treated with respect.
Through careful selection of specific objects from far-away places,
the giver shows the receiver and the people with whom the receiver interacts how much the giver values the relationship with the
receiver.

Careful attention to department store rankings shows respect for the recipient and also links the recipient to a larger hierarchical system of value. Careful attention to selection of travel gifts conveys respect for the recipient and at the same time aligns the recipient to a larger cosmic process, allowing the recipient to both experience and dominate difference. Attention to notions of auspiciousness and inauspiciousness shows respect for the recipient and emphasizes reproduction predicated on encompassment at these major points of transition.

A twenty-year-old woman told me once that she was not yet experienced enough to give "important" gifts (gifts related to seasonal and life cycle events), and that the thought of participating in formal giving intimidated her. Giving can, according to this larger system of symbolic meanings, either positively or negatively influence major times of transition. Emphasis on choosing an auspicious day, for example, ensures that happenings on earth are synchronous with the rhythm of the heavens. Ignorance of the celestial cycle of days could, following this logic, result in an unhappy marriage or a second death at a funeral. The cosmic processes reflected and reinforced in practices of giving are fundamental to the rites of passage of almost all individuals.

Rites of Passage

BIRTH

On the day of the dog in the fifth month of a woman's pregnancy, her natal household, usually her mother, traditionally gives her a *fukutai* (long band of cloth) to bind around her abdomen. This cloth is wrapped in paper and tied with mizuhiki, the special cords used for gifts. In Warabi, some families also attach dried abalone or a symbol of dried abalone and the glutinous rice with red beans eaten at auspicious events. Most of these bands have been made from red and white cloth. From 1942 to 1945, the city government gave fukutai to expectant mothers (Kodama 1993: 78–79). The day of the dog is chosen for presentation of this band because dogs are said to give birth easily; at shrines dedicated to fertility and childbirth, there are often statues of dogs. Some women noted that their mothers taught them the complicated process of wrapping the band of cloth around their abdomens; in other cases, although the cloth came from their own households— in particular, from their own mothers—it was their mothers-in-law who taught them how to wear fukutai. Many women who do not have the patience for wrapping themselves up with a cloth band generally wear a girdle from the fifth month onward. Covering the stomach, whether it is with a traditional cloth band or a modern girdle, is considered important for keeping the baby warm and protected. The giving of the band and the gift itself is called *obiiwai*. It is at this point that the woman's pregnancy is officially recognized, and wearing of the band is said to ensure a healthy child and safe birth.

Often a friend or relative of the expectant mother will go to a shrine or temple, sometimes a local one and sometimes one farther away that specializes in pregnancy and childbirth, and will obtain a protective charm that will be placed inside the band, next to the woman's stomach. In some cases, the contents of this charm can be dissolved in water and then drunk once labor has begun. Another common practice is for a friend or relative of the expectant mother to obtain pieces of paper said to contain gods, usually from the shrine of the tutelary deity of the pregnant woman's area. These papers are placed on the household's Shintō shrine, or, if from a temple, on the Buddhist altar, in hopes of a safe delivery. Women who do not go to shrines or temples and who do not believe in such charms or pieces of paper may still receive them from relatives, and there is usually a great deal of reluctance to simply throw these things away; they are kept in a drawer somewhere (see also Reader and Tanabe 1998: 37–53).

In Warabi, some births are still overseen by midwives, who supervise births in hospitals. The routine delivery of babies in hospitals represents a big change from fifty years ago; in 1947, only 2.4 percent of Japanese women gave birth in hospitals (Kodama 1993: 88). In some of the older households along the Nakasendō, midwives may deliver successive generations of children. The eldest daughter of Mr. Hoshino (the fuel dealer who held the house-building ceremony) recently gave birth to her first child, his first grand-child. The midwife who delivered Mr. Hoshino and then his daughter also delivered his daughter's daughter, and participated in the rites of passage surrounding this birth. Until recently, expectant parents and their families held a small party for the midwife (sometimes combined with the celebration of the cloth band in the fifth month) in order to ask her favor and assistance in the upcoming birth.

Throughout pregnancy and birth, a woman's ties to her natal household are emphasized. In Warabi until World War II, it is said that a woman would tell her mother she was pregnant, and her mother, bearing gifts, would visit her daughter's husband's family to inform them of the good news and ask them to treat her daughter favorably. The woman's mother would come to stay with her daughter during the labor, delivery, and recovery. The woman's mother brought enough rice to feed her daughter and herself during the time she would be staying, and she did all the cooking of the meals for her daughter, sometimes as many as six times a day. The period after childbirth was one of pollution, and a woman who had given birth was forbidden from eating from the food of the rest of the household. Many women today return to their natal households shortly before their babies are due to be born, and stay with their own families for a month or so after childbirth.

In times now past in Warabi, while the midwife was bathing the newborn baby, the rest of the family would make an offering of a rounded bowl of rice to the paper containing the spirit of the household's tutelary deity. The water from the baby's first bath would be buried near the well, and the father of the baby would make an offering of sake to the god of the well, as water was considered the underlying force of all new life. Until the third day of a baby's life, it was kept naked, either on its mother's stomach or on old kimono. On the third day after its birth, it would be dressed in a baby's *yukata* (a simple kimono.) This yukata and the futon the baby slept on were gifts from its maternal grandmother (ibid.: 82–90).

Most doctors expect to receive a gift of money when they deliver a child. This is in addition to payment of fees for their services. The amount of money of the gift depends on the kind of delivery and the extent of the medical procedures performed. For Cesarean sections, it is about 100,000 yen and for vaginal deliveries it is less, but at least 10,000 to 30,000 yen. The amount of money also depends on the rank of the hospital and the rank of the doctor; this information usually emerges from discussions with friends, relatives, nurses, and other patients. Sometimes this money is given with a box of sweets directly to the doctor. At hospitals where there are signs prohibiting doctors from receiving such gifts, a letter of thanks and gift certificates worth the proper cash amount are often sent to the doctor's home. Nurses do not usually receive money, but rather boxes of sweets that they share among themselves.

Many families still observe a naming ceremony held on the seventh night after the birth of an infant. It is at this time, according to some people, that the child is recognized officially as a human being. This occasion is called *shichiya* (seventh night), and it often takes place in the home of the paternal grandparents. The name of the child is written on a white piece of paper and hung in the Shintō shrine, Buddhist altar, or in homes without, on the wall above the child's bed or in the room where the naming event takes place. Close relatives and sometimes friends gather for a meal of auspicious foods such as red beans and white rice and fish with both head and tail still attached. In some places, a tray containing a small portion of this food is offered ceremonially to the baby. Guests will bring various gifts for the baby, such as clothing and toys, money (usually 5,000 to 10,000 yen, depending on the relationship and other circumstances), sake, and sometimes food such as custard for the new mother. In the past, sugar and rice were common gifts. Return gifts given to the guests will usually include auspicious items such a bonito flakes, or pink and white rice cakes. Some families celebrate the seventh night up to a month or so after the birth, as in some cases the mother and child are kept at the hospital for over a week, and the first days and weeks at home are hectic. (See also Beardsley 1959: 291; Embree 1939: 179–83; Hendry 1981: 201; Iwashita 1993a: 46, and 1996: 60–61; Kodama 1993: 92; Norbeck 1954: 167; Yoshizawa 1989: 41.)

Friends, neighbors, and relatives who do not attend the seventh night ceremony also give baby gifts, known as *shussaniwai*. They will also bring gifts to the mother and to the grandparents. One new grandmother reported receiving a special brand of sake known by the brand name Hatsumago (first grandchild). Gifts of special foods for the mother are given directly to her or to her mother or mother-in-law. Gifts specifically for the baby are reciprocated about one month after the birth with gifts known as *uchiiwai*. Uchiiwai are given because a celebratory event has occurred within a family; they are technically not return gifts. However, in practice, they are nowadays given only to those who have given baby gifts, and are often calculated to be half to a third the cost of the original gift. The baby's name is written under the characters for uchiiwai on the paper that is attached to the gift. In the past, gifts given at this time were often food such as red beans and white rice; today, they have become more elaborate.

Uchiiwai are sent out at the end of the period of impurity connected to birth. The period of impurity for girl babies is slightly longer than the period of impurity for boy babies; usually, in the case of boys, it is for thirty-one days, and for girls, it is for thirty-three. The number of days differs slightly from one region to the next; for example, in some places it is thirty days for boys and thirty-one days for girls. At the end of this time of impurity, the baby, dressed in festive clothing given by its maternal grandparents and carried by its paternal grandmother, visits the local tutelary deity. This is called *miyamairi* (shrine visit). The color of the baby's under-kimono is white, the same color as the kimono worn by brides and corpses. Sometimes everyday baby clothes are substituted for traditional clothing, and recently, special outfits are rented specifically for the occasion. Often the baby is made to cry so that the deity will be sure to recognize the baby and will continue to protect it. Today, at many shrines, a Shintō priest conducts a special ceremony of purification for a fee. Often the visit to the shrine coincides with a woman's return, after staying with her parents, to the home she shares with her husband and possibly his parents. After the miyamairi, family members hold a small party. If the doctor or midwife is close to the family, as in the case of the midwife who delivered Mr. Hoshino's granddaughter, she or he may attend the party. Some families, at the end of this month after birth, will give a small gift to the doctor or midwife who delivered the child.

There are parallels between the end of the period of pollution from childbirth and the visit to the shrine about a month after a baby's birth and the end of the mourning period forty-nine days after a person's death. Embree writes that the day on which the visit to the shrine occurs and the event itself are called *hiaki* (in standard Japanese, *hiake*). The same term, he states, is used to signify the end of the forty-nine day period of mourning for the dead. During the first month of a baby's life, its soul is not well fixed in its body, and so hiaki marks the end of a period of danger and uncertainty. From now on the child can be carried on the back and across water, "for he is now recognized by the gods as well as by the people of his world" (Embree 1939: 183). Hendry notes a similar word that signifies the end of the pollution period after birth (*hi no hare*: day that clears). Most people I interviewed were not familiar with the belief that a child's soul is not firmly attached until a month or so after its birth, although they did know the term *kiake* (end of mourning) in connection with the passing of forty-nine days after a person's death. At that time, the soul of the deceased is completely separated from the body. However, in the past in Warabi, it was a practice both to effect and to mark the end of the period of pollution after an infant's birth by giving out white glutinous rice and red beans to families with infants and small children with whom the baby would eventually play. This event was known as *hiawase*, and it was through the offerings of food that the period of pollution was lifted (Kodama 1993: 93). White glutinous rice cakes still mark kiake, the end of the forty-nine-day period of mourning.

The hundredth day after the birth of a baby is known as *kuizome* or *momoka*. On that day, even though the infant is not actually able to eat, a small tray with small chopsticks and assorted delicacies, including red beans with glutinous white rice, is offered ceremonially to the infant. Some of the foods that may be offered are fish with head and tail still attached, vegetables, and meat. This celebration is smaller than the seventh-night festivities, but grandparents or close friends may attend.

FIRST BIRTHDAY AND FIRST STEPS

In present-day Japan, it is customary to celebrate the birthdays of small children, although it is less common to make much of the birthdays of older children or adults. Before 1945, in Warabi and in other parts of Japan, the first birthday was celebrated but other birthdays were not, as everyone was considered to be one year older every New Year. In general, the first birthday was not nearly as important as the first *sekku*, a seasonal celebration either on the third of March for girls or the fifth of May for boys, as the next chapter explores in detail.

If a baby walked before its first birthday, a special ceremony called *ashi no iwai* (celebration of the legs) was held, in which rice cakes were added to a furoshiki tied to the toddler's back until the toddler fell over.[18] Early walking was feared as well as celebrated, especially in the case of the first son. It was said that a child who walked early would leave his family's house once he grew to be an adult, and a first son was expected to take over as head of household when his own father died. The rice cakes added to the furoshiki not only physically forced the toddler to the ground, but also were said to exert a magical power that would keep the child from leaving home (ibid.: 97).

7-5-3

On November 15 of each year, children aged three, five, and seven years go with their families to shrines and temples in order to give thanks for their growth and their health, and to pray for the continued favor of the Shintō or Buddhist deities. Until the age of seven, children were considered not quite firmly planted in the world of humans; they were known as *kami no ko* (children of the gods). The celebrations at three, five, and seven years of age marked and effected the progressive distance from the other world and immersion in this world. Cutting ties to the world of deities was begun already in the offering of the rounded bowl of rice when the child was born, but it continued in these rites marking the third, fifth, and seventh years of life. When the child safely turned seven and conclusively severed the relationship with the other world, the probability that it would suddenly become ill and die was believed to be greatly reduced. Most parents who take their children to shrines or temples on November 15 do not necessarily believe in such dangers, but they nevertheless celebrate these rites of passage, usually with their parents and other friends and relatives.

Which genders celebrate which years varies according to family, region, and historical period. For example, until the Meiji era, in Warabi, it was the practice for boys of five and seven and girls of three and seven to have 7–5–3 on November 15. In other places, all children aged three, five, and seven took part in this event. Now, because people no longer recognize the age of seven as the final point at which a child moves permanently from being a child of the gods to being a child of the human community, these practices have undergone further change. In Warabi, three- and seven-year-old girls and five-year-old boys now observe 7–5–3, although this varies slightly from one household to the next. Several parents claimed that girls celebrate both at ages three and seven, and boys celebrate only at age five because it is more fun to dress little girls up in kimono. Three is a number usually associated with girls, and five with boys, as the girls' most important seasonal festival is on the third day of the third month, and the boys' is on the fifth day of the fifth month.

Traditionally, a child wore adult clothing, kimono with *obi* (band or sash) for the first time when it reached three years of age. Because Warabi was a town of weavers, many women made these special kimono for the eldest boy and girl of their daughters. (Subsequent sons and daughters wore ordinary clothing; the practice of celebrating 7–5–3 in the same way regardless of birth order started only after 1945.) The backs of the yukata that infants wore had no seams, because the width of one bolt of cloth was enough to cover that area. Adult kimono consist of two bolts of cloth stitched together. The kimono of three-year-old children have seams that mimic adult kimono. The back section is, like the infant yukata, made from only one piece of cloth; the seam is added to mark it as different from a baby's clothing. Today, it is most often the child's maternal grandparents who buy or rent the kimono worn for this occasion.[19]

Most families visit shrines on 7-5-3, although some, mostly devout Buddhists, go to temples. Now it has become popular in cities such as Tokyo to go to very famous shrines, such as the Meiji shrine, rather than to the tutelary deity of the area in which one lives. Many families in Warabi still take their children to the Warabi shrine, undergo a special purification rite, and leave with paper bags containing long red and white candied sugar sticks known as *chitoseame*, which symbolize a long life of a thousand years. In the past, offerings of red beans and white glutinous rice were made to the shrine, but now these have been replaced for the most part with money. Often a small party for friends and relatives is held after the visit to the shrine, and guests bring celebratory envelopes containing money. The butterfly knot, indicating that this occasion is a happy one that may be repeated, is used. In the case of close relatives, the amount given is usually 10,000 to 20,000 yen; more distant relatives and friends generally give from 5,000 to 10,000 yen. Of course, these amounts vary according to region, class, and individual family. Return gifts of auspicious items such as bonito flakes and white and pink rice cakes may be given to guests on their departure. Some people interviewed compared 7-5-3, especially in the case of girls, to a small version of a wedding celebration.[20]

Before leaving in the morning for a shrine or temple, children visit neighbors to show off their kimono. Neighbors may also gather on the street shortly before the family is ready to leave for the shrine or temple. Gifts from neighbors are usually under 5,000 yen; in the neighborhood where I lived, 1,000 yen was the most common, but this is unusually low. In higher income areas, gifts from neighbors at 7-5-3 are usually at least 3,000 yen. This money is inserted into an envelope, and because it is a relatively small amount, drawings of the slice of dried bonito and the butterfly tie are printed with red ink directly on the paper. Return gifts to neigh-

FIG. 3.3. Two girls at shrine on 7-5-3. Photograph by author.

bors include bags of chitoseame (with the number of sticks in each bag sometimes corresponding to the age of the child), red beans and white glutinous rice, or some kind of auspicious sweets.

ENTERING SCHOOL, GRADUATING, AND SIMILAR RITES OF PASSAGE

While each new level of schooling a child begins may be marked by the giving of gifts and small-scale celebrations, perhaps the most attention is focused on a child's entry into elementary school. Parents buy the standard backpack, usually black for boys and red for girls, carried by elementary school students; other school-related items, such as a desk, pencil holder, and other supplies, may also

FIG. 3.4. Gifts for students on the first day of first grade. Photograph by author.

be given to the child. Friends and relatives may also give presents of money, school supplies, or gift certificates for books.[21] It is unnecessary for return gifts to be made for gifts given to children, although some families still make return gifts.[22] A special ceremony is held on the first day of school, which is in April, usually just as the cherry blossoms open. These ceremonies are extremely festive and elaborate; a Japanese woman I know whose daughter entered the first grade in an American school was shocked at how little attention was given to the event in this country. The entire school assembles to welcome the new first graders. In one such ceremony I attended in Warabi, the second graders escorted the first graders to seats in the school auditorium, and afterward, both the school principal and a sixth grade student made speeches welcoming the incoming students. After the program in the auditorium ended, the students went to their respective classrooms. On each desk of the first grade students lay a pile of wrapped gifts (Figure 3.4). The students' mothers and some fathers stood in the back of the room. Everyone was formally dressed; some mothers wore kimono, all fathers wore suits, and even the little boys and girls wore their best clothes. The first hour of class involved unwrapping the textbooks and other school supplies in the order instructed by the teacher. Included was a special gift from the local government.

Gifts given upon entrance to middle school, high school, and university, and gifts given upon graduation from those various schools, as well as gifts given upon entry into a company, are similar. People with close personal ties to the child or young adult give these presents, and there is technically no need to make immediate return gifts, although over time neighbors and relatives will give to each other's children on these occasions. When a person enters a company, often a portion of the first salary is used to buy gifts for those people to whom the young person has become indebted, such as parents and a favorite teacher. At this time, small presents may also be given to the people who gave money or other presents at the time of graduation or entrance into the workforce.

BECOMING AN ADULT

Ceremonies symbolizing and effecting transition to adulthood were instituted in the Meiji era. Perhaps 60 percent of young Japanese people actually attend the January 15 ceremonies organized by local governments to congratulate twenty-year-olds on their adult status, their right to vote, and to remind them of their various responsibilities. Many young women wear long-sleeved kimono (only unmarried women wear this particular style) and men wear suits. It is common on this day to pay visits to shrines and sometimes temples. Especially in the case of young men and women who live with their parents, neighbors who have known the young person since he or she was a small child may gather and give gifts, usually of cash. Depending on the income levels in the neighborhood and the depth of relationship between the neighbors and the young person and his or her family, the amounts vary from 3,000 to 20,000 yen. Twenty-year-old women receive more attention and money for clothing than twenty-year-old men. In 1996, the average cost of a woman's kimono for this occasion was 300,000 yen, and some families spend 1,000,000 yen or even more.

Renting such a kimono and the accessories costs 100,000 yen for one day. It is usually the parents who give their children the clothing that is worn on January 15. In the case of daughters, this clothing is extremely expensive. I have known women who have asked to have the money instead of the kimono, and who have used this money to go on trips overseas. On the other hand, suits for men rarely cost more than 50,000 yen. Relatives such as aunts, uncles, and grandparents will also give money on this day, usually between 10,000 and 50,000 yen, depending on the relationship. Young men and women who attend the official coming of age ceremonies also receive token gifts from their local governments.

Before these coming of age ceremonies started by the Meiji government, becoming an adult was something altogether different. In Warabi, this process started when a girl was seven and a boy was thirteen. An aunt gave a girl an undergarment like those worn by adult women, and an uncle gave a boy a loincloth like those worn by adult men, similar to the type still worn today at festivals by men carrying portable shrines. This time of transition was when the aunt or uncle explained about sex, including masturbation, and, in the case of boys, nocturnal emissions. Parents were considered ill suited for talking about such topics with their own children. Entrance into the community's young adult group was contingent not on age but on ability to perform certain kinds of work in certain amounts of time. In one day a man needed to carry 60 kilograms of rice a certain distance, or prepare a field for planting equal in area to 600 tatami mats, or husk 50 kilograms of rice, or harvest 120 kilograms of rice, or make 10 pairs of straw sandals, or make a rope of 540 meters. Women were supposed to be able to do 70 percent of what a man could accomplish in the same time. Further tests included whether a woman could, in one day, spin thread equivalent to one large rice ball or weave a piece of cloth 34 centimeters by 20 meters (ibid.: 101–2; Tokoro 1986: 191–92). However, the coming of age ceremony that was marked by the giving of an undergarment was the informal one related to sexual maturity; attainment of adulthood in pre-Meiji times marked by entrance into the young adult men's or women's group did not necessarily involve the giving and receiving of objects.

MARRIAGE

There have been tremendous changes in practices of betrothal and marriage over the course of Japanese history. In the Nara (710–784) and Heian (794–1185) periods, despite the marriage politics practiced by the elite, there were not usually formal engagements. Weddings recognized relationships that already existed: a man simply began sleeping at a woman's house and eventually was incorporated into her family. Engagements became important in the Edo period (1600–1868), particularly among samurai. In order to find a partner of the appropriate rank, searches were conducted across feudal domains, and the practice of both formal engagements and marriages conducted in the home of the groom, with the subsequent incorporation of the bride into the groom's family, became the rule. These practices then spread from the samurai to other social classes. Prior to the Meiji period, the actual marriage ceremonies were simple affairs involving the bride and groom drinking sake from the same cup, and perhaps sharing some rice cakes. The Meiji government, in order to strengthen imperial Shintō as a national religion, promoted an official Shintō wedding ceremony starting with the marriage of the Emperor Meiji. After World War II, when shrines lost much of the government's financial support, they began performing wedding ceremonies in order to bring in revenue. It was therefore not until after 1945 that it became common for marriages to occur outside of people's homes (Minami 1994: 113–16).

Numerous exchanges are made in connection with marriage. In some areas, gifts may be exchanged when a decision is reached for two people to marry. In almost all areas, the presentation of betrothal gifts both marks and reinforces the promise to marry.[23] Most couples today buy sets of lucky items to accompany the cash that constitutes the main portion of the betrothal gift. Department stores sell these sets. In the past, there was no such standardization, and some elderly people smile at the elaborate sets in the department stores.

The sets that the department stores sell come in groups of nine, seven, five, and, very rarely, three items. The most elaborate one has nine items. It contains a piece of dried abalone wrapped in white paper. Abalone lives for many years in the ocean, grows to a very large size, and is thus symbolic of a long life. The second item the set includes is a pair of white fans that unfold in the same way the couple's happiness and good fortune will unfold. The third is a pair of two dolls depicting an old couple, or it may be a kind of seaweed that looks like long, white hair, indicating that the couple will grow old together. The fourth is dried squid, because the more you chew it, the more flavor comes out; the implication is that the closer the husband and wife become, the more each will appreciate the good qualities of the other. The fifth is the kind of dried seaweed known as konbu, auspicious because it sounds like the word to rejoice, yorokobu. It is labeled not with its usual characters but rather with ones that can be pronounced konbu, but which mean "a woman who will bear children." The sixth is dried bonito (*katsuobushi*), also an auspicious food, reddish in color. Katsuobushi can be written with characters meaning "victorious warrior." Before this fish is dried, the head and tail are cut off and the underside containing the belly region is cut from the top side containing the back. These two parts are wrapped in white paper. As was mentioned in the section on auspicious objects, the bottom and top parts of the bonito, the different halves that make up the whole, are analogous to the male and the female together composing the marital unit. Katsuobushi is grated and used in cooking; it is often given as a return gift at weddings (Figures 3.5–3.7). The seventh item is a cask made from willow for holding sake; *yanagidaru*, the name for this container, is written with characters meaning "lots of happiness within the house." The eighth item is an inventory of the various gifts, written with pen and brush on high-quality paper in a specific format. The ninth item is an envelope containing cash. These auspicious objects are displayed in the bride's home until after the marriage. They are then either saved or taken to a shrine to be burned. Throwing the set into the ordinary trash is considered disrespectful and unlucky.

The cash amount of the groom's betrothal gift is technically supposed to be equivalent to three months of the groom's salary. In

FIG. 3.5. Grated *katsuobushi* is a popular gift item for auspicious occasions. Photograph by author.

the rare cases nowadays in which the groom assumes the bride's name and enters the bride's family, the money is given by the bride's family to the groom's family, and it is usually at least twice as much as would be given if the situation were reversed. I found that 1,000,000 yen was what most grooms gave. Surprisingly, this amount did not seem to vary as widely as I thought it would according to occupation and income level. For example, a man in his midtwenties who worked in a small shop making teriyaki chicken, a doctor in his early thirties, and a man in his midthirties who owned his own film production company all gave 1,000,000 yen as part of their betrothal gifts. In none of these cases was half of the original gift returned, although that is the practice in some areas and in some families. According to a 1992 survey by Sanwa Bank, roughly 40 percent of men gave their fiancées 1,000,000 yen (the amount was higher in the Kantō area than in the Kansai area), 20

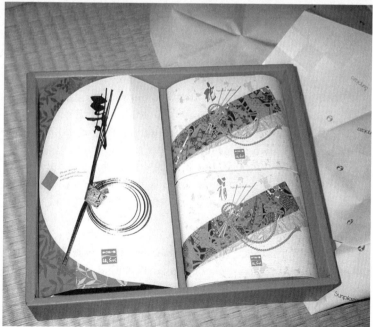

FIGS. 3.6–3.7. Wedding return gift (shown both open and closed) containing *katsuobushi*. Photographs by author.

percent gave 500,000 yen, and 20 percent reported not giving anything at all (Iwashita 1993: 23). Older people I interviewed said that the practice of giving cash occurred even before World War II, although the amounts of money were considerably lower. One elderly grandfather in Warabi grinned and told me that many people simply handed over a beautifully decorated but empty envelope, for they were too poor to put any money inside. What was important, he maintained, was the formality of giving the envelope.

The way the groom's family presents betrothal gifts to the bride's family varies greatly according to region, class, and individual family. The male go-between (nakōdo) presides over the presentation of engagement gifts.[24] If he is too busy to attend, a favorite uncle or family friend familiar with the various procedures may substitute for him. Sometimes, this event occurs in the home of the bride, very rarely in the home of the groom, sometimes in a hotel, or sometimes in a private room of a restaurant.

Etiquette books for these ceremonies describe words to be spoken, ways of presenting and receiving the gifts, and so on. Many of these instructions are similar to those found in manuals for tea ceremony, especially the guidelines for sitting, bowing, offering, unfolding papers, and moving within tatami rooms. It is usually the go-between who does most of the talking and the mothers of the bride and groom and the wife of the go-between who do the complicated maneuvering, to spare the couple from having to remember which way to turn, how to present certain items, what to say, and so on. The instructions in each book, television program, or video are slightly different, but it seems that what is important is not so much exactly how these motions are carried out, or exactly what kinds of formal language are used. Rather, the words and actions should emerge in a particular way with particular care, thus demonstrating that one is putting one's whole heart into this ritual. Many people smiled and told me that they could not really remember any details from their own betrothal ceremonies, but added that if they ever had to act as go-betweens, or if their own children ever married, they would probably study in order to do a good job. However, there is a great deal of variation in preoccupation with these rules; Edwards, in his work on Japanese weddings, describes a go-between whose wife laughed so hard when he began speaking in formal language that he simply gave up and carried out the remainder of the ritual in everyday Japanese (Edwards 1989: 80).

Roughly one-third of the time, a return gift will be made from the bride and her family to the groom. This return gift is usually something to wear, such as a suit or a watch. In most cases, this gift is a token worth a relatively small fraction of the original present. In some cases, however, the bride's family will make a return gift of half the money, although such a return gift is usually not made nowadays; instead, the amount of the original cash gift is halved. Often the present to the groom mirrors a present of an engagement ring or some other personal item that he gives to the bride.

The money the bride receives as part of the betrothal gifts is used to buy furnishings and other items for the couple's new home. Even when the bride moves into her husband's parents' house, she usually brings such items as chests of drawers and bedding. In Nagoya, a city in Chūbu famous for its elaborate weddings, wealthier families arrange for the transportation of the trousseau in small trucks whose sides are covered with glass. In the business families among whom anthropologist Matthews Hamabata conducted his field research, the selection of items for the trousseau (including Western porcelain and silverware, Japanese dinnerware, linens, chests, kimono) was an important act performed by a mother for her outmarrying daughter in order to ensure that the bride would be accepted into her new household. Positive reception of the trousseau by the bride-to-be's future mother-in-law was met with great relief, for it meant recognition of the bride-to-be's good upbringing (Hamabata 1990: 144). Only one of the many families I interviewed adhered to such formal customs concerning the trousseau; most women purchased necessary items such as stoves, refrigerators, storage chests, and so on, and the ritual viewing of the trousseau was often skipped altogether. In many cases, future in-laws, in particular future mothers-in-law, make some evaluation based on the trousseau of the taste and refinement of the bride-to-be and her family. But this level of scrutiny is most prevalent in wealthy families and in families in which the groom-to-be is the oldest son and the newlyweds will live with the husband's parents. Lebra recounts the enormous expense of dowries for brides marrying into the imperial family (Lebra 1993: 229–31).

In urban areas in the period immediately after the end of World War II, many weddings were held at shrines. As the emphasis shifted from inviting primarily relatives to inviting some relatives but also including many superiors and colleagues from the workplace, shrines could no longer accommodate the increasing number of people. Even in the countryside, where some weddings were still held in homes in the postwar period, as modern houses were built without the sliding doors that enabled smaller rooms to be converted into one large room, more and more weddings were held in *kekkonshikijō* ("wedding palaces"). As ties with people at the workplace became progressively more important in terms of social interaction and career advancement than ties with extended family members, the wedding reception, which was attended by all guests, eclipsed the actual marriage ceremony, which was attended only by relatives. Edwards (1989) and Goldstein-Gidoni (1997) offer extensive analyses of the wedding productions orchestrated in marriage palaces and hotels.

The core of the wedding ceremony is a ritual exchange of sake between the bride and the groom, and between the family of the bride and the family of the groom. The sake is served in the same kind of lacquerware set with the three nested cups that people drink from at New Year's celebrations. Drinking of sake is one way of forging ties (*en o musubu*) with another person. In daily life, this connection is made because one person pours for another, and the receiver lightly places fingertips on the cup as the sake flows in; there is in this way a link between giver and recipient. Often, but not always, there is a hierarchical component to this connection; the junior person first serves the senior person, or the host first serves the guest, and then later, this action may be reciprocated. At marriage ceremonies from the Heian period (794–1185) onward, the connection between groom and bride has been formed by their drinking sake from the same cup. This ritual was formalized in the Meiji period (1868–1912), and today the bride and groom drink three times from each of the three cups (*sansankudo*, 3×3, the auspicious Chinese totality). The next chapter will explore how New Year's rituals of visiting, giving, and receiving, including the drinking of sake, bind people together and reinforce relationships of hierarchy. In the Shintō marriage ceremony, there is a hierarchical order in which the participants drink. First the groom drinks, and then the bride. When it is time for the parents to drink, the groom's parents drink before the bride's parents, and the fathers drink before the mothers.

The wedding industry in Japan is a vast service sector, highly commercialized and elaborated (Edwards 1989; Goldstein-Gidoni 1997). Many of the rituals within the reception originated in manufacturers' campaigns for market expansion. For example, the candle ceremony, in which the bride and groom move from one table to the next to light the candles on the tables and converse briefly with their guests, was created by the Kameya candle company in 1974. Its sales were declining because of consumers' preference for electric lights on altars for safety reasons, as well as the general decline in household altars (Minami 1994: 118). Rentals of the traditional kimono, wedding gown, and Western evening dress worn by the bride at various points in the reception cost between 1,000,000 and 2,000,000 yen, depending on the kind of hotel or wedding palace and the type of clothing selected. Wedding palaces reached the peak of their popularity in the mid-1980s, and the current preference seems to be for hotels.

The more sumptuous displays of light shows and dry ice of the 1980s and early 1990s have been streamlined, but most receptions still resemble a theatrical production punctuated by segments of a fashion show. The main elements are speeches by high-ranking guests, followed by speeches by lower-ranking guests and possibly skits or singing by friends of the bride and groom, a cake cutting ceremony (artificial cakes are rented to guests with prices determined by the height of the cake, and a single piece of actual cake is cut by the bridal pair), "candle service," presentation of bouquets from the bridal pair to their parents, and a speech by the father of the groom and possibly also by the father of the bride, which concludes the celebration.

The gifts to wedding guests as they depart from the reception are usually selected from thick brochures or catalogues prior to the wedding. In some cases families procure the gifts themselves, and they are placed in a bag bearing the logo of the hotel or wedding hall. The kinds of gifts vary greatly from one wedding to another, but as mentioned in the section on auspiciousness and inauspiciousness, they tend to include one item that will serve as a reminder of this happy event, as well as auspicious foods and other less permanent objects. At one wedding I attended, I received a bag full of very heavy, traditional gifts. These included glutinous white rice and red beans, dried bonito flakes, pink and white rice cakes, sea bream, a set of dishes, as well as smaller items, such as a telephone card with a photograph of the bridal pair. There is a recent trend in large urban areas such as Tokyo to give a small bag containing a catalogue from which the guests can select the gifts they prefer. Sometimes disagreements emerge between the families of the bride and groom as to what kinds of return gifts are appropriate. For example, at the marriage of a woman whose parents lived in Tokyo to a man whose family came from Niigata, the family of the woman preferred a few compact, light, expensive gifts, whereas the family of the man preferred many bulky, heavy, cheaper gifts. The woman's mother said with exasperation, "All those country bumpkins care about is that the bags weigh as much as possible." Some families I interviewed actually had two different sets of bags to give out to the guests, one kind for those guests connected to the groom and another to those related to the bride.

Some gifts, as noted in the first chapter with the example of the weddings of Mrs. Ueda's children, are sent through the mail after the wedding, or are brought in person to the recipient's house. Much of the honeymoon is spent purchasing further gifts for friends, relatives, and others; in 1989, Japanese newlyweds in Hawaii spent an average of $2,111 per couple on gifts (Tobin 1992: 205).

DEATH[25]

Until the mid-1960s, wakes and funerals in Warabi were held in the homes of the deceased. When a person died, close family members, in order of hierarchical position within the family, wiped the deceased's mouth. They flexed the limbs of the corpse to keep them pliable as long as possible, so that the tasks ahead, such as bathing the body and inserting it into a barrel-shaped coffin, would be easier. The household's Shintō altar was covered with long, white pieces of paper to protect it from the impurity of death. It would remain covered for forty-nine days, until the soul of the dead person went to the other world. Although sleeping with one's head to the north is avoided in daily life, the dead body was laid out with its head pointing toward the north (yin). On the chest of the deceased, a knife, scissors, or other sharp instrument was placed in order to protect it from evil spirits, or perhaps to facilitate cutting ties with the living. A small table with offerings of incense, candles, and flowers was set in front of the body.

The family of the deceased quickly informed the head of the neighborhood association, who organized the necessary helpers. The bereaved family itself did very little work; almost all preparations were in the hands of friends and neighbors, who came to help in pairs of husbands and wives. Two men were selected to walk from door to door to spread the news of the death. These men avoided greetings and conversation with any people they passed on their way. They would give this news either at the entrance way or the veranda, and even if they were offered food, they would eat only on the veranda; they would not enter the house. For this reason, still today in Warabi it is considered inauspicious for two men to walk with one another side by side. They or other men took care of notifying all relatives who lived far away. Other jobs the male helpers performed included contacting the temple, the local funeral company, making a program for the funeral, and digging the grave. Many of the necessary items were borrowed from the temple or rented from the funeral company. One person kept track of money used for funeral expenses and money received as funeral gifts; any costs in excess of the money taken in were borne by the neighbors, although today these remaining expenses are covered by the family of the deceased. Before World War II, most mourners brought food such as rice or sugar rather than money, and because most of the labor was provided by people living in the neighborhood, there were few instances when money actually changed hands. Today in Warabi, professionals at the local funeral company, Isecho, handle most of the work of wakes and funerals.

The women who came to help did all of the cooking and serving of food, including the preparation of food to be offered to the corpse and also the food given as part of the return gifts to the parting guests. *Makuradango* ("pillow rice balls"—rice balls placed at the pillow of the corpse) were offered to the deceased in two sets of four.[26] A bowl of mounded rice, *makurameshi* ("pillow rice") was also offered to the corpse. In contrast to daily practice, this rice was not rinsed before cooking. As described in the beginning of this chapter, two bowls were filled with the cooked rice, and one rice bowl was put on top of the other, and then removed. In this way, the offering had a rounded, complete shape. Two chopsticks were inserted perpendicular to the top of the rice, which was then offered to the corpse on a tray with miso soup. A living person usually eats from the rice bowl to the left of the soup; when presenting a tray of food to the corpse, however, the orientation was reversed, with the rice bowl to the right of the soup.[27] Both inserting chopsticks upright into a bowl of rice and offering rice to the right of soup are practices considered extremely inauspicious in daily life.

Two of the male helpers then went to Isecho, the funeral company, which in prewar days was more of a specialty store for funeral items. They ordered a coffin, ancestral tablets, and long, slender pieces of wood pointed on both ends on which the name of the deceased would be written. Until the mid-1950s, almost all corpses in Warabi were buried. Only those who were thought to be carriers of contagious diseases were burned. Most families buried their dead in coffins shaped like barrels, although wealthy families used coffins so that the bodies could be laid out in sleeping position. After cremation became common, all families began using the larger "sleeping-style" coffins for the actual wake and funeral, because as bodies were no longer buried in coffins but were rather reduced to bones and ash and placed in ceramic containers, space no longer was an issue.

Four men dug the grave. The neighborhoods were organized in a circular pattern, and with each death, the job of digging the grave moved counterclockwise from one house to the next. If a man's wife was pregnant, he was excused from this responsibility until after she had delivered their child. Before beginning to dig, the workers each ate a block of tofu and drank chilled sake. The grave had to be four *shaku* (slightly less than four feet) deep, and digging was very arduous work. Warabi has a high water table, and so there was much lifting of wet, rocky earth. It was unnerving work as well, for diggers often uncovered coffins whose sides had burst open because of water damage. Because of the unpleasantness of this task, the grave diggers sat in the positions of highest honor at the dinner given after the funeral.

While neighbors helped with these various preparations, the family of the deceased readied the body. The tatami was taken out of the room in which the corpse had lain, and a deep wash tub was set out. The most senior male relative supervised the washing of the body, although many people participated in this task. First, cold water was put in the tub, followed by hot water—that is the opposite of how water is put in the bath in daily life. Literally, this drawing of water was called *sakasamizu* (inverted water). The body was washed and the face was shaved if it was a man; light makeup was applied in the case of a woman. After the bath was finished, the bath water was thrown out in the northern (yin) part of the garden, and everyone drank chilled sake to purify themselves.

The body was then dressed in a white kimono, which was usually made by close female relatives. The thread used to sew it was not knotted at the end, and it was important that a group of women all sewed on the kimono simultaneously. The right (yin) side of the kimono was laid over the left side, something never done in daily life. The right and left *tabi* (cotton socks shaped like mittens for feet) were reversed, and straw slippers were tied to the feet of the deceased. The corpse was then put in a cross-legged position;

if the limbs had hardened too much, the bones were broken. Then the body was eased into the barrel-shaped coffin.

A small table containing incense, candles, flowers, rice cakes, and a mounded offering of rice was placed in front of the coffin. At this point, the wake began. Before 1945, relatives sat with the body and kept candles and incense burning throughout the night. After 1945, this ceremony became much more structured. At first, people simply gathered to read sutras, and then it became customary to ask a priest to lead the service. Today, the wake is a time for people who cannot come to the funeral to pay their last respects; they make offerings of incense, give gifts of money, and receive return gifts in the same way that guests at a funeral do.

The funeral began in the morning and continued on into the afternoon, following roughly the same pattern as the funeral of Mr. Ishiyama's father, which was described in the first chapter. The Buddhist priest read sutras, and then the family, in order of hierarchical relationship and closeness to the deceased, offered incense; then the other mourners offered incense. After the last farewells were said to the corpse, the coffin was nailed shut using a stone instead of a hammer.

The coffin was not taken out through the front door of the house, but rather through the veranda (*engawa*). The coffin was placed in the garden, with four bamboo branches surrounding it. The priest walked counterclockwise around the coffin, chanting sutras; the family of the deceased followed the priest, forming a kind of procession. As they left to carry the coffin to the burial ground, they burned two bundles of straw in the garden of the house; the ashes from this fire were not cleaned up until the forty-ninth day after the person's death. A Buddhist priest came to conduct special services on the seventh, twenty-first, thirty-fifth, and forty-ninth days after death.

Funeral rites today are more similar to those at Mr. Ishiyama's father's funeral, described in Chapter 1. However, most families still adhere to the tradition of memorial services to ensure the dead person a place in paradise. These are called the one-, three-, seven-, thirteen-, seventeen-, twenty-five-, and thirty-three-year ceremonies. At these anniversaries, sutras are read, offerings are made to the deceased, and modest feasts are held. Guests bring gifts of cash and return home with bags of gifts; the way in which gifts and return gifts are determined is very similar to the practices governing giving at funerals. The thirty-third anniversary is considered the official transition to ancestorhood, after which the deceased is remembered at *obon*, the festival of the dead, at which offerings are made to all ancestors as a group (Hamabata 1990; Smith 1974; Beardsley et al. 1959; Norbeck 1954; Embree 1939).

In death, the normal order of hierarchical relations of universal principles is overturned. In the wrapping of incense money before it is inserted into the envelope, right (yin) is folded over left (yang), and bottom is folded over top.[28] The cash itself is placed face down. Water used to bathe the corpse is drawn opposite from the usual fashion: first cold (yin) and then hot (yang). The kimono of the deceased is closed with the right side lying over the left side; right and left foot coverings are reversed, as is the order of offerings presented to the deceased on a tray, with the most important dish, the rice, placed on the yin rather than the yang side. Rice balls are offered to the deceased in even (yin) numbers.

There is a clear demarcation between what is pure and what is impure; in this state of death where yin is dominant, the deceased and close family members are considered polluted. It is not until the forty-ninth day after death, when the deceased is reborn into paradise and forms a clear break with the world of the living, that in Tokyo and many other areas the bereaved family sends return gifts for incense money received at the funeral. This period of delay is similar to the practice of waiting until the impurity of childbirth has passed before sending return gifts for presents received at a baby's birth; both in death and in childbirth, it is the female principle of yin that is strongest, and it is only when yin has been subordinated to yang that normal social relations can be resumed.

At auspicious events such as weddings, events crucial to the reproduction of human beings and of society, yang is stressed in the wrapping of money (left over right, top over bottom), the emphasis on odd numbers, the wearing of kimono (left side over right side). Opposing sets of rules govern auspicious and inauspicious events. However, even though there is a clear line between events related to life and events related to death, the parallels between life cycle rituals centering on death and those centering on life demonstrate that there are certain ways in which the two overlap. Babies, brides, and corpses all wear white. They all sever their ties with the worlds from which they come. In particular in the case of corpses, an effort is made to ensure that these ties are completely cut. For example, the thread used to sew the funeral garment is not knotted, perhaps in order to avoid tying the soul of the deceased to the world of the living. A dead person's soul may eventually be reborn as a baby, and with the child's birth, the connection with the other world, the world of spirits, is severed. In some areas of Japan, when a bride left her natal household, she wore her kimono with the right side over the left side, symbolizing her death to her uterine family; upon reaching her husband's home, the left side was laid over the right side. Babies, brides, and corpses all partake, at least symbolically, of the bowl of mounded rice, rice that because it is spherical in shape and consumed entirely, severs ties completely. The seven-day intervals by which the souls of babies become attached and the spirits of dead people become more distant, and by which pollution associated with death and childbirth disappears, indicate that rituals surrounding death and birth share structural similarities.

Giving at life cycle events requires alignment with this larger process of yin's submission to yang. The number of strands in the cord that ties the envelope, the odd numbered units of bills the envelope contains, the way the envelope is folded, are all material embodiments of the encompassment of yin by yang, of female by male, and the life that flows from that hierarchical ordering. Precise measurement, both in terms of the emphasis on odd units of bills and on the cash value given, enables and underscores this encompassment. Gifts to male employees are of considerably higher cash value than gifts to female employees. Unequal treatment of male and female itself underscores the importance of reproduction, because within this symbolic system, it is through the combination of male and female in unequal relationships that life is believed to be created and sustained. This is why, for example, in the giving of ceramic bowls to a married couple, it is important that they be a pair of two unequal parts, with the bowl for the husband larger than the bowl for the wife.

Practices of giving and receiving at key points in the life cycle reflect and reinforce this encompassment of female by male. Except in the rare event of adoption of the son-in-law into the wife's family, the naming ceremonies and gift exchanges associated with them that identify the child as a social being and the member of a particular family are held in the home of the baby's paternal grandparents. During the child's first visit to the tutelary deity, it is the paternal grandmother who holds the baby. When participants at Shintō weddings exchange sips of sake, the groom drinks before the bride.

As the next chapter will demonstrate, ideas of encompassment and alignment are also central to seasonal giving. In *The Rites of Passage*, Arnold van Gennep suggests that celestial changes, such as the changeover from month to month, as in ceremonies related to the full moon, from season to season, as in festivals associated with the solstices and equinoxes, and from year to year, as in New Year's Day, should "be grouped together, though all the details of the proposed scheme cannot be worked out as yet" (Van Gannep 1960: 3–4). Chapter 4 will discuss seasonal cycles and how seasonal giving and life cycle giving are interconnected.

4 ⌒ Seasonal Cycles

This chapter describes what kinds of seasonal cycles there are, how they have developed historically, how they intersect, and how they relate to the giving of gifts. Gifts given in Japan are, in a large percentage of cases, related to seasonal cycles. Year-end (winter) and midyear (summer) gifts (seibo and chūgen) represent the largest proportion of total gifts given; these alone account for 60 percent of the annual profits of most department stores.[1] Scores of temporary workers are hired to assist customers in selection, to pass out samples, wrap, sort, and deliver gifts (Figures 4.1–4.4). Giving is also significant at the vernal and autumnal equinoxes, certain annual observances known as sekku, and on some Western holidays.

Major Seasonal Events

There are four major seasonal events: seibo (year-end giving), chūgen (midyear giving), *shōgatsu* (New Year's), and bon (festival of returning ancestral spirits).[2] Chūgen (literally, "middle origin") was in China one of three *gen*. The other two were *jōgen* (literally, "upper origin") and *kagen* ("lower origin"). These three annual events were rooted in Taoism and celebrated on the fifteenth days of the first, seventh, and tenth lunar months. Jōgen and kagen were lantern festivals, with jōgen associated with New Year's and kagen connected with thanksgiving for harvests and ancestor worship. Chūgen in many parts of China was a day when large fires were built to honor various gods, and gifts were given in order to remove sin and inauspiciousness. In Japan, jōgen and kagen merged with

New Year's and harvest celebrations, respectively, and thus were forgotten. Chūgen became confused with bon, and eventually the Chinese religious elements fell away and it was seen as an occasion for gift-giving (Ding 1988: 44–45; Iwashita 1993a: 89; Okada and Akune 1993: 100–101).

Seibo and chūgen are not generally considered related to shō-gatsu and bon. People often mention seibo and chūgen in the same breath because it is at these times that people give presents to such people as company superiors, teachers, doctors, accountants, land-lords, and sometimes relatives. Most people I interviewed did not consider bon and shōgatsu to be directly related either to one another or to seibo and chūgen.

It seems, however, that these four seasonal events were once closely interconnected (Yanagita 1970: 55–85; Smith 1974: 17; Tokoro 1986: 55–58; Okada and Akune, 1993: 89–90). Ancestors returned at six month intervals, both at shōgatsu and bon. Chūgen and seibo were offerings made to returning ancestors shared among friends and family members after the ancestors had partaken of the gifts. Shōgatsu and bon practices differ from place to place, but there are generally common elements despite geographical differ-ences. Practices of celebrating shōgatsu and bon are also similar to one another in their structure of events.

Historical Change

One very elderly woman in Warabi vividly remembered a time in her childhood when people were ordered not to make offerings to the Buddhist altars during the period of New Year's celebrations. She said, "We were supposed to shut up the Buddhist altar, and not offer any food or drink at all. . . . [At] New Year's, we were taught, only the Shintō altar could be honored. . . . [It] seemed very cruel, and of course some people went ahead and made offerings to the Buddhist altars anyway." Yanagita Kunio writes about this same trend:

The idea of worshipping [at New Year's] the national ancestral shrine is being promoted now, but it did not exist formerly and it is a new devel-

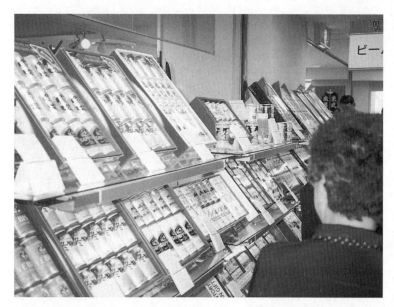

FIG. 4.1. Year-end gift display of beer. Photograph by author.

FIG. 4.2. Department store employees take orders for year-end gifts. Photograph by author.

FIG. 4.3. Temporary workers sort and load gifts. Photograph by author.

FIG. 4.4. Computer-controlled conveyer belt drops gifts into appropriate chute depending on delivery address. Photograph by author.

opment. It was not desirable to have distributed such venerable imperial representations to each house in the past, and it is not fitting now. . . . [T]here surely have been changes in the views of our people, but there never was a time when they believed that the revered great national *kami* [god] would visit each household at New Year. (Yanagita 1970: 50)

The Meiji government (1868–1912), in order to instill a sense among Japan's population of unity and subservience to the emperor, began the process of changing New Year's rituals. The New Year deities of returning ancestors and agricultural spirits became instead the national Shintō god.[3] No longer were special shelves to be constructed for worship of souls of the deceased and of agricultural spirits; rather, all attention was focused on the Shintō altar of Japan's new imperial religion.

In Warabi, many families had prepared their traditional New Year's broth without using bonito flakes or anything containing fish or meat, because Buddhist deities and returning ancestors would not eat of anything that was once a sentient being. But then the Meiji government purged from New Year's rituals anything connected with Buddhism or death.[4] Shōgatsu came to be associated with auspiciousness, purity, and Shintō; bon came to be connected with death and Buddhism. Some families continued to prepare food for the Buddhist altars during the New Year despite pressure to cease these practices.

In some areas, the Meiji government tried without success to abolish rites for bon. But the Meiji government did succeed in establishing a calendar of rites centered on Japan as a nation and the Japanese imperial house, thereby drastically altering most people's experience of ritual life. The majority of the population had mostly ignored imperial rites; now the emperor assumed center stage as the high priest of the nation (Hardacre 1989: 100–102). The reconfiguration of the New Year's deities as one national Shintō deity was one part of this larger process. The many different interpretations as to what the New Year's deity is, and whether it is singular or plural, are related to these historical and political events and popular acceptance of or resistance to policies implemented by the Meiji government. Most people today are not aware of the intense effort to change Japanese ritual practices. Even when asked about the elderly Warabi woman's recollection of being ordered not to feed the spirits of the Buddhist altar during New Year's, many people who taught me about gift-giving, including a famous author of books on giving and receiving, told me emphatically that shōgatsu is connected with Shintō and auspiciousness, whereas bon is connected with Buddhism and death, and it has always been this way.

Examination of the particular practices of giving at these major seasonal events reveals an underlying ritual system similar to one Hocart outlines in his work *Kings and Councillors*. In describing a Hindu ceremony "creating the world," Hocart writes: "And so it goes on, and as it goes on, it renovates the real world for the benefit of the sacrificers; it puts vigour into the animals, puts milk into the females, provides the body with head and limbs, organizes society, making the commons subservient to the king" (Hocart 1970: 67). As the accounts that follow demonstrate, at certain key points in the seasonal cycle, the dead return to the world of the living. Notions of deities, conceptions of deceased spirits, and ideas of the divinity of the emperor are interrelated. The offerings to these spirits provide a paradigm for other kinds of giving and receiving, and it is in part this giving and receiving that revitalizes human beings and their relations with each other, renews the world of nature and that of gods, and aligns individual events with a larger cosmic order. This ritual system is in some ways very old, and in other ways a modern creation of the Meiji state for specific political ends. These aims include the elevation of the emperor to divine status and the reinforcement of a patriarchal hierarchy.

The following pages describe first shōgatsu and then bon rituals. No two families celebrate these occasions in the same way. The descriptions that follow are based on information gleaned from participant observation, interviews, and literary sources. I constructed these typologies to convey basic components present in many families' practices, some of the ways in which these practices have changed, and some of the ways in which these practices differ from one region to the next.

The timing of seasonal events varies from one place to another. For example, in Warabi, many seasonal celebrations occur one month later than they do in Tokyo. People in Warabi explained to me that this is because Warabi residents follow the old lunar calendar, whereas Tokyo inhabitants use the Western solar calendar. One cannot calculate a lunar date by simply adding a month to a solar calendar date. The lunar date would depend on when the solar year began, and every eight years a shift of three months in the lunar calendar would be required to keep some correspondence with the solar calendar. However, most people in Warabi believe that since the lunar calendar is roughly thirteen months, adding one month to the solar calendar is a way of approximating when a festival would have been celebrated had the lunar calendar been used.

The New Year

New Year's preparations are said to have begun on the thirteenth day of the twelfth month, but now they are generally postponed until later. At the end of December, women clean their homes thoroughly, including all the parts of Buddhist altars and Shintō shrines. In Warabi, as far back as most people can remember, New Year's cleaning always took place between December 26 and 30. This was known as *susuhaki* (literally, "purification of soot," a term stemming from the time when wood fires were used). A broom was made from very new bamboo. As it would be used to clean the Shintō and Buddhist altars, it was very important that the bamboo be considered pure. All of the furniture and the tatami mats were moved out of the house before susuhaki began (Kodama 1993: 378–79). Today, in many homes, very thorough house cleanings still take place (without bamboo brooms!), although some younger people omit this practice altogether. Television news programs are full of various tips on end of the year cleaning.

In the past, before the New Year, the men of a particular extended family, led by their most senior representative, collected pine or branches from other green trees for the New Year decorations (Yanagita 1970: 49; Tokoro 1986: 56). Yanagita describes the ritual for cutting down and transporting the pine tree, in which the tree is offered sake, prayers, and carried carefully with a new rope (Yanagita 1970: 55). *Kadomatsu* (literally, "gate pine") are pine boughs and bamboo cut diagonally, tied with rope, and placed outside the gates of homes in pairs. Kadomatsu originated in China, where they were placed at house entrances in order to drive away evil spirits and ensure long life and happiness (Tokoro 1986: 56). In Japan, evergreen trees such as pine were considered to be inhabited by gods, and the kadomatsu, like other pine decorations, served as the temporary resting place for the New Year's deity and as a symbol that a household was properly welcoming in the New Year. Bamboo was added to kadomatsu in the Kamakura era (Okada and Akune 1993: 90; Tokoro 1986: 58).

Branch family members were to assist the main family in these various preparations, and although they did not always do so, it was usually the case that the most senior male member of the oldest branch family placed the kadomatsu in front of the main family's gate.[5] Additional branches were placed in the kitchen, well, toilet, and on the four corners of a special board hung in the main room according to the direction in which the New Year's god would come, as determined by someone familiar with principles of yin and yang. A sacred rope with white paper markers was hung over or around the board (Kodama 1989: 79; Yanagita 1970: 52–53). Sometimes this rope was hung across the entryway to the house, marking the area a sacred space, the temporary dwelling of the New Year's deity.

In Warabi, especially devout parishioners of Warabi Shrine, Sangakuin Temple, and the group of people who worship the mountain Ontake-san bring sets of paper called *kamajime* (the standard Japanese term is *heishi*) to their friends and family. These papers contain gods, and every year people receive a new "set" of gods and burn the old ones in the New Year's fire at the shrine. There are usually seven or eight such pieces of paper in a set, and each has a different name. There is a god for the well, toilet, Buddhist altar, kitchen, as well as many others whose exact roles I was not able to learn. Some people put each of these papers containing a god in the appropriate place; the well god goes by the well, the toilet god in the room with the toilet, the kitchen god in the kitchen, and so on.

Sometimes a single paper will contain many different gods. In the past, many families placed the New Year's altar to the left of the Shintō altar, and lined up all the different pieces of paper on these two altars rather than spreading them all over the house, but today few homes have New Year's altars. Little porcelain and brass bowls contain the offerings to these gods. At New Year's, some households buy a new spoon for putting the offerings into these little bowls, and add the old year's spoon to the flatware used daily by people in the household (Kodama 1993: 383–89).

There are many variations in these preparations according to geographical area and family. Most people in Tokyo no longer procure and make their own New Year's decorations, but buy them at special end-of-the-year markets. In general, only wealthy households and shops put elaborate, store-bought kadomatsu by their gates. In Warabi, the families who have lived there for generations still make very simple kadomatsu, taking bamboo and pine from their gardens. (See Figure 4.5 for a sketch of the kind of kadomatsu seen in Warabi.) Nowadays most people no longer construct special altars for the New Year deity, and New Year's offerings are made to the Shintō (and sometimes also Buddhist) altar of those houses that still have altars. There are quite a few families in Warabi who make offerings to two or three different altars and to many different gods.

Before December 30, groups of neighbors or extended families once made the rice cakes for offerings and human consumption during New Year's festivities. In Warabi, this task must not be performed on a date containing the number nine, as the Japanese pronunciation of the Chinese character for "nine" sounds like the word for pain and suffering. People in Warabi used to rise at two in the morning and work until the early evening to prepare all the rice cakes necessary for the New Year's holidays. This practice is rare now, although in the neighborhood where I lived, we neighbors made rice cakes together in a vacant lot near the temple. This custom had actually lapsed for many years until Mr. Ishiyama, the rice cracker maker, revived it. He cooked up large quantities of sticky rice in his shop, and the men in the neighborhood used a

FIG. 4.5. Many Warabi families make their own simple *kadomatsu*. Drawing by Chika Sato MacDonald.

FIG. 4.6. Neighbors make *omochi* in vacant lot by Warabi temple. Photograph by author.

large wooden mallet to pound rice against a stump whose top had been slightly scooped out (Figure 4.6).

Rounded cakes called *kagamimochi* (mirror rice cakes) for offering to the New Year's god are shaped from the very first batch of rice that is pounded with the wooden mallet.[6] (See Figure 4.7 for a depiction of the two-layered offering of round rice cakes.) The rice cake that forms the base is larger than the rice cake that is on top. In Warabi's past, each family made seven or eight of these double-layered cakes to offer to the different Buddhist and Shintō gods present in their homes. Nowadays, most people purchase vacuum packed New Year's rice cakes at the grocery store. Kagamimochi are placed on the Shintō altar by December 31.

Auspicious decorations surround the kagamimochi. Two of these were described in Chapter 3's section on auspiciousness and inauspiciousness. One is the daidai, which is put on top of the

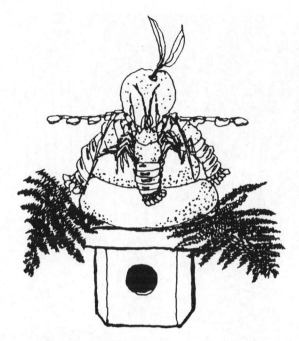

FIG. 4.7. *Kagamimochi* with auspicious decorations.
Drawing by Chika Sato MacDonald.

kagamimochi. It is a kind of small tangerine whose name is a homonym for the phrase "generation to generation." A common interpretation of the significance of daidai is that the family will flourish from one generation to the next. The second is dried seaweed or konbu (as mentioned in Chapter 3, yorokobu, the word for rejoice, sounds like konbu, and therefore konbu is auspicious). Another auspicious adornment for kagamimochi is *urajiro* leaves; known in English as the New Year fern, the urajiro is considered lucky because the small segments of each frond join each other, suggesting good relationships between the married couples of a family (Iwashita 1995: 165).

A big bottle of *toso* (literally, "slaughter" and "revive"; ceremonial spiced sake) is prepared and also placed next to the shrine. Drugstores sell packets containing the necessary medicinal herbs to

FIG. 4.8. White zigzag paper attached to stick and inserted into ground next to curb. Drawing by Chika Sato MacDonald.

brew toso, and some families use *mirin*, a kind of sweet rice wine, rather than sake. On the evening of December 31, a little bottle is filled with the toso and presented to the Shintō altar. In some families, it is the senior man who presents this offering. He takes a bath and puts on clean clothes before doing so.

In some more traditional homes it is customary to place the winter gifts delivered throughout the month of December on a small table in front of the household's Shintō shrine. Some families also place some gifts in front of the Buddhist altar, although the majority of oseibō presents, particularly such gifts as sake, are presented to the shrine rather than to the altar. Many families living in modern apartments and houses simply store their winter gifts in whatever part of their homes can accommodate the boxes. Although the gifts are offered to the altars, givers choose items according to the likes and dislikes of family members, conceiving of their presents as primarily for the living members of the household rather than for the spirits who will be returning.

In Warabi as in other parts of Japan, all accounts must be settled biannually, before the beginning of shōgatsu and before the beginning of bon (this practice is known as *kaketori*.) While some people (mostly women) are cleaning and cooking in preparation for the New Year, others (mostly men) collect various payments due to them at this time. As all business must be straightened out before the start of the New Year, everyone is extremely preoccupied. Many in Warabi perform a purification ceremony on December 31 (*misokapparai*: New Year's Eve purification). In the set of papers containing various gods received from shrines and temples before the end of the year there is a small piece of white paper (*heigami*). Heigami is cut and folded in such a way that it has a zigzag shape, much like that of pieces of paper hung on ropes to mark sacred spaces. The head of the family takes the heigami and removes impurities from each member of the family by waving the paper over each family member two or three times, and then sets it outside. In some families, one family member will purify himself or herself with the heigami, throw it in the air, and another family member will catch the paper, purify himself or herself, throw it up into the air, and so on (Kodama 1993: 393). When walking around

Warabi during the New Year's holidays, one sees many of these white zigzag papers attached to sticks that have been inserted into the ground next to street corners and sidewalks (Figure 4.8).

On December 31, parishioners of the local shrine build a fire (*kagaribi*) to welcome the god or spirits of the New Year.[7] This large bonfire is thought by some both to attract (one person compared it to a lighthouse that guides ships into a harbor) and also to contain the New Year's god or spirits. The many people who come to worship at the shrine on New Year's Eve (*hatsumōde*) stand around this fire. Parents tell their children to bathe (*abiru*) their bodies in the smoke and heat of the fire, which is seen to have a protecting and purifying effect. In some places, foods such as dried squid are roasted in the fire and then eaten; consuming this food that has come into contact with the fire is thought to bring good luck.[8] Old items of magical and religious nature from the last year, such as the papers that contained gods, special rakes to bring good luck in business, *daruma* dolls, arrows, and so on, are burned. In the old days, the candle on the Shintō altar would be lit with fire from this fire, but now most families have a small electric lamp on the Shintō altar instead of a candle.

In many places, sake known as omiki ("honorable god wine": sake that has been offered to the shrine altar) is given to the New Year's worshippers to drink. In Warabi, it is at the local temple that sake offered to the temple's Buddhist altar is shared with the people who come on New Year's Eve. First the sake is heated, and then it is passed out in paper cups to the throngs of cold people. This sake, like the bonfire, is considered to have protective and purifying properties.

Around one or two in the morning, families return to their homes. Branch family members may stop by the main family homes in order to pay their respects to the Buddhist and Shintō altars. The gifts that branch families gave to the main family during the winter gift-giving season are sometimes, as previously mentioned, laid out on low tables in front of the altars. If branch families present further gifts on New Year's Eve, they are usually very simple ones (these tokens are called *nenshimairi*, literally, "year," "begin," "visit/worship/come humbly." Before going to bed, family members may eat noodles together. These are *toshikoshisoba* (literally, "year-crossing noodles," meaning noodles eaten as the old year passes). They are auspicious because if one eats them one's life and one's family fortunes will extend like the long noodles.

On New Year's Day, there are a variety of offerings to the altars in a family home. In the past, these offerings were made to the special New Year's altar, to the Shintō altar, and to the Buddhist altar. Now, depending on the family, the offerings are made to the Shintō and Buddhist altars, or more commonly, only to the Shintō altar. (There are more and more families who have no altars at all. Sometimes these families make offerings to photographs of deceased parents. Sometimes they skip the offerings altogether.) In the old days when people drew water from wells, the most senior man in the family drew the first water of the New Year (*wakamizu*, literally, "young water") and offered this water to the altars. This water was used to make the special New Year's broth (Kodama 1993: 395; Iwashita 1995: 164). The flame that lit the fire that cooked the broth, vegetables, and rice cakes came from the shrine bonfire lit on New Year's Eve (Tokoro 1986: 58).[9]

Toso, the spiced sake, is usually offered to the Shintō altar on the night of December 31. On New Year's Day, the family gathers together and drinks toso from a special set of lacquered cups, similar to the cups used in a Shintō wedding ceremony (Figure 4.9). The family drinks in order of rank; in some families, first males drink in order of seniority and then women drink in order of seniority; in others first the older men drink, then the older women, then the younger men, then the younger women, and so on. Children do not generally like the taste of toso (many adults also find the medicinal flavor unappealing), but are told to drink it because it will bring good luck.

The senior male of the house makes offerings of a soup, which is made from broth, rice cakes, and vegetables, to the various altars. Then the family partakes of this special New Year's delicacy. Eating this soup to some means internalizing the power of the god of the New Year (Iwashita 1995: 164). It also signifies receiv-

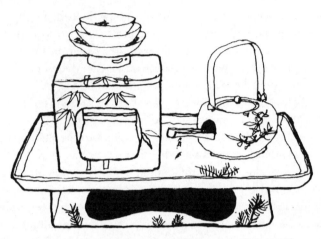

FIG. 4.9. Lacquered cups for drinking *toso*. Drawing by Chika Sato MacDonald.

ing good luck and blessings from the New Year's deity (Tokoro 1986: 58). After the presentation to the altars, one or more family members consume the offerings of soup. Elderly people remembered that in their childhood offerings to the altars were made repeatedly and were not removed, but were piled on top of one another through January 3. On the evening of January 4, the family ate all of these offerings.

The god of the New Year was said to stay within the household through January 3. This period is known as *matsu no uchi* ("within the pine"), because during this time the god resides within the pine branches of the New Year's decorations. When Warabi was a small village of farmers and weavers, for the first three days of January people in Warabi did not work.[10] Even household tasks such as cleaning were not performed; sweeping, for example, could sweep out good fortune. Some residents of Warabi now commute to offices in Tokyo that open for the New Year as early as January 2, but many people still do not work until January 4. The broth with rice cakes is offered to the altars and eaten for the first three days of January. New Year's decorations are taken down on

January 7 in most homes, and for some people, matsu no uchi lasts until January 7.

On January 1, children and young adults receive *toshidama*[11] (literally, "year" and "gem" or "spirit"). Toshidama are given by adults to children. In some small family-owned companies, the president may give toshidama to employees. In the past, in many places, toshidama were rice cakes and other kinds of food. Yanagita Kunio describes how in the southern regions of Kyūshū, the New Year deity is believed to take the shape of an old man who brings rice cakes to good children. In some communities, a man dressed up as the New Year's deity knocked on the doors of houses late at night, bringing New Year's gifts to children. By eating the rice cake brought by the deity, one's life would be extended another year (Yanagita 1970: 59). Donations of food and alcohol to temples and shrines that were offered to the New Year's deities and then distributed among parishioners were also once known as toshidama. As the word *tama* (*dama*) means "spirit," it is widely interpreted as the spirit of the New Year's deity received by the head of household and then passed on to the children. Now, however, few people think of these religious meanings. In almost all parts of Japan, money is inserted into small, colorful envelopes, and is then given to children by parents, grandparents, other relatives, close friends, and neighbors. Older children may receive as much as 10,000 yen in each envelope, sometimes even more. If a New Year's gift of money is given to a superior's child, such as the child of a boss, it is not called toshidama, but *nenshi* (literally, "year" and "beginning," a gift given at the beginning of the year).

On January 2 and 3 in Warabi, and toward the middle of January in other places, dancers dressed up as lions, gods, and demons, visit people's homes.[12] These costumed performers are variously interpreted as New Year's deities and returning ancestral spirits. They will often inquire whether there is a lazy or disobedient child in the house, and issue warnings to that person. They receive rice cakes, sake, or money when they depart. (See Yan 1996: 60 for a similar account of this practice.)

On January 11, *kagamibiraki* (opening of the mirror) takes place. By this time, the two stacked, rounded rice cakes known as kagamimochi have become hard and stale. Most people now soften them with a little water and then cut them to pieces with a large, sharp knife; however, technically the *mochi* should not be cut,[13] but rather broken with a mallet or pulled apart with one's hands (Iwashita 1995: 170). These pieces of rice cake are roasted or eaten with sweet red bean soup. The small bottle of the spiced sake that was offered along with the kagamimochi on New Year's Eve is also consumed at this time. Children who resist eating the stale rice cake pieces may be told that for the sake of good luck, they should eat. A few people explained that by eating kagamimochi, one receives the power or the spirit of the god of the New Year.

The two rounded rice cakes are similar to the two bowls of rice that are put together to create the mounded bowl offered to babies, brides, and corpses. In the same way that consumption of mounded bowls of rice cuts ties, so does consumption of mounded rice cakes. Just as the mounded rice bowls are formed by packing in as much rice as possible, rice cakes are made by pounding large quantities of rice into smaller masses. Eating completely of these round, dense foods emphasizes total consumption, and signals the departure of the New Year's deity. But whereas the mounded rice bowl cuts ties completely, the mounded rice cake does not. The connection with the New Year's deity is maintained in the sense that it is through eating the mounded rice cakes that humans receive the power of the deity. The fact that the rice cakes should be pulled apart rather than cut might indicate that the connection between humans and gods is not and should not be completely severed.

The people participating in these events and rituals are mostly members of particular families. Families make various preparations together, go to temples or shrines together, make offerings or witness the making of offerings, and consume those offerings together. These New Year's rituals reinforce hierarchical relationships between family members. The spirit and the power of the New Year deity is internalized first by the senior male of the family, and then is passed through him to the other members of the family.

Some people explained that when elder relatives give the gifts of money called toshidama to children, they are passing on the spirit of the New Year deity. In the past, it was senior men who led in the selection of the pines used for the dwelling place of the New Year's deity, the pounding of the first rice cakes that are later offered to the deity. It is still the case that the most senior male makes the offerings to the New Year's deity and is the first to consume these offerings. At shrines and temples where sacred sake is served on New Year's Eve, it is men who take the sake that has been offered to the returning deities and distribute it among the throngs of worshippers.

New Year's practices underscore hierarchical relationships between main families and branch families. On New Year's Eve, branch family members may stop by the main family's house to pay their respects to the shrine and altars. In the past, various preparations were undertaken together, such as the placement of the pine decoration kadomatsu in front of the main family's gate by the most senior member of the most senior branch family. On the second and third of January, branch family members will visit the main family, usually with sake, beer, or food, to extend their New Year's greetings.

Company employees will visit their superiors on January 2 or 3, as will teachers, doctors, and many other working people. In cases where the company is relatively small, employees will gather at the president's house and drink, eat, and talk. The first refreshment guests consume is the special spiced sake toso, the offering to the New Year deity. As the superior pours toso for his subordinates, the spirit of the New Year's deity is passed from superior to inferior.

Hierarchical relations between main families and branch families, company presidents and employees, senior teachers and junior teachers, and so forth are reinforced by the visits that social inferiors pay to the homes of social superiors. Similarly, the visits of various people to the home of the emperor underscore the hierarchical relationship between the emperor and all other human beings. On January 5, important people in the government, aristocracy, and foreign embassies come to say New Year's greetings to the emperor. This custom came from China in the Heian period (Tokoro 1986: 60). On January 2, the general population is allowed onto the inner palace grounds.[14] The imperial family appears before the public and issues New Year's greetings. These rites of homage emphasize the emperor's symbolic control over the nation of Japan as well as over other countries. A hierarchical framework encompasses both the domestic and the foreign.

There are other rites the emperor performs in connection with the New Year. In the early morning of January 1, the emperor rises at dawn and performs a rite called *shihōhai* (worship of the four quarters). This rite is performed once with the crown prince and once alone. He worships in the directions of various shrines and imperial tombs, worships the gods of the four directions, thanks the gods and spirits for their generosity in the last year, and asks for their continued good favor (ibid.: 59). These acts represent the emperor's close relationship with various deities, including his power to intercede with them.

As the New Year is born, society, including the hierarchical relationships that compose it, is re-created. Scattered families are reunited, as many people return to their native homes. The spirits of ancestors long deceased also make the long journey from the other world to be with their descendants. Material offerings are presented from inferiors to superiors; spiritual offerings are then given from superiors to inferiors. The branch families give gifts to the main families, workers to bosses, patients to doctors, students to teachers, living people to ancestral spirits and deities. When elders give money to younger family members, they pass on the power they have received from the New Year deity. When people partake of the offerings to the New Year deity (or deities, depending on the viewpoint of the person), they internalize some of its spirit and power.

Giving at the New Year not only reflects and reinforces relations of hierarchy but also renews them. This is one reason why symbols of life and reproduction associated with New Year's celebrations are also central to the rituals surrounding marriage. Plum blossoms emerging from snowy branches, bamboo and pine, green despite the winter cold, are both wedding and New Year's decorations. (Remember the sugared sweets in these shapes Mrs. Ueda served the guests who brought wedding gifts to her home.) This is why the cups and pourers for sake at wedding ceremonies are the same as those used at the New Year. At these times, as the New Year is born and the relationships in society are reaffirmed, or as a man and woman are joined in marriage, their offspring anticipated, and their relationships with their families and the rest of the world recast, symbols of life and fertility are present.

New Year's giving among humans could be considered an extension of a divine ritual system of offerings to gods. In the same way people give tokens to deities, inferiors give gifts to superiors. At one level, humans make offerings to gods as a sign of appreciation and recognition for the life and livelihood bestowed on them, gifts that can never be repaid. On another level, offerings are made in order to ensure the gods' protection and the reception of power and other benefits. Seasonal giving from inferiors to superiors is often represented as a similar combination of gratitude and self-interest.

The Meiji government reshaped important events in life and seasonal cycles in order to bolster State Shintō and the emperor's position at the apex of Japanese society. These Meiji changes used powerful ritual symbols of hierarchy and reproduction to foster conceptions of national identity based on imperial rule. The state now encompassed important rites of passage (weddings, coming of age ceremonies, New Year's rituals) that until this point had been the primary domain of families and communities.

Bon

Partly because of Meiji government policies to discourage practices related to Buddhism, the first two days of shōgatsu are national holidays, but bon celebrations vary from one place to the next. The bon festival of returning ancestral spirits is in the seventh month of the year. People in Warabi, like many Japanese, believe they celebrate bon according to the lunar calendar, in mid-August rather than mid-July. Bon is a time of summer vacation when the Tokyo skies are clear and the streets relatively quiet, as more and more workplaces close for a ten-day period.

The preparations for bon are similar to the preparations for shōgatsu. In the past, the same thorough cleaning that women gave their houses before New Year's was also performed before the start of bon. Nowadays, many people simply clean as usual, although those living in more traditional homes may do a very thorough cleaning. In addition to cleaning the house, the family gravestones are scrubbed thoroughly. As is also customary before the start of the New Year, debts should be settled prior to the beginning of bon, and summer gifts are given in advance of the bon holiday. In homes that have the space, these gifts may be placed mostly in front of the Buddhist altar and the special bon altar, although some are given to the Shintō altar. In the same way pine branches are gathered before the start of shōgatsu, flowers and leaves are placed by the altars in the home, and by the gravestones in the graveyard.[15] At bon, as at shōgatsu, family members travel far and wide to be together in their natal homes.

By the late afternoon on the thirteenth day of the seventh month (July 13 in some places, August 13 in those areas using a rough approximation of the lunar calendar to determine the start of bon), all preparations should be finished. The altar is opened, and food and incense are added to the flowers that are offered. Many families in Warabi place a small table in front of the Buddhist altar, the *bondana* (bon altar),[16] which contains flowers, leaves, the ancestral tablets normally kept in the Buddhist altar, and various foods such as seaweed,[17] fruits, vegetables, and rice cakes. (See Figure 4.10 for melons often offered to bon altars.) Lanterns are placed outside the home. In the past, a fire was built outside the door to the home. In Warabi, many people build these fires, similar to the one made at the shrine for New Year's, near the graveyard or in fields or empty lots. These fires are known as *mukaebi* (meeting fires).

In Warabi, it was customary in some families for the head of the family and the eldest son to take baths and then go alone to meet

FIG. 4.10. Melons often offered to *bon* altars. Photograph by author.

the returning ancestors (Kodama 1993: 444). These practices were similar to the bath taken by the head of the family before making New Year's offerings. Nowadays, the entire family will go to the graveyard together. The head of the family and some other members of the family will carry lanterns.[18] When they arrive at the grave, they will offer prayers and incense, and as they light the lantern or lanterns, the spirits of the ancestors will either follow the flame or actually jump into the flames. The family will return to the home, but those living in traditional homes will enter through the side door that leads into the garden,[19] rather than through the main door. The candle on the bon altar will be lit with the flame from the lantern held by the head of the household, and with this act the ancestral spirits are transferred to the altar from the lantern. Tea and steamed balls made from rice flour and water, arranged in the shape of a pyramid, are offered to the altars. The rice balls are known as *mukaedango* (literally, "meeting rice balls"). In Warabi, there are supposed to be thirty-five of these balls, arranged in a pyramid (ibid.: 444).

The spirits receive offerings of food three times daily. Some families have particular menus for each meal of bon. These menus have been passed from one generation to the next, and include rice, noodles, seaweed, boiled pumpkin, tempura, and rice cakes. No meat or fish is offered to the ancestors, who will not eat of anything that once was a sentient being. Offerings are also made to a small altar below the bon altar or next to the Buddhist altar. This altar is for the *muensama* (literally, honorable ones without ties), spirits who have no family of their own to return to. Family members consume these offerings to the altars after the spirits have had their fill, and the food offered to the altars and then later eaten by human beings is considered to have protective and auspicious properties.

During the days in which the ancestors have returned home, they are supposed to be able to relax in a peaceful environment. Children are told to play quietly. They are also warned not to kill any insects, because the killing of living things offends the spirits. Buddhist priests may come to say special prayers for the ancestors. In some cases, because it is expensive to pay a priest to come to one's home, families will instead go to the temple near the ancestral graves and have prayers and sutras read there.

The first bon (niibon: literally, "new bon") for a recently deceased spirit is a turning point for that spirit and that spirit's family. As Robert Smith writes in his work *Ancestor Worship in Contemporary Japan*, "With the conclusion of the rites of the first bon, the spirit is thought to have begun the long process of becoming an ancestral spirit. Over the years, on occasions marked by successive memorial rites, the dead person becomes more and more remote and fades from the memories of family members" (Smith 1974: 72–73).

Friends and relatives bring gifts for the spirit on his or her first bon. In many places, including Warabi, these gifts are traditionally noodles. In Warabi, it was customary for these noodles to be carried in the giver's hands without any wrapping. Noodles extend in length, indicating the desire for a continued relationship; carrying noodles with bare hands indicates intimacy and connection of the living with the dead. The family of the spirit who would return for its first bon would make rice cakes in the same way rice cakes are made for New Year's. These rice cakes were finished by August 12 and then distributed to the friends and relatives who came bearing gifts. The rice cakes were placed in small boxes, and given only in even numbers of six, eight, and ten (Kodama 1993: 432–33). Many people nowadays bring money, melons, or other delicacies, and return gifts can take various forms, but are usually some kind of food.

On the evening of the sixteenth, the spirits return to the other world. Little horses are made from eggplants and cucumbers, using the vegetables as the bodies and straw or toothpicks for the legs. Warabi residents make saddles for these horses with raw noodles. Rice balls (*omiyagedango*: rice balls given as a parting gift) are again piled into a pyramid and then offered to the altars. A fire is lit by the entrance to the house. The flame from the candle on the altar is transferred to the candle in the lantern, and the family walks back to the graveyard. The candle in the lantern is then placed in the grave, and when the candle dies down and the flame disappears, the ancestors are said to have returned to the other world (ibid.: 447). In some areas, people go to a mountain, river, or seashore to see their ancestors off (Smith 1974: 100–102).

There are many parallels between ritual practice at bon and shōgatsu. There is an emphasis on preparing for these holidays by cleaning and purifying. The decorating of the altars with leaves and flowers resembles the gathering of pine boughs. Debts and gift-giving obligations are discharged before the start of shōgatsu and bon, and these gifts are traditionally offered to the household altars. Fires are lit to both welcome the spirits and to send them off. The ancestors are thought to be both attracted to and contained in these fires. There are similarities between the bon altar and the New Year's altar (Yanagita 1975: 47 and 1970: 55). Offerings made to the ancestors and then consumed are considered beneficial and auspicious because the power of the spirits or deities who first ate of the foods is transferred to the humans who consume them. At both shōgatsu and bon, there is emphasis on purification and renewal; on the transmission of life, of power, and of benefits. The divine economy of offerings to gods is a paradigm of a larger system of giving and receiving among humans.

In addition to the shōgatsu and bon giving to humans and

deities, there are two other seasonal kinds of giving that must be explained. One is the gifts to departed spirits at the vernal and autumnal equinoxes. The other is the giving associated with the five annual observances known as sekku.

Higan

Higan means, literally, "other shore," and it is a religious observance during the seven-day periods surrounding the vernal and the autumnal equinoxes, intended to help souls pass to the world of enlightenment. The days on which the equinox falls are official holidays, and are called *shunbun no hi* (March 20 or 21, depending on the year) and *shūbun no hi* (September 23). During these times, families visit graves, clean them, and offer flowers, incense, and *hagi*, a special sweet made from glutinous rice and covered with red bean paste. Spirits are said to return at higan, and relatives and friends send gifts of melons and other foods to be offered on the Buddhist altar to the souls of friends or family members who have passed away.

Higan is observed by all Buddhist sects in Japan but is unheard of in India, China, or other Buddhist countries. It is possible that higan was originally a celebration of the return of ancestral and agricultural deities. People believed that these spirits came to the fields in spring and left for the mountains in the fall. Farmers prayed to these spirits in spring for a good harvest, and when their prayers were answered in fall they gave thanks (Tokoro 1986: 66–68).

It is also possible that higan was originally pronounced the same way, but was written with the characters for "sun" and "ask," referring to sun worship. In Tango and other parts of the Kansai area, there are ceremonies performed during the seven days of higan in which worshippers go to temples and shrines in the east in the morning, temples and shrines in the south in the afternoon, and temples and shrines in the west in the evening. There are also rituals related to the worship of the god of sun and god of fire performed in the Kantō and Tōhoku areas during higan (ibid.: 69–70).

Thus higan has almost certainly evolved in the course of Japanese history. With the arrival of Buddhism in the sixth century, the practice of praying for the repose of the spirits of loved ones gradually gained importance at higan. Since 1878, the eleventh year of Meiji, the emperor has worshipped his imperial ancestors at higan, and from this time until 1945, at the vernal and autumnal equinoxes, schools began with a reading of the Imperial Rescript on Education and bowing to the emperor's portrait.[20] The Meiji government thus appropriated the central days of the higan observances by making what had long been times of exclusively Buddhist worship into national holidays for obeisance to imperial ancestors (Smith 1974: 52; Tokoro 1986: 70).

Higan, like shōgatsu and bon, emphasizes life and fertility, purification and renewal. Higan is the time to anticipate the growing of crops or give thanks for the harvest; it is time to worship the sun, the giver of life, when the hours of sunlight are longest. The light of the outside world corresponds to the enlightenment of the souls of the deceased who are reborn into paradise. Like shōgatsu and bon, there is the cleaning of the graves, the offerings to spirits, and the consumption of those offerings.

Gosekku

The Meiji government's creation of a new national ritual calendar, one which included the emperor's performance of New Year's and equinoctial rites, meant a decrease in emphasis for the five annual observances known as gosekku (Hardacre 1989: 101). *Go* means "five." Sekku, the second character, can also be read *sechi, fushi*. Together the *kanji* for gosekku mean the making of offerings at five ordered divisions. These are the seventh day of the first month, the third day of the third month, the fifth day of the fifth month, the seventh day of the seventh month, and the ninth day of the ninth month. The consecutive odd numbers were almost too propitious and therefore terrifying (Iwashita 1993b: 320).

Although gosekku were an integral part of Tokugawa popular religious life, after the Meiji reforms in ritual occasions, they gradually faded in importance. All of the gosekku, perhaps with the exception of 9/9, are now celebrated in one form or another, but most individuals are no longer aware that the five were once all connected. When I asked people (with the exception of some elderly individuals, flower arrangement teachers, and Buddhist priests) what gosekku were, most would say that one sekku was a girls' day festival on March 3, and another was a boys' day festival on May 5. The fact that 1/7, 7/7, and 9/9 are part of gosekku is no longer widely known.

1 / 7

The seventh day of the first month is known as *jinjitsu* (day of the human). In parts of ancient China, the first day of the first month was the day of the chicken, the second day was the day of the dog, the third day was the day of the pig, the fourth was the day of the goat, the fifth the day of cow, the sixth the day of the horse. These are the animals of the Chinese zodiac (with possibly the exception of the rabbit) that can be bought and raised by humans; they seem to be arranged roughly in order of size, with the smaller animals toward the beginning of the first week of January and the larger animals toward the end of that week. On the day of the chicken, no chickens were killed; on the day of the dog, no dogs were killed, and so on. The seventh day is the day of the human,[21] and on this day, no criminals were put to death. It was also on the seventh day that the fortune for the coming year could be predicted; if the weather was good, the coming year would be too; if the weather was bad, the year would be horrid (Okada and Akune 1993: 102).

In some areas of China, on the day of the human, it was customary to eat a rice gruel containing seven herbs in order to ward off disease and evil spirits. One source (Campbell and Noble 1993: 1047) claims this practice was imported to Japan in the Muromachi period (1392–1568); another (Okada and Akune 1993: 112) writes that it was in the Edo period (1600–1868) when this custom was brought to Japan. It was in the Edo period that the Tokugawa *bakufu* made the seventh day of the first month one of the gosekku. On this day, the shōgun and all the people under him ate the rice gruel mixed with the seven herbs.[22]

It is the practice in some areas of Japan—Kyūshū, for example—for seven-year-old children to receive rice gruel with seven herbs from seven sets of neighbors. In Warabi, the child would walk with a tray from one house to the next, and then would eat all seven bowls of gruel. As explained in Chapter 3, all people were thought to turn a year older at New Year's. The seven-year-old had finally left the world of young babies and children, who in fact belonged partly still to the other realm of spirits, and had entered the community of human beings. At this pivotal moment, the seven-year-old child needed extra protection and strength.

Regardless of whether the seven-year-old children in a particular area follow special rituals, it is the practice for families in almost all parts of Japan to eat of this rice gruel with seven herbs on January 7. The emphasis of this ritual is on the gruel's protective and purifying qualities. As will become clearer in the following discussion, each of the gosekku emphasizes purification.

3/3

The third day of the third month, together with the fifth day of the fifth month, are in Japan the two most important of the gosekku. During the Wei dynasty (220–265), it became customary on this day for people to enter rivers or oceans in order to cleanse themselves of impurities and ward off disease. This practice became popular among the Japanese aristocracy in the Heian period (794–1185). Instead of bathing themselves, though, people fashioned paper dolls, transferred impurities to the dolls by blowing,[23] placed the dolls in boats constructed from bamboo leaves, and floated them in pools of water. Eating, drinking, and other merriment accompanied this occasion, which was referred to as "Banquet of the Crooked Water" (Iwashita 1993b: 320; Okada and Akune 1993: 102–3).

Observance of the third day of the third month as it is celebrated today is based on changes made during the Edo period (1600–1868). Dolls were made from cloth rather than paper, and arranged in hierarchical order on tiered platforms. The emperor and empress sat on the top step, and various attendants were arranged on the lower steps. Originally, the emperor was placed on the left side of the empress, because left according to some interpretations of yin/yang theory is considered superior to right.[24] During the Meiji era, the European concept of right being superior to left entered Japan, and the emperor was sometimes switched to the right side of the empress (Tokoro 1986: 183).

The celebration of the third day of the third month is also known as *momo no sekku*, *jōshi no sekku*, and *hinamatsuri*. Momo no sekku (peach blossom festival) alludes to the blooming of the peach trees in the third lunar month. Peach is considered purifying and auspicious, because demons are said to fear peaches, and peach water was once used to wash corpses (Iwashita 1993b: 320). *Jōshi* (literally, "top serpent") *no sekku* referred to the first day of the serpent.[25] Originally, this 3/3 festival was held on the first day of the serpent of the third month. Thus the actual date of the festival changed from year to year. In Wei dynasty China, it was finally determined that the third day of the third month would always be considered the day of the serpent. In the Edo period, 3/3 was called *jōshi no harae*, purification on the day of the serpent (Okada and Akune 1993: 102). Hinamatsuri refers to the dolls (*hina*) at the focus of this celebration. Serpent is a homonym for three: although the characters are different, both are pronounced *mi*.

In present-day Japan, the doll festival has changed its focus to a celebration for girls. At the birth of a couple's first female child,[26] the maternal grandparents give a set of dolls to their granddaughter. Sometimes the father's parents will give dolls, but most often the gift comes from the mother's side. These dolls must be faithfully displayed every year (the dolls are otherwise said to cry), and when the girl grows up and marries, she takes them with her to her new household. She may pass the dolls down to a daughter, but not to a daughter-in-law; they form a link with the mother's natal family, and even in families where there are no daughters, a wife may display her dolls and in doing so remember her own parents. The dolls are taken out sometime in mid to late February and are put

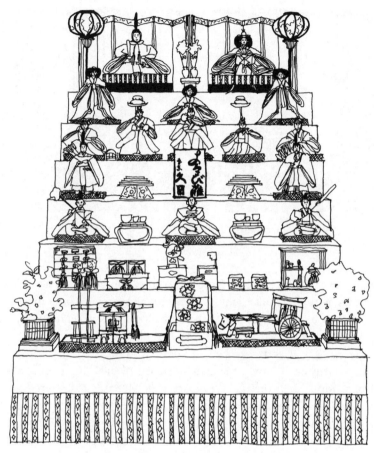

FIG. 4.11. Elaborate doll set for 3/3. Drawing by Chika Sato MacDonald.

away promptly on March 4; if the dolls are kept out longer than March 4, it is believed that the girl may have difficulties in getting married.

These dolls are either elaborate sets arranged on tiered plat-forms covered with red felt, consisting of emperor, empress, and assorted attendants, or they are simpler pairs of an emperor and an empress (see Figures 4.11 and 4.12). The dolls are very expensive,

FIG. 4.12. Simpler doll set for 3/3. Drawing by Chika Sato MacDonald.

with sets ranging in price from 85,000 to 600,000 yen. As older homes with spacious alcoves (*tokonoma*) become less common, people instead strive for smaller numbers of dolls of high quality.

At a baby girl's first 3/3, friends and relatives may be invited for a party. Delicacies are cooked and offered to the dolls on little lacquered trays and bowls; the guests also eat of these foods. A traditional food eaten on 3/3 is *chirashisushi*—literally, "scattered sushi." In the Kantō area, cooked and uncooked vegetables and seafood are mixed with vinegar rice and sliced omelet; in the Kansai area, generally these ingredients are spread on top of the vinegared rice. Another special food for 3/3 is a soup made from clams associated with female genitals. *Hishimochi* (diamond-shaped rice cakes) and *kusamochi* (rice cakes made with mugwort) may also be offered and eaten, although nowadays hishimochi are often made from wood or plastic and are laid out just for show. *Shirozake* (literally, "white sake," a drink made from sake and rice malt) is also offered to the dolls and consumed by the people present.

In Warabi, there are several past practices related to 3/3 worth noting. The maternal grandparents provided the emperor and empress dolls, the paternal grandparents gave the three maidens serving sake, and other relatives brought the various attendants. After the party to which friends, relatives, and neighbors were invited, lacquered boxes containing diamond-shaped rice cakes were presented to the guests. These rice cakes are difficult to make, because they have white, pink, and green layers, and today most people give *sakuramochi* (rice cake containing bean paste wrapped in cherry leaf) instead. Other auspicious foods some families give as return gifts for the guests' presents include bonito and sticky rice with red beans. In the past, when these foods were given in lacquered boxes, the boxes were washed and then returned with a box of matches inside (Kodama 1993: 95).

5/5

In Japan, the fifth day of the fifth month is a festival for boys in the same way the third day of the third month is a festival for girls. In many areas of China, this day was for repelling bad spirits and illness. The fifth month was considered to be especially dangerous for transmission of disease (possibly because of the long rainy season). In order to prevent illness, people went into the fields to gather medicinal herbs, hung mugwort and irises from the gates and doors of houses, and drank a wine made from iris plants (Ding 1988: 94). These practices were transmitted to Japan in the Heian period (794–1185). Both mugwort and iris leaves were hung from the eaves of houses, and *chimaki*,[27] triangularly shaped steamed rice wrapped in bamboo leaves, and kashiwamochi,[28] rice cake wrapped in oak leaves, were eaten. (See also Okada and Akune 1993: 102–3.)

In the Kamakura (1185–1333) and Edo (1600–1868) periods, 5/5 began to be associated not only with processes of purification and the warding off of illness and disease, but also with militarism. In the homes of boys, wind socks in the shape of carp were flown. (See Figures 4.13 and 4.14 for carp banners in Warabi.) As the previous chapter noted, the carp is one of few fish that swims against currents, even up waterfalls. In Chinese legends, it is said to turn into a dragon once it has climbed a waterfall. In Japan, the carp symbolizes bravery, strength, and virility because it swims up-

FIG. 4.13. Carp banners
flying over homes in
Warabi. Photograph by
author.

stream to spawn. In addition to carp wind socks, dolls dressed in
armor holding swords and spears were placed inside homes. In
some families, the decorations were simply armor and weapons
without dolls.

The iris, the flower of 5/5, had always been considered a plant
that could prevent illness, and in the Kamakura and Edo periods it
came to be associated with military prowess. *Shōbu* ("iris") can
also mean "warlike spirit" and "fight" or "contest." The shape of
an iris before it blooms is also very much like a spear. The iris

FIG. 4.14. Carp banners for 5/5 displayed in front of Warabi shop. Photograph by author.

plants bloom right around the fifth lunar month. In the Edo period, it became common for people to take a bath that had been filled with iris leaves; at public baths, this practice still continues today. (Figure 4.15 shows a poster advertising such a bath.) Soaking in iris water is supposed to make a person stronger and ward off disease.

In the past, there were 5/5 events involving iris stalks. One of these is called *shōbuuchi* ("striking with irises"), in which boys would wear helmets and fight one another using iris stalks as

FIG. 4.15. Sign for 5/5 iris bath. Photograph by author.

spears. In Hachinohe of Aomori Prefecture, people celebrated 5/5 by bundling irises and beating them against the ground until they fell apart, and then throwing these bundles onto the roofs of houses. In the first part of the eighteenth century, this same practice was popular in the Tokyo area (ibid.: 104).

The fifth day of the fifth month is also known as *shōbu no sekku, tango no sekku,* and *kodomo no hi.* Shōbu no sekku means the festival of the iris. Tango no sekku refers to the first day of the ox. The character for ox can also be pronounced *go,* the Japanese word for "five." Kodomo no hi is translated as "Children's Day." On May 5, 1948, Children's Day was made a national holiday for both boys and girls, and it is the official name for 5/5. Only the festival for boys was designated as a holiday, with the festival for girls on 3/3 officially subsumed within 5/5.

The gift-giving practices connected with 5/5 parallel those of 3/3. As in the case of 3/3, it is technically the maternal grandparents of the boy who make gifts of carp banners or warrior dolls. However, sometimes all kinds of friends and relatives will give gifts, especially carp wind socks, and the rooftop of a home or its garden will be filled with these decorations. These banners mark a family's pride both in having a male heir and in an extensive network of friends and kin. In Warabi, the banners were much more common than the dolls until after World War II, when the dolls became more popular; now the pendulum is swinging back to the carp banners (Kodama 1993: 95). In the same way as on 3/3, a small party is held for friends and relatives. The return gifts usually given by the family of the boy who is being honored are kashiwamochi, rice cakes wrapped in oak leaves.

7/7

Japanese observances on the seventh day of the seventh month have their origins in a Chinese festival transmitted to Japan in the eighth century that celebrates the annual meeting of the herdsman star (Altair) and the weaver maiden star (Vega) in the Milky Way on the evening of 7/7. This Chinese legend became entwined with stories about a Japanese goddess named Tanabatatsume who wove the garments of the gods. During the Nara period, on the night of this festival, known as Tanabata (literally, "seventh evening"), young girls in court circles prayed to the weaver maiden deity for success in weaving, sewing, needlework, calligraphy, and penmanship, making offerings of summer fruits and vegetables to the star. Eventually this practice spread to other classes of society, with the addition that bamboo branches were placed in courtyards and decorated with slips of paper. These papers were of five colors, corresponding to the five Chinese elements.[29] On the slips of paper, the girls would ask the goddess for help in becoming more skilled in the aforementioned arts. In the Edo period, both boys and girls would write wishes and poems on the slips of paper (Okada and

Akune 1993: 104–5). At the end of Tanabata, the branches decorated with slips of paper and origami ornaments would be washed
away in rivers.

In many areas, Tanabata is closely connected with cleaning
preparations for bon.[30] It seems that the emphasis on purification
is Japanese rather than Chinese in origin. Thus 7/7 was a day for
washing hair, washing children, horses, and cows, cleaning graves,
and cleaning wells. The bamboo branch decorated with the slips of
paper was often placed by the well of a household, and offerings of
salt and sake were made to the god of the well. Also, the ink with
which children in Warabi wrote their wishes was supposed to be
made from dew they gathered early in the morning of 7/7 from the
leaves of sweet potatoes (Kodama 1993: 433). In many parts of
Japan, it is considered auspicious to have rain on Tanabata, as the
rain is considered part of the overall processes of purification and
cleansing before bon. This rain is referred to as *kiyome no ame*
(rain of purification). In some parts of China, rain is considered
unlucky on Tanabata, because it is believed that the two lovers will
have difficulty in finding each other in the Milky Way (Okada and
Akune 1993: 105).

Today, Tanabata is celebrated primarily in nursery and elementary schools and by families with small children. Teachers usually
tell a story about Tanabata to nursery school and primary school
classes. Oftentimes the teacher will explain that there were once a
weaver maiden (Orihime) and a cow herd (Hikoboshi) who each
labored very hard. Then they fell in love and neglected their chores.
The god of heaven became angry, put a big river between them, and
decreed that they could meet once a year, but on all other days they
had to work as hard as possible. In some versions, white magpies
build a bridge with sticks to enable the lovers to meet. After the sto-
rytelling, children construct ornaments and write wishes on strips
of paper. In the past, classes would walk to rivers to dispose of the
bamboo branches and decorations at the close of Tanabata, but
because of the littering problem these practices created, most teachers now burn the branches and paper instead.

Tanabata is a very special holiday in Warabi, because weaving
used to be the primary occupation of many of its inhabitants. It is

FIG. 4.16. Tanabata in Warabi; note the bamboo plants on right.
Photograph by author.

celebrated according to what people in Warabi believe to be the
lunar calendar, thus in August of the solar calendar. The main street
going up to the train station becomes a pedestrian zone, and there
are many decorations (Figure 4.16). There are stalls selling all sorts
of sweets, little plastic figures, little gold fish, live baby chicks, rub-
ber balls, and so on. A huge bamboo branch decorated with origami ornaments and strips of paper bearing wishes stands in a promi-
nent place in the train station. Residents of Warabi stress fun and
enjoyment during this time. Elderly people reported that in their
childhood years, they were careful not to go into the fields on the
night of 7/7 for fear of disturbing the two lovers.

9/9

The ninth day of the ninth month is known as *chōyō no sekku*
and *kiku no sekku*. Kiku no sekku (chrysanthemum festival)

alludes to the blooming of chrysanthemums in the ninth lunar month. Chōyō no sekku (literally, "pile-up yang festival") refers to the two nines of 9/9. As explained in Chapter 3, in the system of belief known in Japan as Ommyōdō,[31] odd numbers are considered yang, and therefore auspicious. This particular system is based on the numbers one through nine. Nine is the highest odd number and therefore a nine for both month and day is extremely auspicious.

According to principles of yin and yang, the end of 9/9 represents both the height and the end of yang, the warm, fertile season. As winter approaches, the spirit of yin will predominate. In China, and later in some parts of Japan, it was customary to climb mountains, and pick fruits, and drink wine made from chrysanthemum petals. By consuming this fruit and wine, it was believed that human beings could internalize the spirit of yang and thus ward off disease and foster a long and happy life (Yoshino 1983: 286).

This festival came to Japan in the beginning of the Heian period (794–1185) and was celebrated widely throughout all classes of society during the Edo period (1600–1868). In the Heian period, the emperor held a chrysanthemum viewing party on the ninth day of the ninth month. This occasion was called *kangiku no en* (chrysanthemum viewing party) or *chōyō no en* (pile-up yang party). Courtiers celebrated the long lives they had led, and prayed for continued good health; they drank sake with chrysanthemum petals and wrote poems. In the Edo period, people feasted on chrysanthemum petals dipped in sake.

For the most part, 9/9 is no longer observed in Japan. Although nine is considered very auspicious according to principles of yin and yang, *ku*, the Japanese pronunciation for the Chinese character "nine," is associated with the word *kurushimu* (suffer), and is often avoided as an unlucky number. Interestingly, in 1966, the national government designated September 15 as Respect for the Aged Day (*keirō no hi*). The origins of 9/9 were in celebrating and praying for long life; it is hardly a coincidence that Respect for the Aged Day follows shortly after the ninth day of the ninth month. Local governments give money and other gifts to senior citizens on this day, and children and grandchildren give presents of warm clothing for the winter, food, flowers, or other items to their parents and grandparents.

All the sekku are concerned with the celebration and preservation of life and reproduction. Thus 1/7 stresses the eating of seven herbs to promote health; 3/3 and 5/5, in addition to various rituals for protection against disease, celebrate the birth of children. The 3/3 dolls embody female reproductive potential. By displaying them faithfully every year (but only for a limited time!), offering them auspicious foods, including a soup made from clams that are said to look like female genitals, girls and young women enhance their reproductive capabilities. Because the dolls embody a woman's fertility, they must be taken by the bride to her new home upon her marriage. Similarly, the iris of 5/5 is the shape not only of a spear but also of a phallus, and the symbolism of 5/5, including the carp that climbs upstream to spawn, emphasizes virility and masculinity. (The wind socks *rise* when filled with air.) The 7/7 holiday is the one annual occasion for the cowherd and the weaver maiden to meet and presumably to make love. And 9/9 venerates long life and good health; it is celebrated at the height of the fertile season, encouraging enjoyment of the bounty of yang.

Holidays Imported from Europe and North America

Most seasonal giving is connected to annual events that originated in China and were transmitted to Japan either directly from China or through Korea. But since the early 1970s, there has been a gradual increase, especially among younger people, in seasonal giving related to Western holidays. These include Christmas, Valentine's Day, Mother's Day, and Father's Day.

CHRISTMAS (EVE)

Christmas in many parts of Japan, but certainly in Tokyo, is a festivity mostly for young lovers and sometimes for families with small children. Christmas is celebrated only until Christmas Eve; on December 25 all decorations, including Christmas trees, are

FIG. 4.17. Tokyo Christmas decorations of hearts with tiny bells inside; hearts are popular decorations because Christmas in Japan is strongly associated with romance. Photograph by author.

removed and New Year's decorations are put in their place. Areas around department stores are decorated with bells, reindeer, Christmas trees, Santa Claus figures, and hearts (Figure 4.17). Some families have special Christmas Eve dinners complete with Christmas cakes and (sometimes) toys given by parents to children, but this practice invariably ceases when the children grow older. Most families, with the exception of the small minority who are Christians, do not celebrate Christmas. (See also Moeran and Skov, "Cinderella Christmas: Kitsch, Consumerism, and Youth in Japan," in Miller: 1993.)

Until the American occupation of Japan, Christian missionaries and Christian converts were the sole observers of Christmas, although in the 1930s, some department stores began holding Christmas sales. After the Tokyo Olympics in 1964, the focus of Christmas became that of a holiday for young couples. Christmas now is a time for love, sex, and consumption. Dates for Christmas Eve are arranged at least several months in advance. For many young people in Tokyo, a Christmas date means dinner at a restaurant and a reservation afterward at a hotel. Women especially may be given expensive gifts, such as jewelry. They may give their boyfriend or male companion a token gift in return. It is not uncommon for a young man to pay over 100,000 yen for a Christmas date. There are stories of women who have contests with one another to see who can receive the largest number of the most expensive Christmas gifts, or of couples who did not make hotel reservations enough in advance and wait in lines outside love hotels where rooms are rented by the hour.

The way Christmas is celebrated in Tokyo and other major Japanese cities is connected with how Christmas is represented in (especially American) movies. One woman in her late fifties told me how as a child living in Tokyo in the immediate postwar period, she longingly watched films portraying American families eating Christmas dinners of turkey, children showered with presents, young couples walking hand in hand as they window-shopped along snowy streets. At that time food in Tokyo was extremely scarce, as were other necessities. Young Japanese today have no similar encounters of visions of plenty amid material deprivation, but they do exhibit a desire to experience Christmas as they see it depicted in the mass media.

Christmas gifts are outside the hierarchical relationships embedded in year-end and midyear giving. Some people deliberately sent Christmas gifts rather than seibo (year-end) presents. One professor explained to me that giving Christmas gifts allowed her to give freely, from the heart. If she sent a seibo gift, she said, she felt it was not a pure expression of gratitude, because seibo presents are embedded in relations of hierarchy. By sending a Christmas gift rather than a seibo gift, she explained, she was making it clear that she really wanted to give.

VALENTINE'S DAY AND WHITE DAY

Valentine's Day took a long time to gain acceptance in Japan. Morozoff Ltd., a Kobe-based chocolate company, introduced Valentine's Day to Japan when it ran an advertisement aimed at foreigners in 1936. Around 1953, Morozoff again began promot-

FIG. 4.18. Crowd of women buying Valentine's Day chocolates. Photograph by author.

ing chocolate contained in red, heart-shaped boxes (*Asahi Evening News*, February 11–12, 1996: 5). The Mary Chocolate Company asserts it started the practice of giving chocolates on Valentine's Day in 1958 (Creighton 1988: 310–11). At any rate, this holiday was tirelessly promoted by manufacturers of chocolate and department stores until it finally gained a foothold in the 1970s. (See Figure 4.18 for a photograph taken close to Valentine's Day of a crowded department store chocolate counter, and Figure 4.19 for a department store display of materials for baking sweets for a more personal "Valentine's Day message from the heart.")

FIG. 4.19. Baking supplies for Valentine's Day treats.
Photograph by author.

Valentine's Day in Japan is a time for women to give men
chocolates. A small proportion of these presents are to men to
whom the women have romantic attachments. In a 1991 survey by
Morozoff Ltd., 84 percent of women gave chocolate to "people
who help them" and only 28 percent of those same women to their
lovers or spouses. Women I interviewed reported giving their
chocolate gifts to their fathers, brothers, company superiors, and

colleagues. The largest percentage of the gifts are to their bosses. For boyfriends and husbands, they sometimes made chocolate desserts by hand. In some work situations, there can be a great deal of plotting that goes along with the giving of chocolates. Female office workers jointly make decisions on which male workers will receive what kind of chocolates and how these chocolates will be presented. The chocolates given to men to whom women have no romantic attachment are known as *giri choko*, or obligatory chocolates.

Many men interviewed about Valentine's Day termed it ridiculous or absurd (*bakabakashii*), but at the same time were secretly delighted at receiving chocolates or embarrassed or envious if they did not receive the same number and kind (different brands of chocolates have their own rankings of prestige) as their friends and colleagues. Five female graduate students at Rikkyo University, with which I was affiliated during my fieldwork, selected a male graduate student they found (in contrast to many of the other male students, who looked down on their female peers) self-effacing and sweet, and arranged to appear at different times on February 14 with gifts of chocolates. Some of these women made special trips to the university (for many, an hour's train ride in each direction) in order to hand over their gifts, to the surprise and pleasure of the embarrassed recipient.

Yuko Ogasawara presents a fascinating account of office ladies' gifts of Valentine's Day chocolates to their male superiors as the manipulation of workplace hierarchies to their own advantage. Ogasawara suggests that stacks of chocolate boxes on a man's desk are indicators of his popularity with office women and his general managerial abilities. Office ladies give men they consider arrogant or inconsiderate fewer chocolates, broken chocolates, or time their gifts so that the men receive them very late in the day. Valentine's Day, Ogasawara argues, is a Day of Judgment: office ladies indicate their likes and dislikes, and men assess one another based on the preferences of women (Ogasawara 1998: 98–107).

March 14 is White Day. White Day originated in Japan; it started in the late 1970s after promotions by department stores and chocolate companies to further increase their sales. On this day, men are supposed to make return gifts of white chocolate or other white sweets to the women who gave them dark chocolate on Valentine's Day. Some more careful men make these return gifts, but many neglect White Day. As previously indicated, it is usually the more senior employees whose wives buy White Day gifts for their husbands' female employees. (See Chapter 1 for the White Day gifts Mrs. Inoue purchased for her husband.) These presents from superiors are usually at least twice the amount of the original gift, and may include even such personal items as white underwear. When I asked a friend who had received a gift of underwear from her boss if this was not inappropriate, she firmly said it was completely acceptable; it had been selected by his wife, and there was therefore no sexual overture involved.

MOTHER'S DAY AND FATHER'S DAY

Mother's Day is held on the second Sunday in May, and Father's Day is observed on the third Sunday in June; these have also taken hold since the 1970s. Both holidays were imported from the United States,[32] and to an even greater extent than their American counterparts, Mother's Day takes precedence over Father's Day. Red carnations are given by children to their mothers on Mother's Day, and white carnations are sometimes offered to Buddhist altars on the behalf of the spirits of mothers who have passed away. On Father's Day, belts, ties and wallets are prominently displayed in department stores as appropriate gifts. A florist told me that when he delivers flowers to mothers from their married children, particularly in the cases where the flowers have been sent from a daughter-in-law on behalf of herself and her husband to her mother-in-law, the mothers often ask how much the flowers cost so that they can make an appropriate return gift.

Many Japanese practices of giving, with the exception of offerings made at the vernal and autumnal equinoxes, are closely tied to seasonal events originating mostly in China but also in Europe and North America. These holidays of foreign origin have been integrated in different ways into the seasonal cycle. Christmas, Mother's Day, and Father's Day, as well as some aspects of Valentine's Day, focus on close, dyadic connections between individuals, whereas those celebrations that are Chinese in origin emphasize a series of (oftentimes hierarchical) relationships. Valentine's Day is the only exception to this general pattern. Although Valentine's Day may have something to do with lovers, the bulk of chocolates are given by women to male superiors at the office. In this sense, Valentine's Day could be considered a modern transformation of the divine economy of seibo and chūgen to the modern business context.

Western holidays still require return gifts unequal to the original gifts, the same as the sacrificial system at seibo and chūgen. On Christmas, men give much more than women. On White Day, women either get nothing back, or gifts worth twice the amount of their original present. Celebrations such as Valentine's Day and Christmas are points at which relations of hierarchy are reinforced. The one-way flow of chocolates from women to men on Valentine's Day fits the pattern of gifts from inferiors to superiors. It is often appropriate in these kinds of gifts, as in the case of year-end and midyear gifts, that no return gifts be made; such presents are tokens of gratitude and therefore no reciprocation is necessary (Befu 1967: 161–67; Creighton 1988: 315). When men accept chocolates and do not make return gifts on White Day, even if they claim they are simply forgetful or uninterested in such frivolous customs, they are putting themselves in a superior position to the women who gave chocolates to them. High-ranking employees may reciprocate on White Day, but such reciprocation does not imply equality. The amount of a White Day return gift is twice that of the original gift, a huge breach of etiquette in most other kinds of exchanges. Because the women are generally so much younger than the senior men, such imbalances are construed as paternal rather than demeaning. Usually, to make a return gift of equal or more than the original gift's value is considered tantamount to cutting a relationship.

At the same time this giving and receiving during Christmas and Valentine's Day emphasizes hierarchical relationships between men and women, it also undermines those hierarchical relationships. During these Western holidays, it is women who have the upper hand. At Christmas, some young women in Tokyo compete with one another to receive as many expensive gifts as possible from as many different men as possible, sometimes pawning the items they receive for cash. On Valentine's Day, women's giving affects men's self-esteem, as in the case of the female graduate students who gave to the one male student in their department they considered especially humble and sweet. In some work places, Valentine's Day can be a happy occasion for some men and a tense and embarrassing one for others, because women may express, by the ways in which they give or do not give, their opinions not only about the men they are romantically involved with but also about their male colleagues.

In contrast, giving at New Year's and bon reflects and reinforces hierarchical relationships without subverting them. Inferiors give to superiors: branch families give to main families, workers give to bosses, married couples give to go-betweens, students (or their parents) give to teachers, patients give to doctors. Senior men are the intermediaries between human beings and gods; it is they who make the offerings, and it is through them that the power of the deities is transmitted. Biannually, at the depths of both summer and winter, when nature is at its most alive and most dead, the living and the dead members of families are reassembled and the hierarchical relations structuring society are reinforced.

When the Meiji leaders sought to unify the inhabitants of the Japanese archipelago under an imperial system, they deliberately fashioned a role for the emperor as high priest of this new nation. In pre-Meiji times, New Year's rituals already reinforced a whole series of hierarchical relationships. The Meiji government did away with the focus on ancestors, and in its place emphasized the national Shintō deity, one of whose manifestations was the emperor himself. Bon, inextricably connected with ancestor worship and Buddhism, was to be eliminated; this policy met with great resistance and ultimately failed. Giving to returning ancestors at the equinoxes had been practiced for thousands of years; the Meiji government designated these two key points in the seasonal cycle as times for worshipping the emperor.

With the new structure of religious life imposed by the Meiji government, those holidays less directly connected with national Shintō gradually lost importance or at least were to some extent diminished. Bon was not expunged, but today it is not celebrated, as it once was, on equal terms with New Year's. The five sekku still remain, but to a large extent have faded in significance. The 3/3 and 5/5 holidays are still observed, as are to a lesser extent 1/7, 7/7, and 9/9, but few people understand how these different days are related to one another.

The sekku emphasize purification and reproduction. However, although the consecutive odd numbers symbolize the encompassment of female by male, sekku giving, unlike New Year's giving, does not for the most part involve offerings to gods or reinforcing human relations of hierarchy. When there are offerings, they are to female figures, often by girls. The giving in conjunction with sekku that is most like the offerings presented at New Year's is the food given to dolls on 3/3, and the wishes written to the weaver maiden on 7/7. In the case of 3/3, the offerings are made almost exclusively by women and girls. In the case of 7/7, many of the skills, such as improved ability in weaving and needlework, were prayed for by girls rather than by boys. On 3/3 and 5/5, it is links through women that are of primary importance; dolls and carp wind socks traditionally come from the maternal grandparents of the child.

When the Meiji government created a system of emperor worship that would assist in the complex process of nation-building, most sekku did not encourage piety to the emperor and to other male figures of authority. It is not a coincidence that 5/5, the one sekku that celebrates male virility and has come to be associated with warriors and militarism, was the one sekku chosen to be a national holiday.

In contemporary Japan, New Year's rituals most strongly bolster hierarchical relationships culminating in the great national Shintō deity and the emperor. Although each main family has direct access to the spirit of the New Year deity, the imperial family creates a single hierarchy from these competing centers. The emperor, through visits paid by foreign dignitaries as well as by ordinary citizens, and through the religious rites he performs, aligns himself to the hierarchies of deities and asserts his position as the supposed apex of human society.

It is through attention to specific details that people align themselves with these larger systems. Specificity plays a major role in giving and receiving in the attention given to seasonal cycles. Flower motifs decorating gifts are plum blossoms toward the beginning of the year, then peach and cherry blossoms, irises, hydrangea, and finally, in autumn, chrysanthemum. Thus a gift given around Girls' Day (March 3) would be decorated with (artificial) peach blossoms; around Boys' Day (May 5) irises would be commonly used. Presents to children entering school are garnished with cherry blossoms, and sweets given in April around the time of school entrance ceremonies are wrapped in cherry leaves. In the same way a careful and knowledgeable giver of gifts is aware of what kinds of things are appropriate from what kinds of places; he or she also knows what kinds of foods and what ways of wrapping and decorating are connected to particular seasonal cycles. Both seasonal gifts and travel gifts relate the giver and receiver to each other and to a larger cosmic system or process.

Seasonal gifts indicate alignment to a process based on relationships of domination and subordination that includes and extends beyond the individuals giving and receiving. Annual gifts to superiors are made in accordance with a seasonal cycle external to giver and receiver. In summer and winter—when nature is respectively at its fullest and most dead—gifts are presented to superiors, marked with appropriate seasonal symbols. These gifts are objects that lend themselves to precise measurement, such as cans of oil, soap, seaweed, beer, gift certificates, and so forth. Most objects are labeled clearly with a code that tells the receiver the price. The giver must not only take care to align himself and his family, or, more usually, herself and her family, with the cycle of seasons, but also with the hierarchical order of society. The cash amounts of these gifts are calculated in accordance with intersecting factors such as strength of relationship, gratitude, and hierarchy. Odd numbered units of cash, objects worth odd numbered units of yen, odd numbers of items contained in a gift, as well as particular methods for wrapping the cash or the gift object, represent encompassment of yin by yang. Finally, seasonal giving expresses alignment with established hierarchies of department stores, specialty items, and name-brand goods, giving high-ranking people gifts from the tops of these hierarchies. Attitudes toward seasonal giving, because it is part of this larger system of relations of domination and subordination, differ greatly from one individual to the next. Chapter 5 will explore this subject in more detail.

5 ⬧ Variations in Attitudes toward and Practices of Giving

Attitudes toward and practices of giving vary according to region, occupation, education, class, family background, gender, religion, and personality. People have different feelings about giving, depending on whether they feel obliged to do so to maintain hierarchical relationships, and whether it is directed toward individuals inside or outside their networks of relations. How do these differences influence orientations toward giving?

The return gifts at Mr. Ishiyama's father's funeral described in Chapter 1 illustrate how giving differs according to region. To summarize the main points: these bags of gifts were handed out just after the ceremony, and the cash value of each bag was 5,000 yen. In Tokyo, guests receive token presents immediately after the funeral, and each small bag usually contains such items as a telephone card, sake, and salt (sake and salt purify from the pollution of death). After forty-nine days have passed and the soul of the deceased has permanently separated from the world of the living, return gifts are made in the amount of half the value of the original gift. When I asked Mr. Ishiyama why Warabi practices of giving return gifts at funerals differ from those of Tokyo, he said:

In Warabi, we don't discriminate against poor people. Whether someone has given only 2,000 yen or 20,000 yen, the return gift is the same. We are not like those people in Tokyo who care about precise calculations. That is the same reason we do not use department stores; when we give funeral gifts, we use the shops from the neighborhood, or in my case sometimes I go to the warehouse where I buy things for my store. We don't worry about finding a high ranking department store. All that concern with rankings and prestige is really ridiculous.

In reality, some families in Warabi do make return gifts from department stores, especially if they have many business connections with Tokyo people, or if they themselves have lived in Warabi for a relatively short time.[1]

Mr. Ishiyama's attitude toward giving at funerals is not only an example of difference according to region but also according to class, occupation, and personality. Mr. Ishiyama graduated from high school, but he did not attend college. Most of his friends and business associates are from the neighborhood where he grew up and where his family has lived for many hundreds of years. From his rice shop, Mr. Ishiyama interacts with many people from various walks of life. He has little regard for especially polite or indirect language, and is known for his energy, drive, generosity, and ability to get things done. An impatience with calculations of value of return gifts, department store hierarchies, and so on was common among people in Warabi who had not gone to college, were middle or lower class, and in their language and dealings with others used direct speech and made few status distinctions.

Mr. Ishiyama's contention that all Tokyo people are concerned with rankings is not true. A family who ran a small meat stand in Tokyo shared an attitude similar to Mr. Ishiyama's. At the anniversary of the death of the husband's father, presents for guests were purchased from a department store. Both the butcher and his wife emphasized that they went to the nearest department store and paid no attention to the department store rankings. They stressed that they were unlike company office workers who worried about selecting the right kind of department store; to them, it really didn't matter. Other similar examples have led me to believe that families with higher incomes and higher levels of education are more likely to focus on rankings of stores and precise calculations of monetary value based on price than are working-class families whose social networks are centered in neighborhoods or other smaller, tighter geographical areas.

The case in Chapter 3 about the woman from Kagoshima who sent tins of green tea to her Tokyo in-laws as return gifts for baby presents raises the issues of region and gender. The man's relatives judged the woman harshly. "What kind of upbringing does this bride have, anyway?" many grumbled. They assumed that something had gone terribly wrong with the baby, as in the Tokyo area tea is associated with death. They did not fault the husband—although he after all had been brought up in Tokyo and might have been expected to be aware of some of the differences in ways of giving between Kagoshima and Tokyo. In general, women are expected to conform to the giving practices of the household they marry into. In-laws and others assess a woman's character and upbringing by the way she gives gifts. Men are generally spared the same degree of scrutiny. A man may be criticized for marrying a wife who does not give properly, but he himself will not be expected to uphold gift relations.

Although women are held responsible for most giving and receiving and are judged by the way in which they carry out these responsibilities, it is relations between men that are of primary importance; it is through women that relations between men are facilitated. This is why in Chapter 2, when Mr. Hoshino gave 5,000 yen at the funeral of his wife's friend's husband, he said that he would have doubled the amount if it had been the wife of one of his friends who had died. At Mrs. Ueda's children's weddings, relatives gave more at the marriage of her son than at the marriage of her daughter, and the boss of her son was given money to thank him for serving as go-between, but the boss of Mrs. Ueda's daughter was not asked to act in this capacity. Mrs. Ueda commented that female employees in her husband's company receive smaller gifts of cash from their superiors at weddings than do male employees; although it is women's work to ensure that proper gifts are given, it is male recipients who are considered more worthy of higher gifts of money. This seems to be true across lines of class and geographic area.

James Carrier, in *Gifts and Commodities*, describes the realms of home and work, gift and commodity, as heavily gendered:

Perhaps the most striking variation is between men and women, who appear to be oriented differently toward the realms of gift and commodity. . . . [K]inship, the core instance of gift relations in industrial societies, is the province of women rather than men, for it is they who arrange the visits . . . [S]imilarly, Christmas, probably the most important celebration of family and kinship, is largely women's work.

Gender is important for understanding the processes and significance of appropriation. . . . [A] household exists in part because its members appropriate the commodities that are circulated and consumed within it. . . . [In] most Western capitalist societies [this need] has to be met if the household is to maintain its integrity in the face of the impersonal economic sphere. . . . [Shopping] is a symbolic task that is important for the maintenance of the household in the face of the world of work. (Carrier 1995: 36–37, 116–19)

According to the model Carrier outlines, it is women who are responsible for the home, for appropriating commodities and turning them into personal things, whether home cooked meals or Christmas gifts. In the distinctions he later draws between practices of giving and receiving in Japan on the one hand and Western Europe and North America on the other hand, Carrier overlooks some fundamental similarities. In Japan there is also a sharp separation between the male world of work and the female domain of home, and in Japan, as in the United States and Europe, it is women who are primarily responsible for giving and receiving. The summer and winter gifts Carrier refers to may seem to be formulaic and very different from the personalized Christmas gifts with which he compares them. However, sensitive selection of these seasonal gifts conveys the importance the giver places on the relationship to the recipient. Often, women living in Tokyo will arrange for specialty items to be sent from their home towns.[2] They will think carefully about what items will be most happily received. In my interviews with housewives, the single most important criterion for choosing a good gift was that it could be used up quickly and would not become a burden. In order to make things easier for the wives of their husbands' superiors, many women sent the same gift every year; in this way, a superior's wife would know ahead of time that she would receive seaweed, or mushrooms, or whatever, and could plan her own purchases of these goods accordingly.

Many people also spoke of the fact that women's maintenance

of gift relations softened gifts to superiors, making them less instrumental. If a wife or mother sent a gift to the superior of a husband or son, the message was explained as: "Thank you for taking care of him, and please continue to treat him favorably in the future." This mediation through women, who exist apart from the realm of work and even send objects strongly identified with their native place, is said to be much gentler than a man who gives his boss a gift. Interestingly, it is women who send objects to women, for the benefit of relations between men. As is described in Chapter 4, this was even the case with the gifts exchanged on Valentine's Day and White Day, when wives selected presents such as underwear, white chocolates, or handkerchiefs to be given to the office ladies who had presented chocolates to their superiors. Many men claimed not to like chocolates, for sweets were seen as something for women and children.[3] They therefore brought the chocolates home to their wives, who ate them and arranged appropriate return gifts for the office ladies.

Gayle Rubin, in her influential essay "The Traffic in Women," restates Levi-Strauss's argument in *The Elementary Structures of Kinship* that women are exchanged in marriage for the purpose of furthering connections between men:

If it is women who are being transacted, then it is men who give and take them who are linked, the women being the conduit of a relationship rather than a partner to it. . . . [T]he relations of such a system are such that women are in no position to realize the benefits of their own circulation. As long as the relations specify that men exchange women, it is men who are the beneficiaries of the product of such exchanges—social organization. (Rubin 1975: 174)

In Japan, from about the sixth century onward, the introduction of Confucianism and Buddhism from China led to a decline in the matrilocal marriage practices of earlier times. For much of Japanese history since the sixth century, male heads of extended families arranged marriages for the benefit of their family units; the exchange of women became an important means of establishing and maintaining connections between male-headed households. Women were expected, in part through the exchange of gifts, to maintain relations important to these families. Today, women, in their practices of giving and receiving, are still primarily responsible for nourishing relationships between their own household and other households. And in some cases, especially in the upper classes, marriages are still arranged in part to strengthen relationships between families. Women enter their husband's families; in a sense, they are given to these families. At the same time, women are responsible for maintaining gift relations with those outside the immediate family unit. They are not only the ones being exchanged at marriage, they are also the ones doing the exchanging after marriage.

Carole Cavanaugh suggests that women in Japan have long been not only exchanged objects but also exchangers of objects. In her essay "Text and Textile: Unweaving the Female Subject in Heian Writing," she argues that some Heian court women, through their production of textiles, were able to exert influence in political arenas that were otherwise inaccessible to them. She writes:

This reassessment revises essentializing views of Heian women as items of exchange in a male economy, characterized particularly by Fujiwara "marriage politics," and focuses instead on the implications of their activity in a web of exchanges made possible by female productivity and expertise. Productivity in the textile arts not only reproduced culture but produced the materiality of social difference. The production of difference, fundamental to the workings of the Heian court where it was institutionalized and advertised in restrictions on clothing, is the defining feature in any systematization of rank and hierarchy. (Cavanaugh 1997: 596)

Cavanaugh depicts the women cloth producers as inferior partners to men in the politics of control and distribution of cloth. She notes, however, that males must request female cooperation, and that "the female possession of goods 'mediates,' indeed softens, the power of the wealth the male owns and distributes" (ibid.: 610). She suggests that the relationship between men as owners and women as producers was vertical in nature, but based on cooperation: "the owner/possessor dynamic of Heian power relations cannot be adequately grasped according to the "either-or" terms of master/servant, or capitalist/manager relationship, where one partner holds real authority and the other provides labor or acts as a substitute or agent" (ibid.).

Ultimately, however, Cavanaugh argues, the female producers of cloth are separated from the object of production. The object, cloth, is fetishized, and the female role in making it is minimized. Rather than being overtly active, the female is passive, hidden. This is also the case in gift-giving. The women exchange for the benefit of men, just as in the past women wove for the benefit of men. Ultimately, the women's expertise should not be revealed except in an indirect manner.

Although women wield influence through their primary responsibility for practices of giving and receiving, their very participation in this system reinforces their subordinate position in relation to men. This is true on a symbolic level, with the emphasis for auspicious occasions of odd numbers over even, left over right, top over bottom. Part of the underlying logic of the life-giving system described in the chapters on seasonal and life cycle events is that it is through these pairs of male and female in hierarchical relation to one another that reproductive qualities are enhanced. The actual monetary calculations people make reflect and reinforce women's inferior status as well, as the discrepancy between Mrs. Ueda's son's and daughter's gifts and the instance of the gift given at the funeral of Mrs. Hoshino's friend's husband demonstrate. Visits paid by branch families to main families privilege oldest sons over other offspring and men over women. Younger brothers go to the homes of their older brothers. Women go to the families of their husbands to pay respect at New Year's and bon before they go to their own families. Sometimes women don't visit their uterine families at all.

In addition to "softening" gifts, especially in making those given to superiors seem more personal and less instrumental, giving by women saves face for men. It is usually not men themselves who offer gifts to the people who hold power over them, but rather their wives and mothers. It is women who must explicitly acknowledge the higher status of the other person and ask for that person's continued favor and assistance.

When a woman makes a mistake in giving and receiving, the male on whose behalf she acts loses face. A newly married Japanese-American wife of a Japanese high school teacher went with her husband to give a midyear present to his supervisor. The gift was in a beautiful bag, and the woman passed the bag containing the gift to her husband's superior. Her husband sharply criticized her in front of his superior for failing to first remove the gift from the bag.[4] The Japanese-American woman felt that because the bag was particularly attractive, the recipient would be happy to have it. She was upset at the behavior of her husband, who was usually relaxed about details of etiquette.

Although women wield some degree of influence because they are responsible for giving and receiving, in the end they are not independent agents, but rather subsumed in their relationships with men. The ideal giver in middle- and upper-middle-class Tokyo should give and receive gifts scrupulously and unobtrusively. She should be a force of unseen strength (*ura no chikara*), building up her husband's face and his connections. Although women are the primary givers of gifts, they give as the subordinate halves of the marital units. Women express deference to the superiors of their husbands through their practices of giving and receiving for the sake of their husbands, thereby sparing their husbands from directly signaling obeisance to their superiors.[5]

Let us turn now to the issue of giving to superiors. Attitudes toward giving to superiors can differ dramatically from one person to the next. The following example of giving demonstrates both a typical kind of giving by upper-middle-class women and a particular orientation toward this kind of giving. In going through her list of gifts sent during the month of July, Mrs. Inoue explained how she brings ochūgen to her landlord every year:

Saying our thanks for being allowed to rent this big piece of land, I bring our summer gift to the landlord. . . . [T]his has continued from Mother's [her husband's mother's] generation; Father and Mother [her husband's parents] lived on this same land, and Mother would go to the landlord, saying how we are indebted (*itsumo osewa ni narimasu to itte*) and would hand over the summer gift; every time we bring a gift, after a few days the landlord's wife comes here, and, thanking us for our consideration, says they just received some gift certificates for beer, and it's not much, just a token of their feelings (*chotto, kimochi dake desu ga to itte*). . . . [W]henever I go over, after a little while she comes over here, saying the other day we received such a fine thing from you, and whether you would call her gift a return gift or a summer gift (*okaeshi to iu ka ochūgen to iu ka*), what's important is that it is reciprocal (*otagaisama*), this consideration [*kokorozukai*: literally, "giving from the heart," but translated as "solicitude, worry, consideration"] is like the oil that makes a machine run. It makes our relations smooth.

At this point in our conversation, I asked Mrs. Inoue whether the monetary value of her summer gift was the same as the monetary value of the gift the landlord's wife brought to her, and she answered sharply, saying:

We have a much stronger feeling of gratitude toward them than they do to us. . . . [We] are humbly receiving the favor of renting their land. Not that we aren't paying a fair price; it's thirteen man [130,000 yen] every month. But in the old days, landlords were very important. The feeling was that they were condescending to let you rent from them. But now things have changed a little bit. They are also grateful to us because the money we pay them makes their lives easier. So both families are thankful. It's like when you borrow a book from the library; the borrower is thankful for being able to borrow the book, and the librarian is grateful that the borrower is using the library. It is the feeling of gratitude on both sides that allows a smooth give and take.

Watching my face carefully, Mrs. Inoue asked me, "Do people in your country feel the same way? You know what I mean. Haven't you given gifts to a teacher? Well, we used to give a lot to teachers. In many places, it's not allowed any longer. But to doctors, of course. If you had to go to the hospital, if you needed an operation, you would give something to the surgeon, wouldn't you?" I shook my head.

"Well, let me tell you about Kuniko's experience." Mrs. Inoue proceeded to explain how her daughter and her daughter's husband gave a present of money to the doctor who had delivered Kuniko's baby by Cesarean section. The amount they gave was 100,000 yen. (If it had been a more serious operation, such as one for cancer, Mrs. Inoue noted, 300,000 yen, 500,000 yen, or even 1,000,000 yen might have been given.) It is not possible to bring this money to the hospital, where there is a sign that reads: "We humbly ask that you refrain from kokorozukai." Patients simply send their gifts directly to the doctors' residences. Mrs. Inoue had determined the proper amount to give by checking with her brother, who is an eye doctor, and various friends who either are doctors or who have connections to hospitals. The money was sent in the form of gift certificates from Takashimaya department store, which Mrs. Inoue explained was the closest store to her daughter's home (although she also admitted that if it had been a low-ranking department store that was closest to her home, she probably would not have used it; Takashimaya is one of the highest ranking department stores in the Kansai area, and is perfectly respectable in Kantō). The type of gift certificate they selected was one that can be used at any department store anywhere in Japan. Mrs. Inoue's daughter wrote a note to the doctor, expressing her thanks for the safe delivery of her son and explaining in very polite language that a small token of her gratitude was on its way. A thank-you note came back from the wife of the doctor.[6]

I asked if a return gift also came back, and Mrs. Inoue said crisply, "That is not the kind of thing for which one receives a return gift. People feel an especially deep sense of gratitude toward doctors, because it is the skill of the doctor that saves or preserves the life of the patient. When you stop and think about it, it is really pretty strange, because after all, it is the doctor's job, and no special gifts should be required. But there you have it. It is a bad custom, maybe, but almost everyone abides by it, even when the hospitals make it clear that such giving is forbidden." I asked if such giving to doctors could be considered a bribe (*wairo*). "No," said Mrs. Inoue. "Bribery is more vulgar (*iyashii*). In the case of sickness, what really enabled one to become healthy again was the doctor's skilled hands, the fact that the operation went well. The feeling of gratitude for the way things turned out becomes money."

This discussion of sending of gift certificates to the doctor who delivered Mrs. Inoue's grandson, especially because it arose from Mrs. Inoue's description of her summer gift to the landlord's family, provides one perspective on giving to superiors. Both seasonal gifts to landlords and gifts to doctors, particularly surgeons, are extremely common. Not all people share Mrs. Inoue's opinion that these kinds of giving are expressions of gratitude and are therefore somewhat appropriate. For example, in his book *Daibyōin no Kaidan* (*Ghost Stories of Major Hospitals*), Yoshio Yanase rails against the practice of giving "thanks money." He begins his discussion describing a scene between a surgeon and the wife of a patient. The wife approaches the surgeon, saying, "Doctor, this is just a small expression of my feeling." The surgeon, as he reaches out for the envelope of money, answers, "No, not at all. For you to do this kind of thing for me, it troubles me" (Yanase 1995: 118). Depending on the rank of the hospital, the rank of the doctor, and the kind of operation, the amount of money doctors expect to receive from their patients differs. Yanase describes what he terms the amorality of doctors, quoting stories of patients who were not able to get a diagnosis or referral until they passed large sums to their doctors. Yanase's position is unusual in the medical community, and he has been blacklisted from working as a doctor because of his writings.

Another example of a person who does not share Mrs. Inoue's more mainstream attitude toward giving to people to whom one is supposedly indebted is Mr. Tanabe. He is the person who sent back the gift of live shrimp, only to have it returned to him again after the shrimp had died. I had asked whether this gift of shrimp was not a good kind of gift, because it was sent despite the fact that the stocks he had recommended performed badly. Was it not therefore an expression of gratitude for his trouble despite the less than perfect result? Mr. Tanabe said it was still not welcome. Chapter 2 explains why he considered this gift to be a burden. In fact, Mr. Tanabe said, he felt this way about most year-end and midyear giving.

Mr. Tanabe stated, "Although there is nothing intrinsically wrong with the customs of summer and winter gift-giving, these traditions encouraged people to become used to receiving things without any resistance. Receiving gifts becomes a habit, and when the amount of money increases, as in corruption (*oshoku*), people accept it indifferently. The people giving the gifts are skillful, for it is to their advantage that their offerings are accepted. This is what is wrong. It is my belief that customs of gift exchange (*zōtō*) are not good."

At this point in the conversation, Mrs. Tanabe asked me if I had seen old samurai dramas on television in which boxes of sweets are given in order to bribe various officials. Under the sweets lies money. This practice is still alive today. Mr. Tanabe talked about the back door enrollment (*uraguchinyūgaku*) in which students who have failed the entrance examination to a school bribe a teacher with money lying under sweets to gain admittance. Mrs. Tanabe used the word bribe (wairo) to describe this practice of giving money hidden in boxes of sweets. Mr. Tanabe did not. I asked him what word he would use to describe such an exchange. Mrs. Tanabe said firmly, "wairo." Mr. Tanabe said, "Well, I guess." I said, "You don't seem very sure." He said, "You mean the money put into boxes of sweets, right?" I nodded. "Well," he said slowly, "usually people don't call that by any special name at all." "But it's a bribe, isn't it?" insisted Mrs. Tanabe. "To put it simply, it's a bribe," said Mr. Tanabe. "What if you put it in a complicated way?" I asked. Both of them laughed. "There is no special word," said Mr. Tanabe, "for money put in a box of sweets."

Why is it that Mr. Tanabe and Mrs. Inoue have such different attitudes toward seasonal gifts and gifts to superiors? And why is it, despite Mr. Tanabe's critical stance toward giving, that he is uncomfortable with calling money hidden in a box of sweets a bribe? Examining similarities and differences in their backgrounds may be helpful in answering the first question. Exploration of the complicated slippage between "gift" and "bribe" will be useful in responding to the second.

There are many characteristics that Mr. Tanabe and Mrs. Inoue share. Both are fairly religious Buddhists, and both are active as volunteers in their respective communities. Mrs. Inoue is the founder of a group of housewives that procures pesticide-free produce on behalf of the members in the cooperative, and Mr. Tanabe volunteers one day a week to bring meals to homebound elderly people. They are roughly the same age: Mr. Tanabe is in his mid-sixties, and Mrs. Inoue is in her late fifties. Both are comfortably off, although Mr. and Mrs. Tanabe live a more frugal lifestyle than do Mrs. Inoue and her family. Both were extremely generous in teaching me many things, and both were always interested in discussing various political and social issues in Japan and other parts of the world.

However, despite these similarities, there are important differences between Mr. Tanabe and Mrs. Inoue that help explain their contrasting stances toward giving and receiving. For example, although both are fairly religious Buddhists, Mrs. Inoue often worships at the Shintō shrine in her neighborhood. I once asked Mr. Tanabe if he disliked Shintō, and he said no, not especially, he just did not particularly care for it. But in other bits of conversation, I detected a critical attitude toward State Shintō propaganda he had learned as a schoolboy. Mr. Tanabe was also deeply unhappy with the way in which schools, teachers, and parents dealt with the issue of bullying. When the news was filled with reports of children committing suicide after being bullied at school, he told me quietly that as a child he had been beaten by bullies, when he and his many siblings had been sent to Kyūshū during World War II. He described how he, small for his age and a newcomer to the school, would be taken into a dark room and attacked, and how despite his cries, the teacher pretended not to see or hear. Finally his elder brother made a knife and slashed the bullies with it. From that point on, no one dared touch him. "Bullies must be stopped," he told me. "One way or another. If the adults in charge do nothing, you have to take matters into your own hands."

Mr. Tanabe's orientation toward bullying and toward State Shintō reflects a distrust of authority figures in particular and hierarchical relationships in general. The Japanese emperor refused to take responsibility for the human suffering the State Shintō and the emperor system generated. In particular, Hirohito failed to acknowledge how these larger structures reflected and reinforced racist notions of Japanese superiority and the acceptability of brutalizing and killing non-Japanese. Similarly, Mr. Tanabe's childhood teacher allowed the insiders to attack a much younger· and weaker outsider. Although Mrs. Inoue would never condone the war crimes committed by Japanese soldiers or bullying in schools, she did not relate these issues— Shintō, military aggression, school bullying—as Mr. Tanabe did.

There is one other way in which Mr. Tanabe seems unconventional to me: He works in the house in a way I otherwise saw only women do. When I first started visiting the Tanabe family, I was very surprised, because Mr. Tanabe jumped up to serve food and drinks while Mrs. Tanabe stayed seated. Mr. Tanabe is the only man I met during my fieldwork who cooked, served, cleared the table, and washed dishes. He started to make meals and do the housework when his wife became ill some years ago, and he continues with much of it now, even though she has recovered.

Mrs. Inoue, in contrast to Mr. Tanabe, seems less critical about such issues as State Shintō, strict gendered divisions of household labor, Japan's educational system, and so on. As an avid giver and receiver of gifts, she could not understand Mr. Tanabe's point of view on the shrimp incident at all. Mrs. Inoue was not alone in her incredulity. Omitting Mr. Tanabe's name, I told the story of the live shrimp to other people, and although many understood what Mr. Tanabe meant by the burden of a gift, most of them felt that he was stubborn and not very gracious in his actions. "What harm would it have done him to accept?" was a common response, and calls to mind the following passage from Bourdieu's *Outline of a Theory of Practice*:

The whole trick of pedagogic reason lies precisely in the way it extorts the essential while seeming to demand the insignificant: in obtaining the respect for form and forms of respect which constitute the most visible and at the same time the best-hidden (because most "natural") manifestation of submission to the established order. . . . [T]he term *obsequium* used by Spinoza to denote the "constant will" produced by the conditioning through which "the State fashions us for its own use and which enables it to survive" could be reserved to designate the public testimonies of recognition which every group expects of its members (especially at the moment of co-option), that is, the symbolic taxes due from individuals in the exchanges which are set up in every group between the individuals and the group. Because, as in gift exchange, the exchange is an end in itself, the tribute demanded by the group generally comes down to a matter of trifles, that is, to symbolic rituals (rites of passage, the ceremonials of etiquette, etc.), formalities and formalisms which "cost nothing" to perform and seem such "natural" things to demand ("It's the least one can do . . .": "It wouldn't cost him anything to . . .") that abstention amounts to a refusal or challenge. (Bourdieu 1997: 95)

Whereas Mrs. Inoue interpreted the gift to the landlord or to her daughter's doctor in the standard language of gratitude, Mr. Tanabe objected to the relations of hierarchy and bonds of obligation implicit in such giving.

Like many of the individuals who participated in my study, neither Mr. Tanabe nor Mrs. Inoue was very comfortable with the word "bribe." Most people describe their own practices of giving and receiving by differentiating between gifts given to people to whom they are linked through social networks and gifts to people with whom they are not connected. The majority of giving and receiving occurs within one's social networks. The giving and receiving among people one knows is differentiated along dimensions of hierarchy and familiarity, and is then further categorized in terms of how welcome or unwelcome the obligation of giving or receiving is.

The giving relationships most upsetting to most people are those with superiors who force inferiors into relationships of giving and receiving. A case of a doctor who would not give a referral or diagnosis until he received thank-you money fits this type of coerced giving. One cannot simply go and see a doctor; one must have a referral from someone the doctor knows, either a friend, relative, or another doctor. In this way, doctors not only control information about patients' conditions, but also control access to other doctors. If a patient does not give the expected money, a nurse may suggest an appropriate amount. I know of only one case, a woman from the former East Germany married to a Japanese, in which a patient refused to give money to a doctor: she prevented her husband from paying thank-you money to a surgeon who performed a major operation on her. According to this woman's daughter, once the doctor and hospital staff understood that they would not receive thank-you money, the quality of her care declined precipitously, and after a few weeks, this woman died. Many people expressed trepidation about how to know how much to give, how to hand it to the doctor, what to say, and so on. Some were shocked about the callous way in which doctors received offerings of tremendous amounts of cash, tossing them unceremoniously into desk drawers and so forth, seeming not to care that in some cases this was money that the giver could not easily afford.

Another example of forced giving was told to me by Mrs. Ueda. At one of our meetings, she made a comment that although the minister who married her daughter at her daughter's husband's church in Niigata had given a congratulatory present, the minister at their own church who had married her son made it a rule not to give envelopes of money at weddings. A few interviews later I asked her about this difference between the giving of the two ministers. Mrs. Ueda started by explaining that the cost of inviting one person to either her son's or daughter's wedding was about 50,000 yen, and as the minister of her church is married, the cost is 100,000 yen for both the minister and his wife. The fee paid to the minister for performing the wedding is 100,000 yen, and so the total cost of having the minister participate is 200,000 yen. Her daughter, who is employed at the Tokyo YMCA, found the minister who married her through YMCA connections. Even though this minister did not know the daughter at all well, he traveled all the way to Niigata, prepared the marriage certificate, and gave a congratulatory gift of 20,000 yen. In contrast, the minister who married her son gave two books he had written and did not even give the marriage certificate; he had the newly married couple pick it up from the printer's for a cost of 10,000 yen. Both the ministers received the same thank-you money, but the son's minister did not pay travel expenses or printing expenses or give a gift, and so he kept more of the money he had received than did the minister of the daughter.

The younger members of Mrs. Ueda's congregation are angry about this minister's behavior. It is they who set up for weddings and clean up afterward. The minister never shares his thank-you money with them and never says thank you to them. As a result of this situation and some other matters that Mrs. Ueda did not specify, many young people are leaving the church.

Mrs. Ueda discussed this situation with the minister, and at the next meeting of church elders, he announced that it might be better for him not to accept thank-you money for performing weddings. A committee was then formed to discuss church policy for weddings, and one of the responsibilities of the committee was to meet with couples getting married in the church (many of whom are not Christians and not members of the church) to explain how many helping hands a wedding requires, implying that perhaps the young people who set up and clean up should receive some sort of thank-you money. The committee stopped short of recommending that the minister not receive thank-you money, deciding instead to leave that decision up to each individual couple. So of course everyone continued giving the fee, and the minister never refused it.

Mrs. Ueda and her family are extremely active in this church. Her husband is the principal of the Sunday school, and is there every Sunday at eight o'clock in the morning. Mrs. Ueda and her son and daughter are always helping out with church bazaars and other events. When she gave the minister the 100,000 yen for himself and the 150,000 yen they had decided to donate to the church, she felt certain that he would refuse the money for himself, saying, "From *you* I really can't accept anything, after all the work you do for the church."

But the minister simply took the money. Mrs. Ueda says that it feels to her that this church is her family, except when it comes to weddings and funerals. She said, "His heart/mind has stopped being able to listen/respond (*kokoro ga kikoenakunatta*). . . . I thought our hearts were connected, but then when it comes to such an important time, especially within a 'family,' doesn't one respond from one heart to the other? Why is it at these times that everything boils down to money? Because it is a big income for him, so unfortunately he got used to this way of doing things."

There are a number of interesting issues that Mrs. Ueda's story raises. One is the issue of gratitude, which also emerges in the examples of patients upset with the doctors' way of accepting thank-you money. These people do not graciously accept these gifts, but rather they take them for granted. The lack of reciprocity clearly bothers Mrs. Ueda greatly. The 20,000 yen given by her daughter's minister was the bare minimum any guest can bring to a wedding, but it was greatly appreciated because it was an indication of a smooth give and take. In contrast, her own minister gave no money and offered no thanks to the young people and did not even pay for the printing of the marriage certificate.

It also sometimes happens that superiors assert their hierarchical relationship toward inferiors through giving. A woman who heard my account of the incense money given by Ishiyama Tomoyasu to Ishiyama Shūji gave me the following example: An elderly woman was cared for over many years by her middle daughter. The old lady's eldest son and his wife did nothing for her at all, even though the son was the successor to the family and inherited his parents' house. The middle daughter never married, and had trouble making ends meet. When the mother of the family passed away, the eldest son gave 500,000 yen (roughly $5,000) at her funeral. This angered all his brothers, sisters, aunts, and uncles. Many of them had given more standard gifts of incense money at the funeral, but had in addition given even larger amounts of money under the table to the middle daughter. Some relatives gave the middle sister as much as 1,000,000 yen (roughly $10,000). But this was done discreetly, in order to avoid causing the middle daughter embarrassment. The eldest son seemed less concerned with helping his sister and more concerned with asserting his superior position as head of the family.

Giving along hierarchical lines is particularly resented when the person in power has not fulfilled his or her proper role, and has rather used his or her position to extract money or labor from inferiors. Gradually, in the course of my fieldwork, I came to understand the frustrations expressed to me by others about how high-ranking people, using the power of their various networks, unfairly demanded material goods and favors.

People would not take the time and trouble to talk to me until I had been integrated into a network of which they were a part. Attempts to communicate without the benefit of a prior connection were met with unease and sometimes even suspicion. Access to information was made possible only by the intervention of a third party. It required a certain degree of trust for people to reveal the ways in which the giving and receiving of objects was related to their relationships with others, and the starting point of such trust was usually an introduction to a person's social network by a close friend or relative, and then the maintenance of that relationship by the giving and receiving of tangibles and intangibles.

For example, Mrs. Amako, a very wealthy woman, agreed to help me in my research. Mrs. Amako lives in central Tokyo. When a mutual friend introduced us, Mrs. Amako spoke at some length about how extensive her gift practices were. She mentioned the large volume of her giving and receiving, the lengths to which she went selecting appropriate gifts, and the frequency with which she had company employees deliver gifts by hand.

I looked forward to my first one-on-one meeting with Mrs. Amako, but I was disappointed. Her primary interest in me was for the sake of her son. He was applying for admission to graduate school in the United States, and she wanted me to ask people in America who did not even know her son to write him letters of recommendation. It is common in Japan to solicit letters of recommendation from people known only through indirect connections. Nervous, I did not explain that this was not so in the United States. I only turned red and made some noncommittal remarks.

Despite or perhaps because of the large volume of gifts she gave and received, Mrs. Amako did not help me very much. Instead, she asked me to teach her and her husband English. But once we started with the English lessons, Mrs. Amako ceased keeping records of giving and receiving altogether. I began to realize that because she was part of my friend's network, I had to tread very carefully. Many of the other women in this network were participating wholeheartedly in my study, and one of them had told me pointedly once how hard Mrs. Amako was working to help me in my research. Mrs. Amako had complained about me to her because I had not helped with her son's letters of recommendation. I wanted to cut relations with the Amako family. This proved difficult, for cutting my relations with one part of the network would endanger my relations with the other parts. In the end, I continued with the free English lessons, gradually decreasing the hours.

These problems and challenges I encountered in following these networks are themselves important to understanding issues of gifts and exchange in modern-day Japan. In this sense, the methods of my ethnographic inquiry and the object of my ethnographic inquiry were the same. From the beginning, Mrs. Amako made it clear that she expected my networks of personal relations to be used to obtain letters of recommendation for her son. In Mrs. Amako's world, much is accomplished by networks and the exchange of favors and material objects. Rather than explaining these relationships to me, she used them; this was in the end also helpful for my study, although it was frustrating at the time.

These examples of doctors, Mrs. Ueda's minister, the unfilial eldest son who gave the 500,000 yen, and Mrs. Amako portray unwelcome giving and receiving along hierarchical lines. But there is also much giving according to relations of hierarchy that is considered by both sides to be entirely acceptable. The gifts to superiors that Mrs. Inoue described fall into the category of gifts of obligation according to hierarchical relationships that are offered without feelings of resentment. When Mrs. Inoue described her relationship with her landlord, she noted that technically, she is more grateful to the landlord than the landlord is to her. However, the landlord always reciprocates with something, and shows her thanks. The money given to her daughter's doctor was reciprocated with a thank-you note from the doctor's wife; Mrs. Inoue described the language used by the doctor's wife as very polite. Mrs. Ueda's gifts to her son's boss or to the minister who officiated at her daughter's wedding were also examples of giving to superiors in which the superior made a concrete gesture of gracious reciprocation.

There are also examples of giving from superiors to inferiors that is appropriate. The example in Chapter 2 of the party attended by professors and graduate students in which first-year graduate students paid nothing, second- and third-year graduate students paid more, fourth- and fifth-year graduate students still more, and professors the most portrays this kind of giving in which superiors take care of inferiors. Interestingly, the amount of money given out by the graduate students had nothing to do with their ability to pay, because often the fourth- and fifth-year students were by far the poorest. In the same way older students were expected to help and advise younger students, they were also supposed to take some care of them when it came to paying for meals marking boundaries, like this one celebrating the beginning of the new school year. When graduate students went out together on an informal basis, in general, the bill was divided up evenly without regard to seniority.

Giving and receiving unconnected with relations of hierarchy may be divided into giving to people within one's network of relations and giving to those outside one's network of relations. People within networks of relations include neighbors,[7] coworkers of the same year, classmates of the same year, and residents of the same apartment building. Giving among close friends, family members, spouses, and lovers may also fall into this category. Sometimes, this kind of giving and receiving is seen as burdensome. Young people who are invited to one wedding after the next may spend much of their discretionary income on the obligatory congratulatory presents of at least 20,000 yen for each wedding. Travelers may avoid bringing back souvenirs for their neighbors. Mrs. Ueda was unhappy that a neighbor she had been trying to disengage from came to her mother's funeral and gave incense money in the attempt to reinsert herself into a relationship with Mrs. Ueda. Some men balk at the huge amounts of money they are expected to spend on their girlfriends at Christmas. For some time there was a trend for women to knit their boyfriends special Christmas sweaters, and knitting schools cropped up in many areas. Some women who did not wish to knit sweaters paid others to knit sweaters for them, which they then passed off as their own handiwork.

Even though there is a sense in which people are pressured with obligations of giving in relationships defined in accordance with dimensions of familiarity rather than hierarchy, much of the giving in such relationships is done with great enthusiasm. In the neighborhood where I lived, we dug for potatoes together and divided our bounty among all the residents of our block; people also handed pots of food back and forth. The continuous stream of giving and receiving between Mrs. Inoue and her friends and neighbors is also an example of welcome exchanges between equals. Many of the Western gifts, such as Christmas gifts, birthday gifts, and Valentine's Day gifts to lovers, are carefully chosen according to the younger generation's formulations of Western notions of the perfect gift. Teenage girls spend hours crafting homemade chocolate treats for their boyfriends to give them on Valentine's Day; these special sweets are very different from the obligatory chocolates they buy for their male superiors and coworkers. Months before Christmas, young men begin planning their Christmas Eve dates, sometimes as much as one year in advance. Just as New Year's is a serious family holiday, Christmas is a time for romance and intimacy, and many young couples seem to enjoy the giving and receiving that accompanies this celebration. Seasonal gifts of Chinese origin and gifts associated with life cycle events are also often given with much happiness; carp wind socks selected for grandsons on 5/5, the special sash given to a pregnant woman by her natal family, New Year's money in small, colorful envelopes given to children all belong to this category.

Giving to people outside one's network of relations is rare, and is usually confined to people who appear to need help. For example, when I once asked Mr. Tanabe if there were any kinds of giving he was comfortable with, he related a story about a cold Tokyo morning in January when he brought cups of hot coffee to a delivery man waiting for a shop to open. I have seen complete strangers gather in a circle around a person who had lost a contact lens, carefully maintaining enough distance so as not to step on the lens by mistake, searching methodically until finally the lens was found. On the other hand, almost no one gives to homeless people in parks or train stations, and people who are homeless do not usually ask for money or food. Although there was an outpouring of donations of food, clothing, and money to victims of the 1995 earthquake in the Kobe-Osaka area, the people I interviewed tended to make gifts to individual friends and family members; some also sent money for repairs to the headquarters in Kyoto of family branch temples in Tokyo.

People like Mr. Tanabe, who by both his own account and those of others is somewhat unusual in his attitudes toward giving, are most comfortable with giving that is unrelated to hierarchy, especially giving involving those outside one's network of relationships. He is one of the few individuals I met, for example, whose volunteer activities are for the most part confined to helping people who are strangers to him. Those like Mrs. Inoue, on the other hand, give almost exclusively within their individual social networks and are comfortable with giving along dimensions of both hierarchy and familiarity. Warabi residents like Mr. Ishiyama also give primarily within their own social networks, along dimensions of both hierarchy and familiarity, although they are critical of many of the status distinctions that giving reflects and reinforces.

There is considerable variation in practices of giving and attitudes toward giving according to region, class, gender, religion, and life experience. People in Warabi, and in other working-class areas both inside and outside Tokyo, are more likely to shun elaborate calculations of value of return gifts, department store hierarchies, and name brand goods. Across all classes and geographic areas, married women are primarily responsible for each household's giving and receiving, and are judged on their performance in these areas. Their participation in giving reinforces their subordinate position to men, as is evident in symbolic notions of yang's encompassment of yin, the higher cash value of gifts to males or gifts through male links, the precedence of visits to husbands' families, and the emphasis on exchange for the benefit of relations between men. Finally, life experience and religious and political views influence individual attitudes toward giving. For example, although most upper-middle-class people like Mrs. Inoue see nothing wrong with widely accepted practices of giving, Mr. Tanabe's perspective is different. Mr. Tanabe's memories of his childhood during World War II as an outsider in southern Japan, his discomfort with State Shintō, and his ideas on the equality of men and women make him critical of all giving, especially giving linked to hierarchies of deities and human beings. The concluding chapter will touch again on this subject of opposition to giving.

6 ☞ Conclusion

So far, I have examined Japanese gift practices within their own historical framework and cultural context. However, any study of giving necessarily engages with an established empirical and theoretical tradition in anthropology, a tradition that ironically often appears unable to escape from certain assumptions generated by the place of gifts in European and American popular ideologies of social life. This final chapter will consider how Japanese practices of giving and receiving relate to this larger body of literature.

Gifts, according to American and European conceptions, exist in a special realm outside the market place. Emerson, in his essay "Gifts," writes: "The only gift is a portion of thyself. Thou must bleed for me. . . . I fear to breathe any treason against the majesty of love, which is the genius and god of gifts, and to whom we must not affect to prescribe. Let him give kingdoms or flower leaves indifferently" (Emerson 1987: 94–96). According to this interpretation, the gift is a part of the donor. The gift stands in opposition to the commodity, which circulates in the world of commercial transactions, where value is calculated on the basis of price, and objects are not exchanged to create relationships between people but rather to turn a profit.

Precisely because gifts exist in this special realm outside the marketplace, they not only should be connected to the person of the donor but also should be devoid of self-interested calculation. Carrying this conception to its most extreme formulation is Derrida's notion of the gift as collapsing in on itself:

At the limit, the gift as gift ought not appear as gift: either to the donee or to the donor. It cannot be gift as gift except by not being present as gift.

Neither to the "one" nor to the "other." If the other perceives it or receives it, if he or she keeps it as gift, the gift is annulled. But the one who gives it must not see it or know it either; otherwise he begins, at the threshold, as soon as he intends to give, to pay himself with a symbolic recognition, to praise himself, to approve of himself, to give back to himself symbolically the value of what he thinks he has given or what he is preparing to give. (Derrida 1992: 14)

Derrida's formulation of the impossibility of the gift because of the impossibility of giving without calculation, without thought of return, without recognition, even from oneself, is itself based on a specific cultural construction of what giving should be.

In the chapters of *Given Time II* devoted to Mauss's classic essay *The Gift*, Derrida criticizes Mauss, saying: "Mauss does not worry enough about this incompatibility between gift and exchange or about the fact that an exchanged gift is only a tit for tat, that is, an annulment of the gift" (ibid.: 37). This statement is not completely accurate, as it is precisely in attempting to understand practices of giving and receiving in societies other than his own that Mauss explicitly recognizes the combination of interest and disinterest in giving. Commenting on this aspect of Mauss's scholarship, Jonathan Parry writes:

The ideology of a disinterested gift emerges in parallel with an ideology of a purely interested exchange. . . . [T]he whole ideology of the gift, and conversely the whole idea of "economic self-interest," are our invention; and the text explicitly acknowledges the difficulty of using these terms for societies such as the Trobriands where prestations—the word itself must have been chosen for its connotations of constraint—are a kind of hybrid between gifts, loans, and pledges. . . . Mauss's real purpose here is not to suggest that there is no such thing as a pure gift in any society, but rather to show that for many the issue simply cannot arise since they do not make the kinds of distinction that we make. So while Mauss is generally represented as telling us how in fact the gift is never free, what I think he is really telling us is how we have acquired a theory that it should be. (Parry 1986: 458)

It is because Derrida writes about giving from his own culture's ideological context that he raises the important issue of the conflation between "gift" and "exchange." The reason Mauss is concerned with the question of interest but takes a different approach from Derrida to the relationship between gifts and exchange is that Mauss is trying to understand giving and receiving from a perspective in which gifts and exchange are not separated.

Mauss proposes that in what he calls "archaic" societies, the separation of the gift from the realm of buying and selling did not exist—in contrast to what he sees as the deeply troubled contract society of his time. His solution to this problem is to reach back into history to bring again to life the intermingling of people and things. He writes that modern European civilization draws a strict distinction between real rights and personal rights, between things and persons, between obligations and gifts. He asks, "Have our civilizations not gone through a previous phase in which they did not display such a cold, calculating mentality? Have they in fact not practiced these customs of the gift that is exchanged, in which persons and things merge?" (Mauss 1990: 48).

As with the European and American idea represented in Emerson and Derrida, the gift for Mauss is extremely personal, infused with the individuality of the donor. He writes: "[A] tie occurring through things is one between souls, because the thing itself possesses a soul, is of the soul. Hence it follows that to make a gift of something to someone is to make a present of some part of oneself" (ibid.: 12). In formulating this implicit, and sometimes explicit romantic critique of modern European life, Mauss attaches particular importance to ethnographic evidence that various Pacific island people conceived of gifts as embodying the identity of the giver. The most famous example he cites is the Maori notion of the *hau*, or the spirit of the gift that compels the recipient to return a matching gift to the giver. The strengths or weaknesses of Mauss's interpretation of this Maori belief have since been debated in literally dozens of further studies by Maori specialists and nonspecialists alike. Here I suggest only that Mauss's appeal to the Maori concept is directly bound up with his romantic critique of bourgeois utilitarianism. Mauss's emphasis on the personal nature of the gift is at once an attempt to describe Maori ideas and an effort to use those ideas to confirm his conviction that there existed a time in our own prehistory when sale was not separated from gifts and exchange, when moral obligation was not isolated from contract, when human beings merged with things—and that Maori life in the present echoes what was once a better and happier period of our own existence.

Recent anthropological interest in drawing a strong contrast between commodities and gifts both reflects and reinforces the conception of the gift as a part of the giver and the related distinction between the realm of the gift and the realm of the marketplace: gifts move between interdependent transactors as inalienable extensions of their donors, while commodities circulate between independent transactors as alienable objects (Gregory 1982).

It is clear that this position, as articulated in different ways in relatively recent writings on gifts and commodities, traces its intellectual lineage to Marcel Mauss's classic essay. Marilyn Strathern, in her highly influential study *The Gender of the Gift*, formulates a radical opposition between gift and commodity worlds. Strathern argues that the pair of terms "gift" and "commodity" provide "an axis for considering a range of contrasts between Melanesian societies and the societies of the Western world. . . . [If] in a commodity economy things and persons assume the social form of things, then in a gift economy they assume the social form of persons" (Strathern 1990: 178). Moreover, she characterizes whole cultures and whole societies by her avowedly heuristic or fictional dichotomy: the West as a commodity society and Melanesia as a gift society.

In doing so, Strathern overlooks the tremendous regional diversity of Melanesia, and uses the Western concept of the gift to explain Melanesian practices of exchange; there is little account of the way local people actually talk about interactions, the words they use or the alienability or inalienability they actually describe. The gift is conceived as the opposite of the commodity, and as the commodity is alienable, the uniqueness of the gift must be in its inalienability. For example, in her discussion of the famous Melanesian regional exchange network known as *kula*, Strathern states that every valuable is someone's *kitoum*, or owned kula shell. She also maintains that the kitoum is "a product of work, and an inalienable part of the male person" (ibid.: 196). She bases these statements on generalizations from Frederick Damon's research on the island of Muyuw, but fails to explain that although Muyuwans actually take shells from the sea, cut, and polish them, this is not the case on other islands, such as Gawa. On Gawa only a small subset of shells obtained through very special kinds of transactional cycles are classified as kitoum and afford their owners the high degree of flexibility associated with this category of valuable (Munn 1986: 148). Strathern highlights only those particular facts from the various ethnographies of areas well adapted to her model of the gift/commodity dichotomy.

I realize that I am making blunt criticisms of a complex work, and am therefore overlooking certain subtleties. However, ultimately, what Strathern claims is that Melanesians are ontologically different from Westerners—that they actually conceive of objects as substantially continuous with themselves, and give themselves away in their objects, while we do not. This idea finds its most memorable expression in Strathern's use of the phrase "partible personhood" as a characterization of all Melanesian social being.

Approaching the work of Strathern and others from a background in the study of Japan, I have been repeatedly struck by similarities between the approach of these gift/commodity theorists and the reifications of difference often encountered in Japanese studies—not to mention in Japan—in the idea that the Japanese as a people are ontologically different from others because of their unique "sense of self."

At a very general level, Japan is a place that challenges the stereotype that Western capitalist societies are characterized almost exclusively by the commodity form, in which commodities circulate between independent transactors as alienable objects, and Melanesian societies are based on gift economies, in which gifts move between interdependent transactors as inalienable extensions of their donors. Japan raises questions about this stereotype because it is a major advanced capitalist society, yet it has an enormously important gift sector that resists any sharp contrasts between gifts and commodities. In Japan, gifts and commodities are not two neat, separate categories. In fact, they are almost always entangled (Thomas 1991). Many gifts are made with cash, the prototypical commodity form. Even when gifts are objects other than cash, in numerous instances it is prescribed that they be readily interchangeable: for example, consumable items such as seaweed, cooking oil, and soap. Trade-in centers for unwanted seasonal gifts pay cash for such items, and then resell them at a profit. The giving of gifts is subject to a calculus of value based on monetary price, for precise attention to monetary cost is integral to the negotiation of certain relationships. When you receive a gift from a department store, for example, there is a code printed on it, and this tells you how much the gift cost. I was even informed in an interview with a florist that when he delivers flowers to people, they ask him how much the flowers are worth. The reason why the receiver is so concerned with the price of the gift is that in many cases, a return gift is called for, and in order to make the appropriate type of return gift, it is essential to know the cost of the original gift.

Although the commodity system is the basis for the gift system, the people who taught me about giving and receiving stated that it is wrong to treat relations of giving and receiving as if they were ones of buying and selling. Yet one leading anthropologist of Japan who has written extensively on Japanese conceptions of gratitude and obligation has misinterpreted this emphasis on calculation, namely Ruth Benedict, in *The Chrysanthemum and the Sword*. Benedict assumes that all processes of calculation are associated with the economic realm, and that the economic realm is lacking in humane values. Benedict explains Japanese relationships of giving and receiving in simple financial terms. These analogies to the realm of buying and selling are misleading. In fact, calculation in the context of Japanese practices of giving can have an entirely different set of meanings.

One of the examples she cites in her chapter entitled "Debtor to the Ages and the World" is of an elderly man whose wife passed away. He did not remarry, a fact his sons and daughter considered virtuous. When the children found out, however, that he had been seeing a prostitute in secret whom he then hired as a maid, they became angry. When the man wrote to the advice column of a magazine asking what he should do, this is the reply he received:

I of course appreciate your long unmarriedness, but you have used this to make your children wear the *on* [indebtedness][1] and also to justify yourself in your present line of action. I don't like this. I'm not saying that you are sly, but your personality is very weak. It would have been better to explain to your children that you had to live with a woman—if you couldn't help having one—and not to have let them wear the on (for your remaining unmarried). The children naturally are against you because you have laid such emphasis on this on. After all, human beings don't lose their sexual desires, and you can't help having desire. Your children expected you to because they expected you to live up to the ideal they had formed of you. On the contrary, they were betrayed and I can see how they feel, although it is egotistical on their part. They are married and sexually satisfied and they're selfish to deny this to their father. You're thinking this way and your children the other way (as above). The two ways of thinking don't meet. (Benedict 1989: 110–11)

Benedict writes:

Americans do not judge a situation in this light. We think that a father who dedicated himself to his motherless children should in later years merit some warm spot in their hearts, not that they are "naturally against him." In order to appreciate it as the Japanese see it, we can, however, regard it as a financial transaction, for in that sphere we have comparable attitudes. It would be perfectly possible for us to say to a father who has lent money to his children in a formal transaction which they have to live up to with interest, "they are naturally against you." . . . Love, kindness, and generosity, which we value just in proportion as they are given without strings attached, necessarily must have their strings in Japan. (ibid.: 112–13)

Benedict misses the point the advice columnist is making. It is precisely because the father cannot expect his children to feel on towards him as a kind of merit to be drawn upon that this relationship is *not* like a financial transaction.[2] The father not only misrepresented himself to his children but also perceived his long unmarried state as a sacrifice for which he expected some recognition or gratitude or at least tolerance. This expectation of return, this forcing of "repayment," is what the person offering advice criticizes. Relations between parents and children should not be as relations between debtors and lenders.

What Benedict perhaps more sensitively portrays is the notion of a whole system of relations of indebtedness in which all people are embedded. At one level, there is a Maussian mingling of love and obligation, a deep awareness of one's relative significance in the scheme of things, of one's constant indebtedness to others. At another level, there is a sense of stress and coercion and exhaustion, especially in the case of inferiors exploited by superiors.

A second and more recent influential study on Japanese ideas of giving and receiving is that of Harumi Befu, who has put forth a model of Japanese practices of giving, suggesting that in addition to on, there are two other types of giving in Japan: *giri* and *ninjō*. Befu, like Benedict, translates on relations as "indebtedness." The *onjin*, or person who has given guidance, favors, or services to the recipient, is permanently in a superior position to the on receiver. The onjin may be a favorite teacher or benefactor. Nothing is adequate to repay the onjin; gifts to the onjin are symbolic of the on debtor and the relationship between the on debtor and the onjin.[3] Social equals, such as neighbors and relatives, stand in giri relations to one another. Giri relations of giving are often between households rather than between individuals, and these households are supposed to maintain balanced exchanges. Befu states that the primary concern is to repay a debt rather than please the recipient with a gift. Ninjō relations are those of personal feeling. A gift of ninjō is typically from one individual to another, and is chosen carefully to fit the recipient. Whereas gifts of giri must be reciprocated in terms of economic value, gifts of ninjō are considered from the heart, and should be devoid of such calculations (Befu 1967: 161–67, and 1968: 445–56).

Befu's categories can be seen as ideal types that are part of a larger framework within which gift-giving takes place. He suggests that people negotiate relationships with others through giving by using conceptions of on, giri, and ninjō as models that may be accepted, rejected, or manipulated. In much the same way that levels of politeness work in language, in which the kind of relationship is constructed in the process of interaction, in the context of giving the intent of the giver is interpreted by the recipient, who, in making a return gift either reinforces or modifies those original expectations.

Although Befu's typology is illuminating insofar as it focuses attention on the kind of relationship between giver and receiver, it is problematic in the sense that the connotations of these terms vary significantly according to each individual context. People rarely describe their own giving practices with the terms on and ninjō. Giri is used fairly frequently, but usually in a way that has an undertone of contempt. It describes someone who gives the bare minimum, who gives reluctantly simply because the person feels forced to out of obligation. "He/she definitely sent that out of giri" was a phrase I heard a number of times, always with negative connotations. When I asked whether something was given out of on, sometimes there was a moment of silence, almost shock.

People told me that on, giri, and ninjō are words usually attributed to the mafia or right-wing activists who drive around in black vans blaring nationalistic songs. After the terrible 1995 earthquake in the Osaka-Kōbe region, the news media reported how gangsters handed out powdered milk and other staples, in their "traditional" role of showing ninjō to the common people. Many are profoundly uncomfortable with these terms because of their dark, feudalistic overtones. On to the emperor led Japanese soldiers to kill and brutalize vast numbers of people in the Asian countries they fought and occupied, and right-wing activists, intent on returning the emperor to his prewar ontological status as god, frequently use this word. Giri and ninjō can be indicative of crooked and exploitative relationships. Ties of giri between the mafia and the construction industry may be partly responsible for the shoddy construction that contributed to the many deaths in the Osaka earthquake.

Conceptions of these terms have changed greatly in the postwar period, and there is sharp disagreement in attitudes toward on, giri, and ninjō. Takie Sugiyama Lebra underscores this lack of consensus, suggesting that on may be "associated with love in a parent-child relationship, with tradition and custom for the relationship between main house and branch house, and with a contractual obligation for employer-employee relationship" (Lebra 1969: 137).

Lebra argues against a single interpretation of the concept of on, noting different ways for construing on relations. These include transference and avoidance of indebtedness, receivers' manipulation of benefactors' needs to be depended on, idealizations of selfless givers that restrain those who demand repayment, and methods for neutralizing or reversing hierarchical pressure (ibid.: 132–36, and 1975: 559–60).

Recent anthropological accounts of giving and receiving in China and Japan demonstrate how the American and European conception of the gift as intensely personal, as well as the distinction between gift and commodity, has influenced anthropologists' understanding of giving and receiving not only in societies of Melanesia and Oceania, but also in those of East Asia. In *Gifts, Favors, and Banquets*, her fascinating study of *guanxi* in urban China, Mayfair Yang writes:

How does gift-giving represent the adding on of personal substance? As noted above, gifts are not alienable from persons in exchange, there is no subject-object dichotomy in gift-exchange as in the owner-property relation in a commodity transaction (Strathern 1983). The lack of disjunction between person and thing in gift-exchange means that the gift remains symbolically attached to and identified with the person of the donor, thus the gift becomes a medium for introducing the personal substance of its donor into the person of the recipient. . . . [F]or the recipient, accepting another's substance is to be "appropriated" or "possessed" by the other in oneself. . . . [T]his is experienced as a softening of her will, as indicated by this saying:

> *Chi ren zui ruan; Na ren shou duan.*
>
> Eating from others, one's mouth becomes soft.
> Taking from others, one's hand becomes short.

The saying has been explained to me in the following way: After one has eaten of other's food, one's mouth finds it difficult to "harden" and purse up to refuse the other's request for help or to say bad things about the other. When one takes a gift from someone, the hand grows short, and so one cannot reach out to push that person away when he or she needs help. . . . [M]ouths that have eaten and hands that have taken become "easy to persuade" (*hao shuo hua*). . . . [T]hus for face, mouth, and hand, accepting a gift is not so much a gain as a loss or reduction of stature and control. It follows that indebtedness is couched in terms of a state of loss, a loss of wholeness of person and independence. (Yang 1994: 195–98)

Identifying the gift with the person of the giver, internalizing and being dominated by that foreign substance, is not the same as the softening of one's mouth or the shortening of one's hand. It is difficult to determine whether the people Yang spoke with actually equated the gifts they received with the person of the giver, and their acceptance of the gifts as part of themselves occupied by another's substance.

A work on gifts by an anthropologist who conducted research in rural China suggests that Yang's interpretation of softening of mouth or shortening of hand as domination by the person of the giver embodied in the gift may be due more to the influence of Strathern's conceptual framework than to the notions of gifts expressed by the people with whom she spoke during her field-work. Yunxiang Yan, in *The Flow of Gifts*, contrasts ideas of gifts in the Chinese village where he did his fieldwork with Weiner's interpretation of the Maori hau:

> Weiner argues that there is a close connection between the hau, the person, and valuables (*taonga*) such as cloaks, fine mats, and shells. . . . [A]lthough this theory of inalienability avoids reducing gift exchange to a simplistic form of dyadic exchange between self-interested individuals, it cannot adequately explain the practice of gift-giving among Xiajia villagers. For the gift is alienable and does not have any supernatural powers in itself. (Yan 1996: 215)

Yan goes on to suggest that it is not the gift object that is inalienable, but rather the relationship between giver and receiver: "The gift creates a spiritual connection between the giver and the recipient, which is generally characterized as *renqing* by the villagers. This is why Xiajia residents always look at how much *renqing* exists between two parties and insist that the offering of gifts be determined by previous *renqing* and *guanxi*. In other words, it is not the spirit of the gift but the spirit of the people that ties the gift transactors together" (ibid.: 216).

Mayfair Yang accepts the thesis that gifts cannot be alienated from persons: "[T]he lack of disjunction between person and thing in gift-exchange means that the gift remains symbolically attached to and identified with the person of the donor, thus the gift becomes a medium for introducing the personal substance of its

donor into the person of the recipient" (Yang 1994: 195). However, the proverbs she quotes to prove this assertion could in fact
also support Yan's point of view. The acceptance of gifts recognizes
the relationship between two individuals, and as the connection
between the two people becomes stronger, mouths become softened
and hands become shorter; it is progressively more difficult to
refuse requests, to push the other away.

In much the same way that Mayfair Yang's understanding of
giving and receiving in urban China seems to have been in part
shaped by Strathern and Gregory, James Carrier, in his work *Gifts
and Commodities*, views gift-giving in Japan through ideas of alienability and inalienability as they relate to separate gift and commodity spheres. He writes:

My argument is that [American practices of] Christmas shopping and giving are cultural activities that spring in large part from the perception of
an alienated realm of work. Support for this argument exists in the giving
of presents in Japan. It is commonplace that economic relations there are
less impersonal than in the West (Abercrombie, Hill and Turner 1986:
121–31). In idealized terms, this means that employees have a durable relationship with the firm that employs them; that employees subordinate
themselves to the firm and its interests; that relations within the firm have
a strong social, as distinct from just utilitarian, element; that employees
derive their social identity from the firm rather than the specific work that
they do (Nakane 1986; Rohlen 1973; see also Dore 1983). While this situation may exist primarily for core employees in larger firms, it reflects a
widespread set of assumptions about how real work ought to be, which
reflects in turn a widespread set of assumptions about what people are and
how they ought to relate to each other (Moeran 1984). Because real work
ought to be unalienated, at least as compared to work in the West, in Japan
there is less likelihood that people will see the economic world as one of
impersonal relations and things, surrounding and differing radically from
the household world of personal relations and things. In saying this I do
not claim that the Japanese do not distinguish between the household in
which they live and the corporations in which they earn and spend money.
I do claim, however, that they do not distinguish these realms in terms of
the personality and impersonality that underlie the American cultural distinction between home and work. . . . [T]he formulaic nature of core
Japanese giving shows that in a society where the economy is not regard-
ed as distinctively impersonal, giving presents does not revolve around the
appropriation of commodities in the way I have said it does in the United
States. (Carrier 1995: 170–80)

Carrier's understanding of the gift in the American context is that the realm of the gift is considered separate from the realm of the commodity. Gifts are supposed to contain within them both the spirit of the giver and the relationship between giver and receiver, and gift relations between people are idealized as different from relations between buyers and sellers in the commercial realm. This dichotomy between gift and commodity both reflects and reinforces the stark separation between home and work. Objects given in the personal and sentimental environment of the home must first be appropriated in order to remove the taint of the market; this is why, Carrier argues, bought gifts must be wrapped, whereas homemade items such as bread or jams can be presented without much decoration. In interpreting practices of giving and receiving in Japan, Carrier notes that gifts are not personalized in the same way they are in Europe and America, and he goes on to imply that the absence of a clear division between gifts and commodities is directly related to a lack of differentiation between home and work.

My own examination of these issues calls into question the reification of whole societies or types of society both by gift/commodity theorists and by students of Japan. In his brief discussion of Japanese practices of giving, Carrier makes both moves simultaneously. He describes the United States and Japan as separate, opposing entities; economic relations in Japan are personal, in the West they are impersonal; in Japan an employee's relationship with the workplace is social, in the West it is utilitarian; work in Japan is supposedly "unalienated," whereas in the West it is "alienated." Carrier is assuming that Japanese have a more personal view of the economic realm, and that they therefore do not need to appropriate commodities to turn them into gifts. But for much of the giving that takes place in Japan, gifts are not supposed to be personal in Carrier's sense of the term; people gain recognition and social standing from their ability to calculate precise amounts of money or to select gifts that are seen as outward oriented, as the dissolving of particularity and lining up with a larger system. The contrast between the "personalized" gift and the "depersonalized" commodity is not useful in understanding giving and receiving in this context.

How might it be possible to think about the relationship between gifts and commodities in more fluid and dialectical terms? Exchanges this book describes assist in formulating a more dynamic model of how gift-giving works. Take, for example, the incense money Ishiyama Tomoyasu gave to Ishiyama Shūji (Chapters 1 and 2). The gift in this case is a lot of money. Money may be considered the paramount commodity form, but the same medium has different uses in different contexts. In this instance the money is used not for purchasing but for giving. The fact that the prototypical form of the commodity is the medium through which a gift is made indicates that there is slippage between gifts and commodities: a clear division between the two does not hold up in this particular act of giving. It is also not the case that the gift object—namely the 200,000 yen—is confused with the person of the giver. Rather, this act of giving represents the importance of the relationship between Ishiyama Shūji and Ishiyama Tomoyasu, between Ishiyama Tomoyasu and Ishiyama Shūji's father, and between the two families. In addition, this gift enacts a transition. It signals that Ishiyama Shūji's father has now departed, that he is no longer in the realm of living people, and that Ishiyama Shūji's position in the family now has changed from eldest son to head of household. And because it is the main family that showed gratitude to the branch family, it can be interpreted to represent a reversal of normal hierarchical relations between superiors and inferiors.

Even though many gifts in Japan are made in cash, there is a strong ambivalence about money and about the calculations gift-giving entails. If you receive a gift of money, the return gift should never be made with money. Chapters 1 and 2 recount Mrs. Ueda's shock when she gave a present of cash and received a return gift in the form of gift certificates; she considered the possibility that the givers wanted to cut their relationship with her. You generally cannot return money with money; to do so would be too calculating. To make a return gift of a gift of cash by changing its form and giving an object is supposed to soften the gift somehow and make it less calculating; even though there are price codes listed on the boxes containing gifts, these objects are still a step removed from money.

In order to examine this complex orientation toward money in more detail, let us return to the example in the first chapter of the ways in which two guests returned the transportation money they received at the wedding of Mrs. Ueda's daughter. Mrs. Ueda was sharply critical of the woman who sent a wallet worth half the amount of the transportation money she had been given, as she had been given a discount on her train ticket. Mrs. Ueda was full of praise for the old man who returned his envelope unopened, stating that he had come as the representative of the dead grandparents of the bride, and therefore could not accept the gift, as kin do not generally receive transportation money. Because the man was connected with Mrs. Ueda's parents and the woman was connected with Mrs. Ueda's daughter, she did not know either very well.

On the basis of the way in which they returned the gifts of kurumadai, Mrs. Ueda made strict judgments about their characters. The man returned the envelope without even breaking its seal. She used the word *isagiyoi* (pure, righteous, manly) to describe his action. Key to her assessment of his character was the fact that he did not open the envelope. "It is human nature to want to look into the envelope," she stated. "But he did not. If you wanted the money even a little bit, you would open the envelope, and then think about it, and then maybe decide to give half back." Mrs. Ueda did not like the calculating behavior of the woman. I asked Mrs. Ueda why she thought it was that the woman didn't return all of the money. Mrs. Ueda pointed out that it is usually rude to return the value of any gift in its entirety; this can cause consternation to the person to whom the gift is returned. Especially when making a return gift for a gift of cash, etiquette dictates that the form of the gift must be changed, so that it is not like one is giving back exactly what one had received. But in this case, a partial return by changing the form of the initial gift was much worse than a complete and total return of the cash, and also worse than no return at all would have been.

Mrs. Ueda called this woman *okatai*. This word describes a person who is especially rigid. It is related to another word, *girikatai* (having a strong sense of duty). People who are scrupulous in upholding their social obligations in giving and receiving are those who, among other things, always make return gifts. These people uphold giri (*gi* is the character for righteousness; *ri* originally meant "to split a jewel" and came to mean "concentrate, act carefully"; giri is variously translated as "duty, integrity, justice, morality, righteousness, social courtesy"). Girikatai has both positive and negative connotations. *Katai* means "hard, solid, stiff, rigid, tough." It can be used to say, for example, that a tight pair of shoes is uncomfortable. It also can describe a building's firm, sound foundation. Girikatai can refer to the social actions of an honest, upright, solid person; it can also describe someone who is rigid, to the extent of being unfeeling. When Mrs. Ueda used the polite prefix "o" and attached it to the word katai, she implied the woman was too strict with her calculations. She was strict to the point of being selfish or petty. What is so interesting about the cases of the man and the woman who returned the transportation money in different ways is that even though the woman did everything in strict accordance with standard rules—she did not send back money, but rather, she sent an object—Mrs. Ueda was offended. It was the man who refused all contact with the money, who returned the envelope unopened, who said, "I am here as the representative of the dead grandparents of the bride, and as their representative, please treat me as kin; therefore, do not give me kurumadai"—this was the person whom Mrs. Ueda admired.

The example from Chapter 5 of the minister's wedding gift further illuminates why there is ambivalence about calculations in giving. As Mrs. Ueda's frustration with the behavior of her minister indicates, two notions that appear to contradict each other appear simultaneously. On the one hand, money is dirty, and the world of money and business stands apart from the idealized church community. People from this "family" should relate from the heart; money should not change hands. This notion of money as dirty may stem partly from Mrs. Ueda's Christian belief system, but Japanese who are not Christian also have an ambivalent attitude toward money. It is rude to give "naked" (*hadaka*) money without enclosing it in an envelope; it is unseemly to speak openly of money. As Marilyn Ivy writes in her description of money showered on performers in itinerant variety theater: "[To] give money in its unmediated form, or even to pick up money lying on the ground, is vulgar in Japanese society" (Ivy 1995: 234). At the same time, the way sincerity is shown is precisely through money. Measurement and calculation are extremely important in giving. For the gift to be perceived as sincere, proper, from the heart, it must be measured and calculated for the benefit of the recipient; it must be oriented outward rather than inward to oneself.

The wallet the teacher sent and the book the minister gave did not meet these requirements. The teacher may have thought that her long letter of explanation about her senior citizen discount conveyed how careful and conscientious she was, as a greedy person would have simply kept all the money, even though only half had been used for transportation to and from the wedding. But from Mrs. Ueda's point of view, the teacher came across as making calculations for her own benefit, as trying to call attention to herself with her many words. The minister's book on Christianity was also full of his own pronouncements. This gift was seen as selfish, inward oriented, as avoiding giving up money that would have been both a material sacrifice and a symbol of orientation to the outside and therefore respect and concern for the bride and groom.

From one point of view, the cash given at these exchanges has nothing to do with buying and selling. The number of strands in the cord that ties the envelope, the odd numbered units of bills the envelope contains, and the way the envelope is folded represent proper alignment with a cosmic order that enables reproduction.

From another point of view, these exchanges are very much connected with the world of buying and selling. Many of these transactions are in cash, and those that are not are often mediated through department stores. Giving is often between people in the workplace in order to enhance chances for advancement or cultivate business connections. Exchangers of gifts use practices of giving in order to benefit themselves and those close to them, but as long as these practices are in accord with a larger system, for the most part they are condoned.

If people fail to conform to their proper roles in the process of exchange, and are perceived as greedy or arrogant, they may be resented as superiors taking advantage of their positions. But as long as superiors align themselves to their proper roles and give the right amount in the right way, their actions are usually interpreted as proper, and the giving of large sums of money to them is viewed as appropriate. This may be why many are hesitant to use the word "bribe" to describe gifts to superiors. An example of this kind of "proper" giving is Mrs. Ueda's gifts to her son's boss. Even though she suggested that the large amounts of cash given to the go-between were because of his high social standing and his busy schedule, there were other people attending the wedding who occupied similarly high social positions and who were also strapped for time. But those people did not stand in direct relationships of power to Mrs. Ueda's son, and those people did not receive such large amounts of money. So while practices of gift exchange use money for their own symbolic purposes, exchangers of gifts use these practices of giving in order to benefit themselves and those close to them. As long as these practices conform to a larger order of reproduction predicated on encompassment, people are extremely reluctant to criticize these gifts to superiors, whereas they express anger over relationships of giving and receiving with superiors that do not conform to this larger order.

Complaints about giving and receiving fall into two categories: criticisms of people for not fulfilling their appropriate roles within the larger system, and criticisms of the larger system itself. Many people expressed resentment toward forms of giving and receiving more concerned with immediate individual profit than with social relationships and proper cosmic alignment. But only a minority of the people who participated in my research refused to give and receive because of the relations of encompassment underlying these practices. Those who did refuse on these grounds to participate in this system were sometimes subject to harsh criticism, though occasionally they were admired and even emulated.

Processes of abstraction and calculation generally associated with the sphere of the marketplace are a fundamental part of gift practices encountered in Japan. It is through careful negotiations of calculations of value and systems of correspondences that givers convey respect to recipients, provide auspicious influence at critical rites of passage, confirm and sometimes change their own social positions or the social positions of others. Givers ideally link each particular instance of giving to more generic considerations, such as cycles of seasons, frameworks of specialty items from far-away places, and hierarchical orderings of human beings, department stores, and numbers. In this context, monetary and quasi-monetary signs are important for giving: they are apprehended as specific quantities that are auspicious because they align with a greater cosmic process.

Models founded on static or essentialist notions of the Japanese sense of self, or models that presume a priori that the gift is a part or extension of the giver, or models of whole societies as gift societies or commodity societies are not very helpful because they say little about the complex details and variations across the many different forms of giving I encountered in my research. There is not one kind of giving in Japan; there have been tremendous changes over time, and ways of giving and attitudes toward giving are extremely diverse. Similarly, there cannot be one simple model for giving. In recent anthropological writings on exchange, what I consider to be a small part of Mauss's thinking—namely, the idea that the gift is the spirit of the giver—has been artificially isolated and blown out of proportion. This study develops what I think has been a neglected theme of Mauss's work: the action of giving itself is an instantiation not so much of a particular person or self, but of the social relationship between giver and recipient. It is not primarily that the gift as an object stands for the giver's identity. Rather, it is a material embodiment of a social and cosmic order. This social and cosmic order both influences human beings and is shaped by them. And though each individual gift act may appear as if it has been determined by this larger context, by its appearance it also projects outward and backward. It situates people, it changes statuses, it builds relationships. There is, in short, ritual efficacy in giving.

Reference Matter

☞ Notes

Chapter 2: Strength of Relationship, Gratitude, and Hierarchy

1. Hendry reports that in Kurotsuchi, Kyūshū, it is desirable when adopting an heir to forge links by blood and marriage to both sides of the family. In one of the cases she presents, the five-year-old son of the husband's brother was adopted as an heir and then married to the wife's brother's daughter (Hendry 1981: 101).

Chapter 3: Life Cycles

1. A woman who suffers a miscarriage, for example, may be consoled by words such as "May the soul of your baby return to you from the other world in a stronger body."

2. A child's soul is not completely anchored in its human body until it turns seven years old.

3. Souls who are in the other world return to the world of the living only at specific points in the seasonal cycle; these will be examined in the fourth chapter.

4. The significance of the parallels between offerings at these different rites of passage will be explored later in this chapter.

5. Omitted rituals include such practices as a bride entering her new husband's home under an umbrella held by her mother-in-law.

6. Smith reports that the presentation of the cash portion of the engagement gift of a young friend of his had to be rescheduled when the bride's mother discovered that someone had folded the right side of the paper over the left side (Smith 1974: 94).

7. This explanation was offered to me by Iwashita Noriko, author of books on giving etiquette. See also Edwards 1989: 107, who agrees with this interpretation, and Hendry 1981: 160, who suggests that the abalone indicates that the giver is not contaminated by death or misfortune.

8. In Kurotsuchi, the village in northern Kyūshū where Hendry did her

fieldwork, tea is also considered auspicious, and is an important element in the wedding rituals. When both parties agree to marry, the groom's family sends a box of tea, decorated with symbols of good fortune, long life, and happiness such as pine, bamboo, plum, crane, and turtle, to the bride's family; the word for betrothal is either *kimeja* ("decide-tea") or *kugicha* ("nail-tea"). The delivery of betrothal gifts is known as *honja* ("main-tea"). Engagement gifts are arranged on separate tables, and the first table is for green tea that has been packed into red and pink cylinders, which are later given to relatives and neighbors. In this region, tea is a symbol of fertility, as it produces as many as four harvests annually. In addition, tea plants in a row gradually grow into one large bush, symbolizing the unity of extended family to be created through marriage (Hendry 1981: 155–59).

9. For further discussion of why it is that in Warabi everyone receives the same return gift, please see Chapter 5.

10. This system of belief is known in Japan as *Ommyōdō* (literally, "the way of yin and yang"), and refers to theories of yin and yang and the five elements.

11. Wing-hoi Chan, who conducted his fieldwork in the southern part of China, states that the number of incense sticks offered to the dead is usually odd, that some people make sure cash funeral gifts are in odd numbers, and that odd numbers, especially three and five, are unlucky numbers for weddings. However, these rules are not all encompassing; for example, sometimes the number one can be acceptable for a wedding gift. One piece of pork would be auspicious, as pork in itself has lucky connotations.

12. Although in most giving in Japan, particularly at auspicious occasions, odd numbers are preferred to even numbers, it is sometimes appropriate to give one pair of something. These pairs are usually things like two cups for drinking tea, two rice bowls, two chopstick holders (in the shape of ducks, such a pair is lucky because it connotes a good relationship between husband and wife). One half of the set is for a man, and one for a woman; the item for the man is bigger. Some people pointed out that the contrasting colors of cords used to tie gifts are also pairs; for example, of white and red, white and black, silver and gold, and so on, as are the lucky combination of red and white found in so many elements of gift-giving.

13. In Mandarin and Cantonese, the pronunciation for "eight" is similar to the word for "prosperity." In an article for the Los Angeles *Times* written on 8/8, Connie Kang describes a complaint lodged against the state utility commission for its plan to change the area code from 818 to 626 in communities in the San Gabriel Valley. Chinese Americans interviewed for this article attributed their phenomenal growth in the San Gabriel Valley to the 818 area code. Kang reports that many residents buy homes with eight in the street number, and pay extra money for telephone and fax

numbers containing as many eights as possible. In Hong Kong, she states, license numbers containing a single eight sell for millions of dollars. The 626 area code that the state utility commission intended to replace the 818 area code with is a very unlucky set of numbers, as they add up to fourteen. Four means death, and fourteen stands for "guaranteed death" (Kang 1996).

14. It is at turning points in the cycles of human lives and seasons, at times of promise and possibility but also of danger, when attention to specific details in giving is so important. At the very auspicious, because of the linked odd numbers, but therefore frightening sekku (1/7, 3/3, 5/5, 7/7, 9/9), there is emphasis on water, washing, purification. These ritual emphases are repeated when the ancestors return in summer, winter, and at the equinoxes.

15. There was a big scandal in the early 1990s when the mistress of a man high up in the Mitsukoshi hierarchy was accused of receiving a house and other very expensive items from suppliers who wanted to have their goods sold at Mitsukoshi. Many businesses in the Tokyo area that had usually sent their seasonal gifts from Mistukoshi instead switched to Takashimaya.

16. Joy Hendry summarizes an unpublished paper by Joseph Kyburz, "*Engimono, Miyage, Omocha*: Three Material Manifestations of the Notion of *En*," in which he states that in the premodern period, a group of people from a village or neighborhood contributed money to send one person on a pilgrimage. Each member of the group was eventually able to travel, but in the meantime could share to some extent in the experience by receiving a gift from the trip for which all had saved. In addition, Kyburz suggests that the gift given on departure and the gift given on return together formed a magical connection that would bring the traveler safely home (Hendry 1993: 36).

17. There is an intense effort to appropriate the outside through such activities as tourism and gift-giving (Field 1994: 15; Ivy 1995: 3). There are similarities here with the ancient Chinese system of imperial tributes. By categorizing and then receiving the specialty items of each far-off place, the Chinese emperor, through mastery of the foreign, both became powerful and asserted his power. It may be that by bringing back meibutsu, the giver expresses high regard for the relationship with the receiver by enabling the receiver to assert control over difference.

18. These rice cakes were known as *isshōmochi* (rice cakes made from one *shō*—1.8 liters—of glutinous rice).

19. Even renting kimono is expensive. Prices for kimono rental at Tokyo's Meiji shrine in 1995 started from 38,000 yen (this price included the cost of putting on the kimono and a commemorative photograph of the child).

20. Most girls wear kimono, but a small minority wear miniature versions of Western-style wedding gowns, complete with veils.

21. These gifts are known as *nyūgakuiwai* (school-entering celebratory gifts).

22. Similar to return gifts given at the birth of a baby, 7-5-3, and other happy occasions, these school-entering return gifts will bear the characters *uchiiwai*, indicating that an auspicious event has occurred within the family that is sending the gift.

23. The betrothal gifts given by the groom to the bride are called yuinō, and the ceremony at which these gifts are given is also called yuinō.

24. The first character of nakōdo means "relationship"; the left-hand radical of this character means "person" and the right-hand radical means "middle," thus person in the middle and by extension a relationship through the middle person involving those on either side. The second character also means "person" (Henshall 1988: 296). Hendry presents a detailed history of the go-between in Japan, a concept introduced from China in the Nara period but utilized widely only among samurai in the Tokugawa era and among the general population starting in Meiji (Hendry 1981: 140–45).

25. This section is heavily indebted to Kodama's research on funeral practices in Warabi and the surrounding areas; please see Kodama 1993: 127–43.

26. As explained in the previous discussion on auspiciousness and inauspiciousness, even numbers are yin, and convey the idea of cutting or separation; four can be pronounced *shi*, which means death.

27. Iwashita writes that rice is normally served on the left because left is considered superior (see previous section on yin and yang), and rice is considered the most important staple food (Iwashita 1995: 27).

28. See Granet 1953: 261–78; and Needham 1973: 43–58.

Chapter 4: Seasonal Cycles

1. Interview with Miura Seiichi of Tobu Department Store.

2. The character for bon was once used to represent a pottery vessel for food, and in present Japanese use it also means "tray," suggesting the central role of offerings of food to ancestors in bon ceremonies. Yanagita Kunio states that a slightly different version of the character now used for bon was common before the medieval period to indicate *bon* or bon offerings (Yanagita 1970: 100).

3. See Harootunian 1988: 415–17 for an analysis of Yanagita Kunio's opposition to the Shrine Merger Act, a Meiji government policy critical to the construction of State Shintō and one that drastically changed many people's traditional practices of religious worship.

4. In order to emphasize the new national religion of Shintō and the Shintō-based divine status of the emperor, the Meiji government implemented a policy of *shinbutsubunri* (separation of Shintō and Buddhism). Before the March 1868 decree, Buddhist priests controlled a large number of Shintō shrines, and there were Buddhist images in many Shintō shrines.

5. As was indicated in Chapters 1 and 2, main families are those headed by an eldest son. In families without sons, the adopted husband of the eldest or only daughter becomes the head of family. The practice of adopting sons-in-law has decreased dramatically, and the relations between main families and branch families are no longer as strict or formal as they once were, at least among working-class families in Warabi. In wealthier families in Tokyo, however, interactions between main families and branch families are more likely to reflect and reinforce the superior status of the main family and the inferior position of the branch family.

6. Kitazawa Masakuni, in his work *Saijiki no kosumorojii*, argues that mochi are in the shape of the bulging mirrors placed in the palace of the Japanese emperor. These mirrors, he stresses, are "purely Japanese," unlike the flat mirrors from China intended for reflecting human faces. The traditional Japanese rounded mirrors were for putting in dark places to reflect the light of the sun. He claims that the rounded mirror symbolizes the sun, the origin of all life. *Kagamimochi*, "mirror rice cakes," symbolize both the sun and the genitals of the female rice goddess (Kitazawa 1995: 66–68). His argument is very sketchy on details, and its heavy nationalistic undertone suggests that his primary aim is to demonstrate that important New Year's rituals are Japanese in origin.

7. Different people have different explanations for what the *toshigami-sama* is. Sometimes, it seems to be a singular god, other times it seems to refer to a host of returning spirits. The historical and political reasons behind these different interpretations relate to the Meiji changes.

8. Warabi residents did not roast food in the bonfire, but a woman who grew up in a small town near Niigata told me that it is a common practice there to roast dried squid in the kagaribi, and to eat of this food that was roasted in the bonfire is considered auspicious.

9. These are *zōni* (rice cakes boiled with broth and vegetables). In Warabi, some families are careful not to make the broth with any meat or fish. This is because the broth will be offered to the Buddhist altar as well as to the Shintō altar (Kodama 1993: 396). Each region has a different recipe for zōni. One commonly used in Warabi for presentation to the altars includes rice cakes, sweet potatoes, and *komatsuna* (a green leafy vegetable similar to spinach) in addition to the broth. Marriages between people of different regions have led to a great variety in zōni recipes from one household to another.

10. In Warabi, the New Year god was said to depart on the day of the

rabbit, the hour of the rabbit. (Yanagita Kunio indicates that this practice was once widespread; Yanagita 1970: 77–78.) Because there are twelve animals in the Chinese calendar, and because the order circulates from year to year, some years the day of the rabbit could be January 1, and other years it could be as late as January 12. If the god departed early, offerings only needed to be made a short time, and the harvest of that year would be good. If the god departed as late as January 12, the harvest of that year would be poor (Kodama 1993: 402).

11. This practice of placing money in small envelopes and giving them to children at New Year's also occurs in China and Taiwan.

12. *Koshōgatsu* ("little New Year") starts with the first full moon of the year, and is most commonly observed in rural areas where the New Year's deities are considered also to be agricultural deities. Sometimes it is an occasion for women to visit their own families, as it is the husband's family who takes priority at New Year's, or for women, who are very busy during New Year's celebrations, to rest and enjoy their own small celebration together.

13. The action of cutting is considered inauspicious. At weddings, also, people refrain from using certain words like "cut," "break," and "separate."

14. The only other day ordinary people are allowed on the inner grounds of the imperial palace is the emperor's birthday.

15. Families who have lived in Warabi for many generations do not put flowers on the graves, but rather *shikimi*, branches of a tree that stays green all year round. It is possible to see quickly by walking through a graveyard at bon which graves belong to more newly arrived families (who offer flowers) and which graves belong to old Warabi families (who offer shikimi). The parallel with the evergreen branches offered at New Year's is striking.

16. Robert Smith, in his work *Ancestor Worship in Contemporary Japan*, quotes Yanagita Kunio as saying that the purpose of the bondana is "to keep the observance for purified souls of distant ancestors from contamination with mourning for the newly dead" (Smith 1974: 72; Yanagita 1970: 116–17).

17. As mentioned in the section on shōgatsu, konbu—because it sounds like the word for rejoice, yorokobu—is auspicious. In the same way that this kind of seaweed is said to make New Year's visiting spirits and deities rejoice, it is said to make the ancestral spirits returning at bon happy as well.

18. More than one lantern increases the likelihood that at least one flame will reach the house without being extinguished. If all the flames die out, the whole process must be repeated until the ancestors are safely carried to the altar inside the home.

19. As is mentioned in Chapter 3, this side entrance is called engawa (literally, "connection side," meaning veranda), the place from which close friends and family members enter the house. The coffin containing the corpse is removed from the engawa. Use of the side entrance indicates a close relationship to the deceased and may also signify avoiding polluting the front entrance with the impurities associated with death.

20. The Imperial Rescript on Education was issued in the name of the Emperor Meiji on October 30, 1890. It states that the Japanese educational system is based on the relationship between the emperor and his subjects, and it exhorts students to be loyal to the imperial house.

21. As discussed in the previous chapter, the number seven is important for Buddhist rituals because gestation periods, periods of a baby's separation from the other world and entrance into the human world, and periods of a soul's separation from the world of the living and entrance into the world of the dead are all measured in seven-day increments. For example, a deceased person is reborn after forty-nine days (seven times seven).

22. These seven herbs are known as *nanakusa*. There are two sets of nanakusa, one set for the spring and one for the fall. The spring set (it is believed that according to the lunar calendar, the beginning of the New Year was also the beginning of spring) is the set eaten with the rice gruel on January 7, and includes *seri* (Japanese parsley), *nazuna* (shepherd's purse), *gogyō* (cottonweed), *hakobera* (chickweed), *suzushiro* (Japanese radish; daikon). The fall set includes *hagi* (Japanese bush clover), *susuki* (eulalia), *kudzu* (kudzu vine), *mominaeshi* (a perennial herb of the family Valerianaceae), *fujibakama* (boneset), and *asagao* (known today as *kikyō*; balloon flower or Chinese bellflower) (Campbell and Noble 1993: 1047). The autumn herbs were used as decorations at bon, indicating again connections between bon and New Year's rituals.

23. In some families, particularly those in which there is a member of *yakudoshi* (an unlucky age), the family members may write their names and ages onto paper dolls, and then breathe on these dolls. The head of the family will take them to a shrine where they are purified and then burned.

24. See Sangren's analysis of Dumont's "encompassment" (Sangren 1987: 172).

25. The day of the serpent could appear twice in any one month. The first time it appeared, it would be referred to as top serpent, the second time, bottom serpent. Sometimes the top serpent was also called original or first serpent.

26. The first child is given dolls by relatives; often, this practice is not repeated with female children that follow. Some parents will buy dolls for their other daughters, but more often, the first daughter's dolls are displayed annually, and other daughters do not have dolls to take with them when they marry.

27. It is said that the origin of eating chimaki comes from China. Ch'u Yuan, a beloved poet of the Warring States period, committed suicide in 343 B.C. by drowning himself in the Mi-lo River of Hunan province. The residents of the area went in their boats to rescue him, but, unable to find him, they threw rice into the waters in order to prevent him from being eaten by underwater creatures. Every year, on the fifth day of the fifth lunar month, the anniversary of Ch'u Yuan's death, people threw rice into the river. Two hundred years later, his ghost appeared and requested that the rice be wrapped in leaves to prevent the monster of the river from eating it. In China, chimaki are known as *tsung tzu*, and the tradition of the dragon boat races and the eating of tsung tzu on the fifth day of the fifth lunar month is said to stem from this story. In some versions, it is the poet's sister who throws tsung tzu into the water (Okada and Akune 1993: 103).

28. Oak leaves are considered auspicious, one woman told me, because they symbolize orderly succession; before the old leaf falls off, a new bud emerges. Like the daidai offered at New Year's, oak leaves symbolize the smooth transition from one generation to the next. Other people were not familiar with this interpretation, and it is not written in any books I have found so far, but it is the case that some varieties of oak leaves can stay on their branches throughout the winter, remaining longer than the leaves of any other deciduous trees.

29. Red is for fire, green is for wood, yellow is for earth, black is for water, and white is for metal (Yoshino 1983: 35).

30. Aomori's Nebuta festival, held from August 3 to 7 (August 7 by the solar calendar is considered July 7 by the old lunar calendar), shows the relationship that exists in some parts of Japan between tanabata and bon. Elaborate images lit from within by lanterns were thrown into the ocean on 7/7 or 7/8 in an event known as *tanabatanagashi* (washing away of Tanabata) or *tanabataokuri* (sending off of Tanabata). The original intent of the Nebuta festival was to remove sins and impurities from human beings before the return of their ancestors at bon (Okada and Akune 1993: 105).

31. Literally, "the way of yin and yang." Originally referred to the philosophy of *I ching*, with particular emphasis on theories of yin and yang and the five elements. See Chapter 3.

32. See Viviana Zelizer's discussion of advertisers' invention of Mother's Day (Zelizer: 1994).

Chapter 5: Variations in Attitudes toward and Practices of Giving

1. Newcomers to Warabi are generally considered to be those families who moved there after World War II.

2. Yunxiang Yan, in his work on giving in the Chinese village of Xiajia,

reports a practice of sending specialty items from the provinces to central bureaus in Beijing at the end of each year. He quotes an official in the ministry of commerce as saying: "Today it is a truck loaded with lamb from Inner Mongolia; and tomorrow it may be apples from Shandong province. All these gifts are tributes from the local bureaus to the Beijing bureau and they are distributed among officers as extra benefits" (Yan 1996: 156).

3. Matthews Hamabata describes how he put this stereotype to use during his fieldwork among women of wealthy business families. In order to win their trust, he had to portray himself as a naïve boy: "In Japan, patterns of behavior that separate the men from the boys are quite clear-cut. . . . [I] developed a keen liking for Japanese sweets, French pastry, and Baskin-Robbins ice cream. Children love sweets in Japan, but boys at puberty learn to detest cakes and candies; and as men, they take to smoking and drinking scotch" (Hamabata 1990: 16).

4. Sometimes gifts can be passed from giver to recipient while they are still in bags, especially if giver and recipient have met at a public place, and the gift is passed over at the end of their time together. But in formal situations such as this one, when an inferior goes to the home of a superior, the gift should be removed from the bag before offering it to the superior. Similarly, before ringing the doorbell, the giver should remove his (or more usually) her coat and fold it in on itself so that the outer part of the coat does not dirty the inside of the recipient's house. Removal of gifts from bags, like unwrapping gifts from furoshiki, signifies respect and care for the recipient in the sense that a pure item, not an item that has been sullied by the outside, is handed over.

5. It is interesting to note that Mr. Tanabe asked his wife not to send gifts to his company superiors.

6. The word Kuniko used for "small token of gratitude" was soshina (trifling gift, inferior goods). The thank-you note that came back from the wife of the doctor used the expression osoreirimasu (osore means fear, terror, or horror, and osoreirimasu means to be overcome with shame or gratitude). In the same way that it is difficult to gloss the many different words for "gift," there are few Japanese phrases uttered when giving and receiving that are easily expressed in English because there are no equivalent set phrases.

7. As Chapter 2 discussed, some relations between neighbors are differentiated according to dimensions of hierarchy. For example, Mr. Tokuguchi, who is from the oldest family of the Nakasendō, stands above Mr. Hoshino's family in the neighborhood hierarchy, whereas the neighbor who rents land from the Hoshino family is indebted to the Hoshino family. However, the relationships along the Nakasendō are unusual in the extent to which they are hierarchically structured; on the street where I lived, in which almost everyone rented apartments, hierarchical relations

between neighbors were much less obvious. (My apartment building was perhaps a two minute walk from Mr. Hoshino's home.)

Chapter 6: Conclusion

1. From roughly the eleventh century onward, on referred to a vassal's obligation to fight for his lord in battle because of land, stipends, or protection received from his lord. The many layers of meaning of this term have developed over time, as will be explored in the pages that follow.

2. Benedict suggests that the primary meaning of on is debt, and that, for example, in parent-child relationships, love is a secondary meaning. However, in her example of the on a man might feel toward his mother, she writes: "[T]he term . . . refers specifically not to his love, but to all his mother did for him as a baby, her sacrifices when he was a boy, all that she has done to further his interests as a man, all that he owes her from the mere fact that she exists" (Benedict 1989: 100). Although she emphasizes the importance of debt in understanding the meaning of on, she also refers to it as "another name for love" (ibid.) and quotes the Japanese saying that one can only begin to return on to one's own parents by caring for one's own children. It is because on to one's parents cannot be repaid and one's gratitude can only be conveyed in words and deeds that the comparison with financial transactions is misleading.

3. Befu does not deal explicitly with the distinctions and continuities between gifts and bribes. He does describe the practice that expects medical students to give exorbitant amounts of money to their advisors upon completion of their graduate work. Befu writes: "The gift is presumably an expression of the student's gratitude, repayment of on, toward his professor for providing special guidance and advice. It is a legitimate, socially sanctioned behavior, although the amount of the gift may be questionable" (Befu 1967: 170).

☞ Bibliography

Ahern, Emily. 1973. *The Cult of the Dead in a Chinese Village*. Stanford: Stanford University Press.

Anonymous. 1996. Valentine's Day in Japan. *Asahi Evening News* (February 11–12): 5.

Appadurai, Arjun. 1986. Introduction: Commodities and Politics of Value. In *The Social Life of Things: Commodities in Cultural Perspective*, edited by Arjun Appadurai. Cambridge: Cambridge University Press.

Baker, Hugh. 1979. *Chinese Family and Kinship*. New York: Columbia University Press.

Beardsley, Richard, John Hall, and Robert Ward. 1959. *Village Japan*. Chicago: University of Chicago Press.

Befu, Harumi. 1967. Gift-Giving and Social Reciprocity in Japan. *France-Asie/Asia* 21: 161–67.

———. 1968. Gift Giving in a Modernizing Japan. *Monumenta Nipponica* 23: 445–56.

———. 1971. *Japan: An Anthropological Introduction*. San Francisco: Chandler.

———. 1977. Power in the "Great White Tower": Contribution to Social Exchange Theory. In *The Anthropology of Power*. London: Academic.

Benedict, Ruth. 1989. *The Chrysanthemum and the Sword*. Boston: Houghton Mifflin.

Bestor, Theodore. 1989. *Neighborhood Tokyo*. Tokyo and New York: Kodansha.

Blood, Robert O. 1967. *Love Match and Arranged Marriage: A Tokyo-Detroit Comparison*. New York: Free Press.

Bourdieu, Pierre. 1997. *Outline of a Theory of Practice*. Translated by Richard Nice. Cambridge: Cambridge University Press.

Campbell, Alan, and David Noble, eds. 1993. *Japan: An Illustrated Encyclopedia*. Tokyo: Kodansha.

Carrier, James. 1990. Gifts in a World of Commodities: The Ideology of the Perfect Gift. *Social Analysis* 29: 19–37.

———. 1995. *Gifts and Commodities: Exchange and Western Capitalism since 1700*. London: Routledge.

Cavanaugh, Carole. 1996. Text and Textile: Unweaving the Female Subject in Heian Writing. *Positions* 4, no. 3 (winter): 595–636.

Cole, Robert. 1971. *Japanese Blue Collar: The Changing Tradition*. Berkeley: University of California Press.

Creighton, Mildred. 1988. Sales, Service, and Sanctity: An Anthropological Analysis of Japanese Department Stores. Ph.D. dissertation, University of Washington.

Crump, Thomas. 1992. *The Japanese Number Game*. New York: Routledge.

Denoon, Donald, Mark Hudson, Gavin McCormack, and Tessa Morris-Suzuki, eds. 1996. *Multicultural Japan: Paleolithic to Postmodern*. Cambridge: Cambridge University Press.

Derrida, Jacques. 1992. *Given Time*. Translated by Peggy Kamuf. Chicago: University of Chicago Press.

Ding, Xiushan. 1988. *Chūgoku no kankonsōsai* (*China's Rites of Passage*). Tokyo: Tōshōsshoten.

Doi, Takeo. 1973. *The Anatomy of Dependence*. Tokyo: Kodansha.

Dore, Ronald. 1958. *City Life in Japan: A Study of a Tokyo Ward*. Berkeley: University of California Press.

Dumont, Louis. 1980. *Homo Hierarchicus: The Caste System and Its Implications*. Translated by Mark Sainbury. London: Weidenfeld and Nicolson.

Edwards, Walter. 1989. *Modern Japan through Its Weddings: Gender, Person, and Society*. Stanford: Stanford University Press.

Ekiguchi, Kunio. 1985. *Gift Wrapping*. Tokyo: Kodansha.

Embree, John. 1939. *Suye Mura: A Japanese Village*. Chicago: University of Chicago Press.

Emerson, Ralph Waldo. 1987. Gifts. In *The Collected Works of Ralph Waldo Emerson*, edited by Jean Ferguson Carr. Cambridge: Belknap.

Errington, Joseph. 1988. *Structure and Style in Javanese*. Philadelphia: University of Pennsylvania Press.

Fair, Janet Kay. 1996. Japanese Women's Language and the Ideology of Japanese Uniqueness. Ph.D. dissertation, University of Chicago.

Field, Norma. 1991. *In the Realm of a Dying Emperor: A Portrait of Japan at the Century's End*. New York: Pantheon.

———. 1993. Beyond Envy, Boredom, and Suffering: Toward an Emancipatory Politics for Resident Koreans and Other Japanese. *Positions* 1, no. 3 (winter): 640–70.

———. 1997. *From My Grandmother's Bedside: Sketches of Postwar Tokyo*. Berkeley: University of California Press.

Frazer, James. 1940. *The Golden Bough: A Study in Magic and Religion*. New York: Macmillan.

Goldstein-Gidoni, Ofra. 1997. *Packaged Japaneseness: Weddings, Business and Brides*. Honolulu: University of Hawai'i Press.

Granet, Marcel. 1953. *La Pensée Chinoise*. Paris: La Renaissance du Livre.

Gregory, Christopher. 1982. *Gifts and Commodities*. London: Academic.

Hamabata, Matthews. 1990. *Crested Kimono: Power and Love in the Japanese Business Family*. Ithaca: Cornell University Press.

Hardacre, Helen. 1989. *Shintō and the State, 1868–1988*. Princeton: Princeton University Press.

Harootunian, H. D. 1970. *Toward Restoration: The Growth of Political Consciousness in Tokugawa Japan*. Berkeley: University of California Press.

―――. 1988. *Things Seen and Unseen: Discourse and Ideology in Tokugawa Nativism*. Chicago: University of Chicago Press.

Heikiba, Yasuyoshi. 1995. *Heisei hachi nen jingūkan unseireki (The Jingūkan Fortune Almanac for the Eighth Year of Heisei)*. Tokyo: Jingūkan.

Hendry, Joy. 1981. *Marriage in Changing Japan*. London: Billing and Sons.

―――. 1993. *Wrapping Culture: Politeness, Presentation, and Power in Japan and Other Societies*. Oxford: Oxford University Press.

Henshall, Kenneth. 1989. *Guide to Remembering Japanese Characters*. Boston and Tokyo: Charles E. Tuttle.

Hiro, Sachiya. 1987. *Bukkyō to shintō (Buddhism and Shintō)*. Tokyo: Shinchōsensho.

Hocart, Arthur Maurice. 1970. *Kings and Councillors*. Chicago: University of Chicago Press.

Holland, James Henry. 1989. Gift Exchange in Japan: The Role of the Foreigner. Master's thesis, Cornell University.

Hori, Ichiro. 1968. *Folk Religion in Japan: Continuity and Change*. Chicago: University of Chicago Press.

Imamura, Anne. 1987. *Urban Japanese Housewives: At Home and in the Community*. Honolulu: University of Hawai'i Press.

Ivy, Marilyn. 1995. *Discourses of the Vanishing: Modernity, Phantasm, Japan*. Chicago: University of Chicago Press.

Iwao, Sumiko. 1993. *The Japanese Woman: Traditional Image and Changing Reality*. Cambridge: Harvard University Press.

Iwashita, Noriko. 1993a. *Zōtōmanā no techō (Notebook of Giving Manners)*. Tokyo: Shōgakkan.

―――. 199b. Subarashii ichinen no sutāto o kiru ni atatte, nenshi no goaisatsu to otoshidamama ni tsuite (Starting a Fabulous New Year, about New Year's Greetings and Otoshidama). *Shio* (January): 324–25. Tokyo: Shōgakkan.

―――. 1993c. Oni ga momo o osoreru? Riyū to, hinakazari de shiru nihon no jōza to shimoza (Are Demons Afraid of Peaches? The Reason [Why They Are Afraid] and Knowing Lower Seat from Higher Seat through Doll Arrangements). *Shio* (February): 320–21. Tokyo: Shōgakkan.

————. 1995. *Oyako no manā ressun* (*Manner Lessons for Parents and Children*). Tokyo: Shōgakkan.

————. 1996. *Keichō omotegaki manā no techō* (*The Congratulations and Condolences Gift Card Manner Memorandum Book*). Tokyo: Shōgakkan.

Janelli, Roger, and Dawnhee Yim. 1982. *Ancestor Worship and Korean Society*. Stanford: Stanford University Press.

Kang, Connie. 1996. They've Got Luck All Figured Out. *Los Angeles Times*, home ed. (August 8): 1.

Keane, Webb. 1997. *Signs of Recognition: Powers and Hazards of Representation in an Indonesian Society*. Berkeley: University of California Press.

Kendall, Laura. 1995. *Shamans, Housewives, and Other Restless Spirits: Women in Korean Ritual Life*. Honolulu: University of Hawai'i Press.

————. 1996. *Getting Married in Korea: Of Gender, Morality, and Modernity*. Berkeley: University of California Press.

Kitazawa, Masakuni. 1995. *Saijiki no kosumorojii: toki no koe o kiku* (*The Cosmology of Saijiki; Listening to the Voice of Ages*). Tokyo: Heibonsha.

Kodama, Sachio, ed. 1988. *Tsukagoshi chiku no minzoku: warabishi shi chōsa hōkokusho daigo shū* (*The People of the Tsukagoshi Area: Warabi Historical Survey Report, Volume Five*). Warabi: Warabi shi.

————. 1989. *Warabi chiku no minzoku: warabi shi chōsa hōkokusho dainana shū* (*The People of the Warabi Area: Warabi Historical Survey Report, Volume Seven*). Warabi: Warabi shi.

————. 1993. *Warabi shi minzokuhen* (*The Ethnographic History of Warabi*). Warabi: Warabi shi.

Kondo, Dorinne. 1990. *Crafting Selves: Power, Gender, and Discourses of Identity in a Japanese Workplace*. Chicago: University of Chicago Press.

Lebra, Takie Sugiyama. 1969. Reciprocity and the Asymmetric Principle: An Analytical Reappraisal of the Japanese Concept of *On*. *Psychologia* 12: 129–38.

————. 1975. An Alternative Approach to Reciprocity. *American Anthropologist* 77: 550–65.

————. 1984. *Japanese Women: Constraint and Fulfillment*. Honolulu: University of Hawai'i Press.

————. 1990. *Japanese Social Organization*. Honolulu: University of Hawai'i Press.

————. 1993. *Above the Clouds: Status Culture of the Modern Japanese Nobility*. Berkeley: University of California Press.

McCormack, Gavan. 1996. *The Emptiness of Japanese Affluence*. New York: M. E. Sharpe.

McGregor, Richard. 1996. *Japan Swings: Politics, Culture, and Sex in the New Japan*. Sidney: Allen and Unwin.

Mauss, Marcel. 1990. *The Gift: The Form and Reason for Exchange in Archaic Societies*. Translated by W. D. Halls. New York: W. W. Norton.

Miller, Daniel. 1993. *Unwrapping Christmas*. Oxford: Oxford University Press.

Minami, Chieko. 1993. Koningirei ni okeru zōtōkōdō no kinō (The Function of Gift-Giving in Wedding Rituals). *Yokohama shiritsu daigaku ronsō* 45, no. 2: 113–37.

Munn, Nancy. 1986. *The Fame of Gawa*. Durham: Duke University Press.

Nakane, Chie. 1967. *Kinship and Economic Organization in Rural Japan*. New York: Humanities.

———. 1970. *Japanese Society*. Berkeley: University of California Press.

Needham, Rodney. 1973. *Right and Left: Essays on Dual Symbolic Classification*. Chicago: University of Chicago Press.

Nelson, Andrew. 1962. *The Modern Reader's Japanese–English Character Dictionary*. Tokyo: Charles E. Tuttle.

Nihon no seikatsu bunka kenkyū purojekuto (Project for Researching Japanese Lifestyles). 1994. *Kankonsōsai no okane jiten* (*Dictionary of Money for Rites of Passage*). Tokyo: Nihon no seikatsu bunka kenkyū purojekuto.

Norbeck, Edward. 1954. *Takashima: A Japanese Fishing Community*. Salt Lake City: University of Utah Press.

———. 1977. A Sanction for Authority: Etiquette. In *The Anthropology of Power*. London: Academic.

———. 1978. *Country to City: The Urbanization of a Japanese Hamlet*. Salt Lake City: University of Utah Press.

Ogasawara, Yuko. 1998. *Office Ladies and Salaried Men: Power, Gender, and Work in Japanese Companies*. Berkeley: University of California Press.

Ohnuki-Tierney, Emiko. 1984. *Illness and Culture in Contemporary Japan: An Anthropological View*. Cambridge: Cambridge University Press.

Okada, Yoshirō, and Akune Suetada. 1993. *Gendai koyomi yomitoki jiten* (*A Contemporary Reading and Answering Dictionary of the Almanac*). Tokyo: Seibundō Shinkōsha.

Parry, Jonathan. 1986. The Gift, the Indian Gift, and "The Indian Gift." *Man* 21: 453–73.

Parry, Jonathan, and Maurice Bloch, eds. 1989. *Money and the Morality of Exchange*. Cambridge: Cambridge University Press.

Picken, Stuart D. B. 1994. *Essentials of Shintō: An Analytical Guide to Principal Teachings*. London: Greenwood.

Raheja, Gloria. 1988. *The Poison in the Gift: Ritual, Prestation, and the Dominant Caste in a North Indian Village*. Chicago: University of Chicago Press.

Reader, Ian, and George Tanabe. 1998. *Practically Religious: Worldly Ben-*

efits and the Common Religion of Japan. Honolulu: University of Hawai'i Press.

Rubin, Gayle. 1975. The Traffic of Women: Notes on the Political Economy of Sex. In *Toward an Anthropology of Women*, edited by Rayna Reiter. New York: Monthly Review.

Sahlins, Marshall. 1972. *Stone Age Economics*. Chicago: Aldine-Atherton.

———. 1996. The Sadness of Sweetness: The Native Anthropology of Western Cosmology. *Current Anthropology* 37, no. 3: 395–428.

Sangren, P. Steven. 1987. *History and Magical Power in a Chinese Community*. Stanford: Stanford University Press.

Schattschneider, Ellen. 1996. Circuits of Discipline: Production, Reproduction, and the Work of the Gods in Tsugaru (Northern Japan). Ph.D. dissertation, University of Chicago.

Schwerdtfeger, Detlef. 1981. Hierarchy and Process: An Involutional Dialectic Model of Social Adaptability in Japanese Contexts. Ph.D. dissertation, Southern Illinois University.

Shimizu, Katsumi. 1995. *Konna toki dō suru gishiki 110 ban (110 Questions as to What to Do in Certain Kinds of Formal Ritual Situations)*. Tokyo: Seibundō Shinkōsha.

Shinoda, Yasuko. 1995. *Manaˉ shitsumonbako: hazukashikunai otsukiai zōtō (Box of Questions on Manners: Relating to Others through Giving without Embarrassment)*. Tokyo: Hikarinokuni.

Shūkyō girei bunka kenkyūkai (Research Association for Religion and Etiquette). 1993. *Kankonsōsai jōzu na okane no tsukaikata (Skillful Use of Money in Rites of Passage)*. Tokyo: Seibundō Shinkōsha.

Smith, Kazuko. 1995. *Makiko's Diary: A Merchant Wife in 1910 Kyoto*. Stanford: Stanford University Press.

Smith, Robert. 1974. *Ancestor Worship in Contemporary Japan*. Stanford: Stanford University Press.

———. 1978. *Kurusu: The Price of Progress in a Japanese Village*. Stanford: Stanford University Press.

Smith, Robert, and Ella Lury Wiswell. 1982. *The Women of Suye Mura*. Chicago: University of Chicago Press.

Strathern, Marilyn. 1983. Subject or Object? Women and the Circulation of Valuables in Highland New Guinea. In *Women and Property, Women as Property*, edited by R. Hirschon. London: Croom Helm.

———. 1990. *The Gender of the Gift*. Berkeley: University of California Press.

Suzuki, Hikaru. 2000. *The Price of Death: The Funeral Industry in Contemporary Japan*. Stanford: Stanford University Press.

Thomas, Nicholas. 1991. *Entangled Objects: Exchange, Material Culture, and Colonialism in the Pacific*. Cambridge: Harvard University Press.

Tobin, Joseph. 1992. *Remade in Japan: Everyday Life and Consumer Taste in a Changing Society*. New Haven and London: Yale University Press.

Tokoro, Isao. 1986. *Nihon no shukusaijitsu (Japanese Festivals)*. Tokyo: Nijūisseskitoshokan.

Valerio, Valeri. 1980. Notes on the Meaning of Marriage Prestations among the Huaulu of Seram. In *The Flow of Life: Essays on Eastern Indonesia*, edited by J. J. Fox. Cambridge: Harvard University Press.

————. 1994. Buying Women but not Selling Them: Gift and Commodity Exchange in Huaulu Alliance. *Man* 29: 1–26.

Van Gennep, Arnold. 1960. *The Rites of Passage*. Chicago: University of Chicago Press.

Vogel, Ezra. 1973. *Japan's New Middle Class*. Berkeley: University of California Press.

Weiner, Annette. 1992. *Inalienable Possessions: The Paradox of Keeping while Giving*. Berkeley: University of California Press.

Wolf, Arthur, and Chieh-shan Huang. 1980. *Marriage and Adoption in China, 1845–1945*. Stanford: Stanford University Press.

Yamaori, Tetsuo. 1993. *Bukkyō minzokugaku (Ethnology of Buddhism)*. Tokyo: Kōdanshagakujutsubunko.

Yan, Yunxiang. 1996. *The Flow of Gifts: Reciprocity and Social Networks in a Chinese Village*. Stanford: Stanford University Press.

Yanagita, Kunio. 1970. *About Our Ancestors: The Japanese Family System*. Translated by Fanny Hagin Mayer and Ishiwara Yasuyo. Tokyo: Japan Society for the Promotion of Science.

Yanase, Yoshio. 1995. *Daibyōin no Kaidan (Ghost Stories of Major Hospitals)*. Tokyo: Kōdansha.

Yang, Mayfair. 1986. The Art of Social Relationships and Exchange in China. Ph.D. dissertation, University of California, Berkeley.

————. 1994. *Gifts, Favors, and Banquets: The Art of Social Relationships in China*. Ithaca: Cornell University Press.

Yi, Eunhee Kim. 1993. From Gentry to the Middle Class: The Transformation of Family, Community, and Gender in Korea. Ph.D. dissertation, University of Chicago.

Yoshino, Hiroko. 1983. *Inyōgogyō to nihon no minzoku (Yin and Yang, the Five Elements, and the Japanese People.)* Tokyo: Jinbunshoin.

Yoshizawa, Hisako. 1989. *Zōtō no shikitari to manā: keichō/nenchūgyōji/otsukiai no kokorozukai ga tsutawaru (Methods and Manners of Giving: Consideration in Relating towards Others as Conveyed through Congratulations and Condolences, Annual Events)*. Tokyo: Shinkōsha.

Zelizer, Viviana A. 1994. *The Social Meaning of Money: Pin Money, Paychecks, Poor Relief, and Other Currencies*. Princeton: Princeton University Press.

☞ Character List
and Glossary of Terms

abiru (浴びる): to bathe

asai (浅い): shallow

ashi no iwai (足の祝い): "celebration of the legs"; event honoring baby who walked before first birthday

bakabakashii (馬鹿馬鹿しい): ridiculous, absurd

bon (盆): Buddhist observance honoring ancestors held either in mid-July or mid-August

bondana (盆だな): *bon* altar

bunke (分家): branch family

butsumetsu (仏滅): "Buddha's death"; one of the *rokuyō*

chikai (近い): close

chimaki (粽): triangularly shaped steamed rice wrapped in bamboo leaves for 5/5

chirashisushi (散らし鮨): "scattered *sushi*" for 3/3

chitoseame (千歳飴): white stick candy symbolizing long life given at 7-5-3

chōmusubi (兆結び): "butterfy tie" for events that happen more than once

chōyō no en (重陽の宴): "pile up *yang* party"; 9/9

chōyō no sekku (重陽の節供): "pile up *yang* festival"; 9/9

chūgen (中元): "middle origin"; midyear giving in July

eki (易): divination

en o musubu (縁を結ぶ): form a connection, a tie, a relationship

engawa (縁側): "connection side," meaning veranda; close friends and relatives enter house from here

fukai (深い): deep

fukutai (腹帯): band for abdomen

furoshiki (風呂敷): wrapping cloth

genkan (玄関): area where you can stand with your shoes before you take them off and step up into the house *giri* (義理): 義 is the character for righteousness; 理 originally meant "to split a jewel" and came to mean "concentrate, act carefully." *Giri* is variously translated as "duty, integrity, justice, morality, righteousness, social courtesy."

girikatai (義理堅い): having a strong sense of duty

gosekku (五節供): five seasonal celebrations; 1/7, 3/3, 5/5, 7/7, 9/9

goshūgi (御祝儀): gratuity and congratulatory gift

hachi (八): the number eight; which is auspicious because the bottom of the character widens out like a fan

hadaka (裸): naked; the word used to describe cash given without any envelope

hagi (萩): sweet made from glutinous rice and covered with sweet red bean paste

harae (祓え): purification

hatsumago (初孫): first grandchild; name of specialty *sake*

hatsumōde (初詣): first visit to shrine at New Year's

heishi (弊紙): standard Japanese term for *kamajime*; sets of paper said to contain gods

hi no hare (日の晴れ): "day that clears"; end of period of pollution after birth

hiake (火明): end of period of pollution after birth; Embree writes *hiaki*

higan (彼岸): equinox

hikidemono (引き出物): bags of gifts given to the departing wedding guests

Hikoboshi (彦星): herdsman or Altair star

hinamatsuri (雛祭): doll festival

hishimochi (菱餅): diamond shaped rice cakes

honke (本家): main family

hotokesama (仏様): "honorable Buddha"; deceased family member's spirit

ie (家): household, family

isagiyoi (潔い): pure, righteous, manly; evokes image of feudal warrior

isshōmochi (一升餅): rice cakes made from one *shō*—1.8 liters—of glutinous rice.

iwai (祝い): celebration, congratulation, congratulatory present

jichinsai (地鎮祭): ceremony of purifying a building site

jinjitsu (人日): day of the human

jōgen (上元): literally "upper origin"; first of three annual celebrations, of which only *chūgen* remains

jōshi no harae (上巳の祓え): purification on the day of the serpent

jōshi no sekku (上巳の節供): "top serpent"; referred to the first day of the serpent

jōtōshiki (上棟式): house-building ceremony

kabu (蕪): turnip; auspicious because of round shape

kadomatsu (門松): literally "gate pine"; New Year's decoration

kagamibiraki (鏡開き): "opening of the mirror"; breaking open of *ka-gamimochi*

kagamimochi (鏡餅): "mirror rice cakes" for New Year's god

kagaribi (かがり火): fire that parishioners of local shrines build on December 31

kagen (下元): "lower origin"; one of a set of three annual celebrations of which only *chūgen* remains

kaishi (懐紙): paper folded so that ends come together

kamajime (竈注連): sets of paper said to contain gods

kami no ko (神の子): children of the gods

kangiku no en (観菊の宴): chrysanthemum viewing party

kansha (感謝): gratitude

kashiwamochi (柏餅): 5/5 rice cakes filled with sweet bean paste and wrapped in oak leaves

katsuobushi (勝男武士): "victorious warrior"; dried bonito, a gift item for auspicious occasions

keirō no hi (敬老の日): "Respect for the Aged Day"

kekkonshikijō (結婚式場): wedding palace

kiake (忌明け): end of mourning; forty-nine days after death, period of pollution ends

kiku no sekku (菊の節供): chrysanthemum festival

kiyome no ame (清めの雨): rain of purification

kōden (香典): "incense money"; envelope of cash presented at wake or funeral

kōdengaeshi (香典返し): "return of *kōden*"; gift acknowledging obituary present received

kodomo no hi (子供の日): "Children's Day," or 5/5

kōhaku (紅白): red and white, an auspicious color combination

koi (濃い): strong, thick

kokorozukai (心遣い): literally "giving from the heart," but translated as "solicitude, worry, consideration"

konbu (子生婦): "a woman who will bear children," auspicious way of writing characters for seaweed (昆布), used in recording formal engagement gifts

kōsai (交際): time of association

koshōgatsu (小正月): "little New Year"

kotobuki (寿): congratulations

kuizome (食初): infant's "first eating" ceremony

kurumadai (車代): transportation money

kusamochi (草餅): 5/5 rice cake made with mugwort

kyōdaidōshi (兄弟同士): fellow siblings

kyokusui no en (曲水の宴): "Banquet of the Crooked Water"; Heian celebration of 3/3

makura dango (枕団子): "pillow rice balls"; rice balls placed at the pillow of the corpse

makura meshi (枕飯): "pillow rice"; a bowl of mounded rice placed at the pillow of the corpse

matsu no uchi (松の内): "within the pine"; time period the New Year's deity is said to be present

meibutsu (名物): a famous or well-known product

mezurashii (珍しい): novel, rare, unusual

miyage (土産): "earth," and "give birth to, produce"; a gift

miyamairi (宮参り): shrine visit; in particular, an infant's first visit to local shrine

mizuhiki (水引): dyed paper cords used to tie gift envelopes

momo no sekku (桃の節供): "peach blossom festival"; 3/3

momoka (百日): "one hundred days"; infant's "first eating" ceremony

muensama (無縁様): "honorable ones without ties"; spirits who have no families

mukaebi (迎え火): "meeting fire" built to welcome back ancestral spirits at *bon*

mukaedango (迎え団子): "meeting rice balls" for returning ancestral spirits to eat

muko yōshi (婿養子): adoption of son-in-law

muneageshiki (上棟式): ceremony of the erection of a house's framework

musubikiri (結びきり): "to tie completely"; knot that cannot be untied, used for gifts at events that should happen only once, such as weddings and funerals

Nakasendō (中山道): major highway linking Edo with Kyoto dating from Tokugawa era

nakōdo (仲人): go-between

nanakusa (七草): seven herbs eaten at New Year's

nenshimairi (年始参り): simple New Year's gifts branch families present to main families

niibon (新盆): "new *bon*"; a departed spirit's first *bon*

ninjō (人情): human feelings, kindness, empathy

nyūgakuiwai (入学祝い): school entering celebratory gift

obiiwai (帯祝い): celebration of sash or band a woman wears from fifth month of pregnancy

omiki (お神酒): "honorable god wine"; *sake* offered at shrine and distributed to worshippers

omiyagedango (お土産団子): rice balls given as a parting gift to ancestral spirits at *bon*

ommyōdō (陰陽道): literally, "the way of *yin* and *yang*"; refers to theories of *yin* and *yang* and the five elements

on (恩): a vassal's obligation to fight for his lord in battle because of land, stipends, and/or protection received from his lord; obligation, debt of gratitude

orei (お礼): thanks; in some cases, thank-you money

Orihime (織り姫): "weaver maiden," the Vega star; name of heroine in Tanabata legend

oshoku (汚職): corruption

osoreirimasu (恐れ入ります): "to be overcome with shame or gratitude"; polite set phrase conveying thanks

oyadōshi (親同士): fellow parents

purezento (プレゼント): "present" written in *katakana*

rokuyō (六曜): "six days," also called *rokki* (六輝); each day designates auspiciousness or inauspiciousness of particular activities

sakasamizu (逆さ水): "inverted water" used to wash corpse, drawn in opposite way from usual practice

sakuramochi (桜餅): rice cake containing bean paste and wrapped in cherry leaf

sansankudo (三三九度): 3x3, the auspicious Chinese totality

seibo (歳暮): year-end giving in December

sekihan (赤飯): glutinous rice with red beans for auspicious occasions

sekku (節供): one of five seasonal celebrations on 1/7, 3/3, 5/5, 7/7, or 9/9

senbu (先負): "haste loses"; one of the *rokuyō*

senshō (先勝): "early victory"; one of the *rokuyō*

shakkō (赤口): "red mouth"; one of the *rokuyō*

shichiya (七夜): "seventh night" after infant's birth

shihōhai (四方排): "worship of the four quarters"; imperial New Year's ritual

shinbutsu bunri (神仏分離): "separation of Shintō and Buddhism" in Meiji Period

shirozake (白酒): "white *sake*"; a drink made from *sake* and rice malt

shōbu (菖蒲): iris; homonyms relevant to this symbol of 5/5 are "warlike spirit" 尚武 and "fight or contest" 勝負

shōbu no sekku (菖蒲の節供): "festival of the iris"; 5/5

shōbu uchi (菖蒲打ち): "striking with irises"; 5/5 contest

shōchikubai (松竹梅): "pine, bamboo, plum"

shōgatsu (正月): New Year's

shūbun no hi (秋分の日): autumnal equinox

shunbun no hi (春分の日): vernal equinox

shussan iwai (出産祝い): baby gift

soshina (粗品): trifling gift, inferior goods; polite word for describing a present one gives someone else

suehirogari (末広がり): spread out like an unfolding fan

susowake (裾分け): distribution of surplus; *suso* (裾) means "end or bottom" as in the cuff of trousers, the hem of a skirt, the foot of a mountain; *wake* (分け) means "divide"

susuhaki (煤掃き): "purification of soot"; New Year's cleaning

tai (鯛): sea bream

taian (大安): "great safety"; one of *rokuyō*

tanabata (七夕): "seventh evening"; 7/7

tanabatanagashi (七夕流し): washing away of Tanabata

tanabataokuri (七夕送り): sending off of Tanabata

tango no sekku (端午の節供): 5/5, or the first day of the ox (午); 端 is the character for extremity, edge, upright, and in this context it means the very beginning of the month

tatemae (建前): ceremony of the erection of a house's framework

temiyage (手土産): visiting gift

tōi (遠い): far

tokonoma (床の 間): alcove

tomobiki (友引): "pull friend"; one of the *rokuyō*

tori no ichi (酉の市): festival of the rooster

toshidama (年玉): "year, gem, or spirit"; adults give children these New Year's gifts of money

toshigamisama (年神様): New Year's deity

toshikoshisoba (年越しそば): "year-crossing noodles"; noodles eaten as the old year passes

toso (屠蘇): "slaughter" and "revive"; ceremonial spiced *sake*

tsukudani (佃煮): preserved food boiled down in soy

uchi iwai (内祝い): celebratory present indicating that an auspicious event has occurred within the family sending the gift

uraguchi nyūgaku (裏口入学): "back door enrollment"

usui (薄い): weak, thin

wairo (賄賂): bribe

wakamizu (若水): "young water"; first water of the New Year

Warabi (蕨): bracken, a kind of mountain grass; town in Saitama prefecture

yakudoshi (厄年): unlucky age

yanagidaru (家内喜多留): *sake* cask as part of formal engagement gift written with characters meaning "lots of happiness within the house"

yuinō (結納): formal engagement gift

zōni (雑煮): rice cakes boiled with broth and vegetables

zōtō: (贈東): gift exchange

Index

In this index an "f" after a number indicates a separate reference on the next page, and an "ff" indicates separate references on the next two pages. A continuous discussion over two or more pages is indicated by a span of page numbers, e.g., "57–59." *Passim* is used for a cluster of references in close but not consecutive sequence.